THE DAF REVOLUTION

Making A Difference in Our Modern World

Ted Hart

The DAF Revolution
Making A Difference In Our Modern World

For information, contact:
TEDHART.COM LLC
Washington, DC
www.tedhart.com

Published via Amazon Kindle Direct Publishing (KDP)

ISBN (eBook): 979-8-9997607-1-5
ISBN (Hardcover): 979-8-9997607-0-8
ISBN (Paperback): 979-8-9997607-3-9
ISBN (Audiobook): 979-8-9997607-2-2
Library of Congress Control Number: 2025916912
Cover and interior design by Jeremy Kahn.

For permissions, media inquiries, or additional resources,
visit www.tedhart.com.

*Printed in the **United States of America.***

DEDICATION

To my children, Sarah and Alexander.
My greatest hope is that you live fully,
give freely, and find joy in uplifting others.

ACKNOWLEDGMENTS

This book would not have been possible without the contributions of over 120 leading experts across the philanthropic, financial, legal, nonprofit, and technology sectors. Their insights, research, and real-world experience shaped the rich and practical material found in these pages.

I am deeply grateful to the many institutions and thought leaders who have provided data, case studies, and best practices, ensuring that this book is grounded in fact-based analysis and practical guidance.

To my colleagues, mentors, and fellow leaders in philanthropy, thank you for your encouragement, your challenges, and your shared commitment to shaping the future of charitable giving.

NOTE ON SOURCES AND METHODOLOGY

Between August 2024 and June 2025, more than 120 leading experts were interviewed for this book. These individuals include DAF sponsors, philanthropic advisors, foundation and corporate leaders, scholars, and technology innovators. All interviews were conducted via video or phone conference by the author.

Direct quotations and referenced insights appear with the consent of each expert interviewed. A comprehensive permission form was signed by each contributor prior to the inclusion of their material, ensuring full compliance with intellectual property and attribution standards.

This cross-sector collaboration has significantly enriched the depth, relevance, and authority of the book's content, grounding it in real-world practice and forward-looking expertise.

DISCLAIMER

The views and opinions expressed in this book are those of the author and individual expert contributors. All quotations and attributions have been reviewed and approved by their respective contributors. These views do not necessarily reflect those of their employers, affiliated organizations, or any companies mentioned.

This book is provided for informational purposes only and must not be construed as legal, tax, investment, accounting, financial, or other professional advice. Nothing in this book creates a tax-advisory, financial-advisory, or other professional-advisory relationship between the reader and the author or contributors. Readers should consult a licensed attorney, tax advisor, Chartered Advisor in Philanthropy (CAP®), Certified Financial Planner (CFP®), or other qualified professional before making any decisions based on the material herein.

The author and contributors assume no liability for any decisions, actions, or outcomes arising from use of the information in this book. Case studies, examples, and scenarios are illustrative; any resemblance to actual persons, organizations, or circumstances beyond the cited sources is purely coincidental.

Laws, tax codes, financial regulations, and best practices evolve over time. This content reflects the best available information as of publication and may not incorporate later developments. Readers are responsible for verifying current rules and guidelines with appropriate professionals.

Discussions of artificial intelligence, data analysis, and predictive analytics describe emerging trends and do not constitute endorsements of specific products, technologies, or methodologies. References to companies, organizations, or entities are for illustrative purposes only and do not imply endorsement, approval, or representation by those organizations.

FOREWORD

When I joined Ren as President and CEO in 2019, I came to a company rooted in the belief that cutting-edge technology can unlock the full potential of philanthropy. Today, we help power more than $140 billion in philanthropic funding, building scalable and efficient giving programs for nonprofits and individuals.

In *The DAF Revolution*, Ted Hart captures exactly why donor-advised funds (DAFs) matter more than ever:

Speed through flexibility: DAFs allow donors to convert complex assets into charitable capital within hours, enabling immediate responses to social crises or new opportunities.

Trust through transparency: As more DAF sponsors publish data and stories of impact, the sector becomes stronger and earns greater legitimacy.

Democracy of access: Many DAFs now offer the option to open an account with no minimum gift amount. This extends philanthropic tools to everyday people like teachers, nurses, and entrepreneurs who once lacked access.

At Ren, we have seen these advantages firsthand. Our Rapid Disbursement Engine has accelerated over 1M grants totaling more than $50 billion. This reflects what Ted describes: DAFs are not passive holding places. They are active vehicles for social good.

Ted does not shy away from tough questions, whether about payout rates, policy, or self-regulation. Instead, he offers a framework for advisors, donors, nonprofits, and policymakers to evaluate DAFs thoughtfully. Most importantly, he never loses sight of the human heart of philanthropy. Across these pages, you will meet parents teaching children generosity, entrepreneurs turning success into impact, and everyday people finding meaning through giving.

In my own public commentary, including in Forbes and CEO Magazine, I have stressed how innovation, speed, and partnerships are changing the landscape of philanthropy. This book gives that momentum substance through clear lessons, practical examples, and a thoughtful path forward.

It is an honor to introduce The DAF Revolution, a timely, insightful, and action-oriented guide for modern philanthropy. May it inspire you to embrace the flexibility, transparency, and democratic values that define today's most effective giving.

Warm regards,
Joe Fisher
President and CEO, Ren

ABOUT THE AUTHOR

Ted Hart is a global philanthropy executive, author, podcast host, and advisor to high-impact donors, foundations, corporations, and nonprofits. He is an Eagle Scout and the proud father of an Eagle Scout, a legacy that reflects his lifelong commitment to service, values-driven leadership, and multigenerational impact. A devoted father, he draws inspiration from the future he hopes to help shape with his two adult children.

From 2012 to 2024, Ted served as President and CEO of CAF America and CAF Canada, scaling global philanthropy from $25 million to nearly $1 billion annually. Under his leadership, more than $4.6 billion in charitable grants were distributed across 135 countries. He previously led major development offices at Johns Hopkins and the University of Maryland Medical Center and, in 2000, founded the International ePhilanthropy Foundation to advance secure and ethical online giving.

Ted holds advanced certifications including ACFRE, CAP®, and CDE®, and is the author of eight books on philanthropy, donor strategy, and nonprofit innovation. A frequent international keynote speaker and respected voice in sector publications, he also hosts The Nonprofit Coach: and Everything DAF! podcast.

A lifelong public servant and community leader, Ted currently serves as Vice Chair of the Howard County Ethics Commission and has led his neighborhood association for more than two decades. He is also an avid cyclist, a volunteer archivist at the U.S. National Archives, and active in the leadership of the Maryland State Chapter of the Sons of the American Revolution.

Is This Really a Revolution?

Is donor-advised philanthropy a revolution or merely the next chapter in a centuries-old story of giving? Traditional charitable trusts, endowments, and foundations have always afforded donors structured ways to give, but donor-advised funds (DAFs) deliver something radically different: real-time, strategic philanthropy that any donor can access, regardless of wealth.

A Fundamental Transformation

Rather than an incremental tweak, DAFs have rewritten philanthropy's playbook. They marry the agility of personal giving with the planning advantages once reserved for the world's largest foundations, empowering donors to recommend grants immediately, respond to urgent needs, and pursue long-range

A donor-advised fund (DAF) is a charitable giving account that lets donors recommend grants and investments over time, with ease and flexibility.

strategies, all from a single account. By collapsing decision-making and distribution timelines, DAFs have made giving more accessible, more strategic, and far more impactful than anything that came before.

The Forces Driving the DAF Revolution

DAFs are reshaping philanthropy through four interlocking forces:

1. **Unprecedented Growth and Scale**
   DAFs now outpace private foundations in both asset growth and annual payout rates, making strategic giving available to virtually any donor.
2. **Technological Innovation**
   Digital platforms, and predictive analytics empower donors to recommend grants in real-time, with data-driven insights, transparency, and precision.

3. **Global Reach**

   By removing geographic barriers, DAFs enable seamless cross-border grantmaking, connecting donors and nonprofits around the world in a truly global philanthropic ecosystem.

4. **Empowered Donor Engagement**

   DAFs transfer decision-making from institutions to individuals and communities, accommodating everything from immediate crisis relief to multi-generational legacy planning, and fostering collaborative models like giving circles.

Total DAF Grants

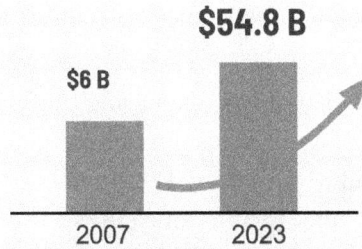

$54.8 B

$6 B

2007   2023

Total DAF Assets

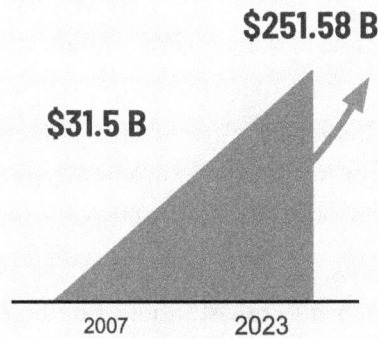

$251.58 B

$31.5 B

2007   2023

Source: National Philanthropic Trust

Together, these forces make DAFs not just another giving vehicle, but a transformational platform that adapts to each donor's unique vision and values. In addition, there is an implicit promise at the heart of every DAF: donors who relinquish legal control of their contribution receive immediate tax benefits, may preserve their anonymity, and retain advisory privileges if they choose. This essential feature helps explain the growing trust placed in DAFs by individuals, families, corporations, and institutions alike.

WHY I WROTE THIS BOOK

Philanthropy stands at an inflection point. DAFs are transforming how dollars reach communities, sustain nonprofits, and empower donors with strategic influence and flexibility. As opportunities multiply at an unprecedented pace, the future of giving has never been more dynamic or impactful.

Yet rapid change can often bring confusion, misinformation, and spark policy debates. This book cuts through the noise by offering clear guidance and a strategic roadmap for using DAFs responsibly. It isn't a defense or a critique, it's a practical guide to unlocking DAFs' full potential for meaningful, lasting impact.

WHO THIS BOOK IS FOR

This book is designed to inform and empower four primary audiences, while remaining accessible to anyone who cares about the future of philanthropy and its potential to shape a better world.

Donors

Donors may include individuals, families, foundations, and corporations seeking to maximize their philanthropic impact. You'll learn how to use DAFs strategically, aligning grants with your values, long-term goals, and community needs.

DAF Sponsors

DAF sponsors are institutions responsible for management, compliance, and distribution of DAF assets. *Chapter 4: Making a Difference: Best Practices for DAFs* unpacks different sponsor types, regulatory obligations, and operational best practices.

Advisors

Financial, philanthropic and legal advisors include wealth managers, tax advisors, estate planners, and attorneys who guide clients through structured giving vehicles. *Chapter 5: The Philanthropic Advisor: Maximizing Donor-Client* Success provides best practices, real-world case studies, and a step-by-step checklist to help advisors integrate DAFs into holistic planning strategies.

Nonprofit Leaders

Nonprofit leaders (executive and board) include organizations aiming to engage DAF donors, cultivate sustainable funding, and adapt to shifting giving trends. *Chapter 6: The Nonprofit Guide to DAFs* offers practical strategies, donor psychology insights, and real-world case studies to help your nonprofit thrive.

Beyond these groups, any reader interested in how philanthropy is evolving will find this book a valuable resource.

BE THE REVOLUTION

We stand in the midst of a transformational moment: the DAF revolution is accelerating, redefining what it means to give and unlocking new possibilities for donors, nonprofits, and communities worldwide.

Whether you're a donor maximizing impact, an advisor guiding philanthropic strategy, a nonprofit leader engaging DAF supporters, or a sponsor stewarding charitable assets, this book offers the insights, strategies, and tools you need to thrive.

But knowledge alone isn't enough; this is a call to action. The revolution continues. Now it's your turn to shape its future.

— Ted Hart

TABLE OF CONTENTS

CHAPTER 1
From Ancient Giving to Modern Generosity

CHAPTER 2
Donor-Advised Funds: Redefining Modern Philanthropy

CHAPTER 3
The History of the Donor-Advised Fund Revolution

CHAPTER 4
Making a Difference: Best Practices for Donor-Advised Funds

CHAPTER 5

The Philanthropic Advisor: Maximizing Donor-Client Success

CHAPTER 6

The Nonprofit Guide to Donor-Advised Funds

CHAPTER 7
International Grantmaking: A Blueprint for Worldwide Giving

CHAPTER 8
Continuing the Revolution: The Future of Donor-Advised Funds

GLOSSARY

FROM ANCIENT GIVING TO MODERN GENEROSITY

EXECUTIVE SUMMARY

Philanthropy has evolved from ancient acts of communal support into a diverse and strategic global system of structured giving. Across cultures and centuries, charitable traditions have reflected the values, needs, and innovations of their time, from religious obligations and civic duties to merchant philanthropy, mutual aid societies, and institutional foundations. This chapter traces that transformation, highlighting how evolving frameworks of governance, motivation, and social responsibility reshaped the flow of charitable capital. In the modern era, new tools like donor-advised funds (DAFs) represent a pivotal advancement, combining flexibility, strategic planning, and accessibility to meet the complex needs of today's donors and the causes they champion.

A TIMELESS HUMAN IMPULSE

"This is a revolutionary moment," says Allison Fine, President of Every.org. "DAFs can unlock so much more generosity, and they haven't yet reached their full potential."[1]

That sense of boundless possibility is nothing new. As Yuval Noah Harari reminds us in his seminal work, *Sapiens: A Brief History of Humankind*,

> Sapiens rule the world, because we are the only animal that can cooperate flexibly in large numbers.[2]

Philanthropy, the instinct to care for others, has been a universal thread throughout human history. From the earliest societies to modern times, giving has remained central to what it means to be human. Harari's insight captures the essence of this impulse: our species' unique capacity for cooperation at scale has enabled us to confront complex challenges through shared effort and mutual support.

> **"Sapiens rule the world, because we are the only animal that can cooperate flexibly in large numbers."**
>
> - Yuval Noah Harari

---

[1] Fine, A. interview by Ted Hart, August 23, 2024.
[2] Harari, Yuval Noah. Sapiens: A Brief History of Humankind. Harper, 2015.

Early Actions for the Common Good

The spirit of cooperation that underpins philanthropy can be traced to the earliest human communities. In hunter-gatherer societies (circa 300,000–10,000 BCE), communal hunting and shared food resources were essential for survival. When a large animal was hunted, its meat was distributed across the group, an early form of resource sharing that reinforced social cohesion and mutual trust.

As societies transitioned to agriculture and urban living, collective efforts became more organized and far-reaching. Agricultural surpluses enabled the construction of granaries, irrigation systems, and storage facilities, public goods that reflected both pragmatic foresight and a community's commitment to shared welfare. These investments often symbolized a leader's responsibility to ensure the well-being of the broader population.

In Ancient Egypt's Old Kingdom (circa 2700–2200 BCE), this sense of continuity extended into the afterlife. Wealthy Egyptians allocated lands and assets to fund ongoing funerary rites for their spirits (*ka*), effectively creating one of the earliest forms of perpetual endowment. These detailed, long-term allocations foreshadow the structured giving models seen in modern philanthropy.[3]

Similar principles emerged in the Indus Valley Civilization (circa 2500–1900 BCE), which pioneered urban planning innovations like drainage and water systems to safeguard public health.[4] In Mesopotamia, the Code of Hammurabi (circa 1754 BCE) encoded protections for widows, orphans, and the poor, an early example of justice-driven social welfare administered through state authority.[5]

Ancient Rome (circa 500 BCE–400 CE) institutionalized civic giving through the munera, elite obligations to fund public works, games, and festivals. While driven by prestige and social pressure, these acts resulted in roads, aqueducts, and entertainment venues that benefited Roman citizens broadly, laying groundwork for philanthropy as a civic duty.[6]

In the Americas, Mesoamerican and Andean civilizations, including the Maya, Aztecs, and Incas, developed sophisticated systems for collective welfare. These included large-scale irrigation, food storage, and clan-based land and education management. Though often state-mandated or tied to religious or imperial

---

[3] Shaw, Ian, ed. The Oxford History of Ancient Egypt. Oxford University Press, 2003.
[4] Kenoyer, Jonathan Mark. Ancient Cities of the Indus Valley Civilization. Oxford University Press, 1998.
[5] Hoffner, Harry A., and Martha T. Roth. Law Collections from Mesopotamia and Asia Minor. Scholars Press, 1997.
[6] Wiedemann, Thomas. Emperors and Gladiators. Routledge, 1992.

authority, these structures embodied the principle of redistribution to sustain the social fabric. Among the Maya, sacred lords (K'uhul ajaw) oversaw temple maintenance and reservoir construction in cities like Tikal.[7] In the Aztec world, calpulli (kinship clans) coordinated land management and ran youth education centers known as telpochcalli.[8] The Inca used the mit'a labor system and qollqa storehouses to redistribute food and resources across the empire.[9]

In East Asia, Confucian ideals shaped charitable norms in ancient China (circa 500 BCE–907 CE). Rulers were expected to act as moral exemplars, funding public works such as flood control systems and supporting kinship-based charitable estates known as yizhuang. Like their counterparts in other regions, these initiatives reinforced social stability through structured care for the community.[10]

Despite the vast differences in time, geography, and governance, these early traditions reveal a shared foundation: the intentional allocation of resources for the collective good. Whether through religious obligation, royal decree, or civic expectation, ancient societies developed frameworks that prioritized community well-being, establishing the earliest roots of organized philanthropy.

Building Blocks of Philanthropy

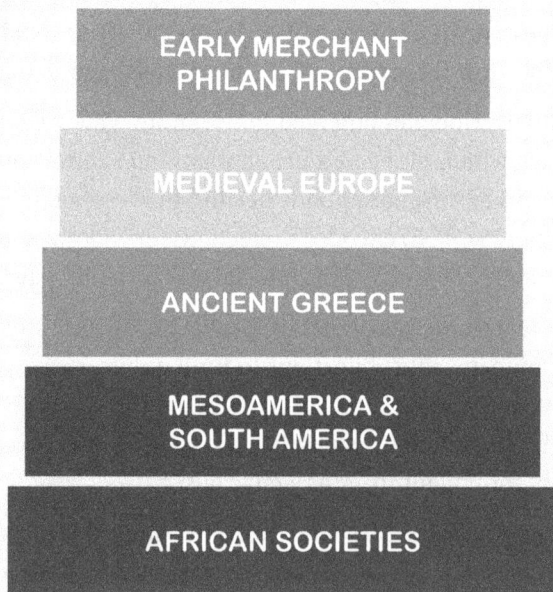

EARLY MERCHANT PHILANTHROPY

MEDIEVAL EUROPE

ANCIENT GREECE

MESOAMERICA & SOUTH AMERICA

AFRICAN SOCIETIES

---

[7] Sharer, Robert J. and Loa P. Traxler, The Ancient Maya, 6th ed. (Stanford, CA: Stanford University Press, 2006).
[8] Maffie, James, Aztec Philosophy: Understanding a World in Motion (Boulder: University Press of Colorado, 2014).
[9] MacQuarrie, Kim, The Last Days of the Incas (New York: Simon & Schuster, 2007).
[10] Ebrey, Patricia Buckley. The Cambridge Illustrated History of China. Cambridge University Press, 1999.

BUILDING BLOCKS OF PHILANTHROPY

Philanthropy, derived from the Greek words philos (loving) and anthropos (humankind), reflects humanity's enduring drive to support others. Across ancient civilizations, communal responsibility and civic duty provided a foundation for structured giving, which has continued to evolve in modern philanthropy.

Early forms of organized giving emerged through public service obligations, taxation, and communal resource distribution. In ancient Greece, civic contributions, such as funding public works, festivals, and warships, were institutionalized through liturgies, which required affluent citizens to finance essential services[11] that benefited society. The concept of redistributive giving was also embedded in many early civilizations.

In medieval Europe, guilds and fraternal organizations played a significant role in philanthropy. These groups pooled resources to provide for members in times of hardship, supporting widows, orphans, and those facing economic difficulty.[12] This model of cooperative giving later evolved into more formalized charitable institutions, leading to the establishment of hospitals, almshouses, and mutual aid societies.

Similarly, many African societies practiced traditional systems of mutual aid and communal sharing. One example is the Ubuntu philosophy in Southern Africa,[13] which emphasizes collective responsibility and interconnectedness, reinforcing the value of community support and resource redistribution. These practices reinforced the idea that the well-being of the individual was tied to the well-being of the group.

A constant across these models has been personal values. Whether through endowments, structured giving, or informal mutual aid, individuals have historically aligned their giving with personal values. In modern times, structured giving vehicles have continued this legacy by allowing donors to align their charitable planning with long-term goals, ensuring contributions are allocated with greater intention and strategic clarity.

By integrating contributions from Asia, Africa, and the West, we recognize the global evolution of philanthropy as a shared human impulse. Across time and geography, these early practices reflect a commitment to social good, establishing

---

[11] Davies, J. K. Democracy and Classical Greece. Harvard University Press, 1993.
[12] Jordan, William Chester. Europe in the High Middle Ages. Penguin Books, 2002.
[13] Tutu, Desmond. No Future Without Forgiveness. Random House, 1999.

principles that continue to shape modern giving models.

These early models of giving, rooted in communal responsibility, state-driven welfare, and cultural or religious imperatives, laid the groundwork for the evolution of philanthropy. As societies grew more complex, so too did the mechanisms of charitable giving. By the 17th and 18th centuries, the rise of merchant classes and the expansion of global trade introduced new dimensions to philanthropy, transforming it into a more structured and influential force in shaping societies.

> **Across time and geography, these early practices reflect a commitment to social good.**

RELIGION, PHILOSOPHY, AND CIVIC GIVING

Throughout history, religious and philosophical traditions provided the earliest moral frameworks for giving, embedding charity not only as a spiritual duty but as a social imperative. In ancient societies, temples and religious institutions managed food, land, and resources, often operating as proto-philanthropic systems.

Across major world religions, charitable giving became formalized as both an ethical obligation and an economic practice:

- Buddhism: emphasizes *dāna* as the first step toward enlightenment, with merit earned by supporting monastics and social causes.[14]
- Hinduism: frames giving as a duty (*dharma*), elevating pure, expectation-free giving (*sattvic dāna*) as spiritually ideal.[15]
- Christianity: evolved tithing from Hebrew law into communal sharing, eventually institutionalizing church obligations and influencing modern tax incentives.[16]

---

[14] Peter Harvey. An Introduction to Buddhism: Teachings, History and Practices, 2nd ed. Cambridge University Press, 2012.
[15] Brockington, John L. The Sacred Thread: Hinduism in Its Continuity and Diversity. Edinburgh University Press, 1981.
[16] Peter Brown, Through the Eye of a Needle: Wealth, the Fall of Rome, and the Making of Christianity in the West, 350–550 AD. Princeton University Press, 2014.

- Islam: mandates *zakat*, a required redistribution of 2.5% of one's wealth to those in need, ensuring social balance.[17]
- Judaism: defines *tzedakah* as a legal and moral requirement, with collective models like *gemach* lending funds and modern Jewish federations reflecting structured, values-based giving.[18]

Alongside religious mandates, philosophical traditions reinforced giving as a civic virtue. In ancient Greece, Aristotle described *philanthrôpia* as a core element of justice and societal well-being. During the medieval period, Islamic *awqaf* and Christian monastic endowments established schools, hospitals, and welfare programs, early examples of durable, community-oriented philanthropy.

Philanthropy is a reflection of society's highest values.

These legacies, sacred and secular, shaped the ethical underpinnings of modern philanthropy. They reinforced the idea that giving should be structured, values-driven, and socially responsive. As Enlightenment ideals emerged and merchant classes gained influence, these traditions gave way to new civic models of charity grounded in reason, responsibility, and long-term impact, paving the way for modern philanthropic institutions.

FROM SACRED OBLIGATION TO SECULAR CIVIC DUTY

As philanthropic traditions matured across civilizations, a pivotal transformation began to take shape in early modern Europe. Religious and philosophical influences gave way to new forms of civic and commercial leadership, as the rise of merchant classes introduced capital, structure, and strategy into charitable giving. This shift marked a transition from obligation to initiative, from spiritual mandate to civic responsibility, laying the groundwork for modern philanthropy's institutional turn.

---

[17] Esposito, John L. Islam: The Straight Path. (Oxford University Press, April 15, 2016.)
[18] Telushkin, Rabbi Joseph. A Code of Jewish Ethics: Volume 1, You Shall Be Holy. Bell Tower, 2006.

17TH–18TH CENTURY MERCHANT PHILANTHROPY

Religious and philosophical traditions had long shaped acts of giving, but the 17th and 18th centuries witnessed a transformative shift: the rise of merchant philanthropy as a systematic, civic-minded force.[19] As Europe's commercial networks expanded, wealthy merchants, armed with newfound wealth and influence, began founding enduring institutions to address social needs, blending medieval charity with early modern pragmatism.

The rise of merchant wealth institutionalized philanthropy, moving beyond ad hoc almsgiving. A pivotal moment came with the 1601 Statute of Charitable Uses, which codified charitable purposes in English law and provided a legal framework that enabled philanthropy to flourish through trusts and endowments.[20] In 1611, London's Charterhouse School was endowed by Thomas Sutton, a merchant whose legacy educated poor boys and cared for the elderly,[21] a model replicated in initiatives like the Marine Society (1756), which trained destitute boys for naval service.[22] Similarly, in the Dutch Republic, merchant elites, including investors in the Vereenigde Oostindische Compagnie (VOC or Dutch East India Company), funded canals, docks, and urban expansions. Amsterdam's 17th-century development, for instance, relied heavily on VOC capital to build infrastructure that served commerce and public needs.[23]

These early efforts laid the groundwork for modern charitable institutions by introducing principles of accountability, governance, and impact measurement, concepts that continue to shape today's philanthropic tools.[24] With the rise of the Enlightenment in the 18th century, philanthropic structures began to evolve again, leading to even more formalized systems.[25]

---

[19] Payton, Robert L., and Michael P. Moody. Understanding Philanthropy: Its Meaning and Mission. Indiana University Press, 2008.

[20] Fishman, James J. "Regulating the Poor and Encouraging Charity in Times of Crisis: The Poor Laws and the Statute of Charitable Uses," Elisabeth Haub School of Law Faculty Publications 406 (2007), https://digitalcommons.pace.edu/lawfaculty/406

[21] Cook, G. H. Charterhouse: A History of the School (London: Hodder & Stoughton, 1951), 22–30.

[22] Rodger, N. A. M. The Command of the Ocean: A Naval History of Britain, 1649–1815 (New York: Norton, 2004), 305–306.

[23] Prak, Maarten. The Dutch Republic in the Seventeenth Century: The Golden Age. Cambridge University Press, 2005.

[24] Bremner, Robert H. Giving: Charity and Philanthropy in History. Routledge, October 27, 2017.

[25] Porter, Roy. The Enlightenment: Britain and the Creation of the Modern World. Penguin Books, 2000.

FROM MERCHANT WEALTH TO MUTUAL RESPONSIBILITY

As wealth from trade and early industrialization began to concentrate, philanthropic responses became more organized. Yet parallel to elite-led giving, community-driven models of mutual aid also gained prominence. Rooted in shared identity and collective support, these societies bridged the gap between traditional charity and formalized philanthropic systems, setting the stage for inclusive, participatory models that echo in today's giving circles and donor collaboratives.

MUTUAL AID SOCIETIES: A BRIDGE TO MODERN PHILANTHROPY

As the Middle Ages gave way to the Enlightenment and industrialization, the foundations of community-based philanthropy evolved with the rise of mutual aid societies in the 18th and 19th centuries. These organizations, often formed by workers, immigrants, and marginalized communities, were established to provide financial and social support in times of need. Mutual aid societies functioned as early safety nets, offering their members assistance for healthcare, funerals, and unemployment, filling gaps left by the lack of formal government welfare systems.[26]

In the United States, African American mutual aid societies, such as the Free African Society, founded in 1787, did more than provide member support. They also strengthened communal ties and laid the groundwork for broader social movements.[27] Similarly, immigrant communities across Europe and North America formed ethnic-based mutual aid organizations to preserve cultural identity while addressing economic and social challenges.[28]

These societies operated on principles of reciprocity, shared responsibility, and collective welfare, echoing themes seen in religious charity but shifting the focus toward secular, community-driven action.[29] The structure and philosophy of mutual aid societies helped inspire later innovations in philanthropy, including fraternal organizations and early foundations.

---

[26] Beito, David T. From Mutual Aid to the Welfare State: Fraternal Societies and Social Services, 1890–1967. Chapel Hill: University of North Carolina Press, 2000.
[27] Nash, Gary B. Forging Freedom: The Formation of Philadelphia's Black Community, 1720–1840. Harvard University Press, 1988.
[28] Salamon, Lester M. America's Nonprofit Sector: A Primer. Foundation Center, 2nd ed., 1999.
[29] McCarthy, Kathleen D.D. American Creed: Philanthropy and the Rise of Civil Society, 1700–1865. University of Chicago Press, 2005.

These cooperative models of giving set the stage for a more formalized philanthropic structure, leading to the rise of modern foundations in the late 19th and early 20th centuries. As wealth accumulated through industrialization, philanthropy became increasingly institutionalized, creating large-scale endowments that would shape the future of structured charitable giving.[30]

The evolution from ancient obligations to modern strategic philanthropy can be seen in key contrasts:

	ANCIENT	**MODERN**
Motivation	Religious duty, societal obligation, royal decree	Driven by personal values, societal impact, and strategic goals
Flexibility	Highly restricted, shaped by societal or religious mandates	High flexibility with donor-driven decisions
Scope	Localized, narrow focus on immediate survival or societal needs	Flexible scope addressing both local and global priorities
Management	Centralized, often hierarchical, under leaders or religious institutions	Decentralized, professionally managed, donor advised
Tax Benefit	None	Substantial tax incentives for charitable giving
Time Frame	Immediate, short-term projects driven by immediate needs	Long-term or immediate, donor-involved planning

This table illustrates the shift from philanthropy being largely driven by religious, political, or elite structures to today's more flexible, donor-driven approaches to giving. Structured charitable tools now offer individuals greater ability to align giving with personal values, strategy, and global impact.

BRIDGING THE ERAS OF GIVING

Between ancient acts of generosity and modern innovations, philanthropy evolved through various structured forms that responded to the societal needs of the time. During the medieval period, religious institutions such as monasteries and waqfs played a central role in managing charitable giving, caring for

[30] Bremner, Robert H. American Philanthropy. University of Chicago Press, 2nd ed., 1988.

the poor, funding education, and supporting community development.[31]

The Renaissance and Enlightenment eras saw the rise of private patronage and early charitable trusts, laying the groundwork for more formalized philanthropy.[32] Wealthy individuals began establishing endowments to fund libraries, universities, and cultural institutions, using philanthropy as a means to create lasting societal impact. The late 19th and early 20th centuries marked a turning point with the creation of structured foundations, such as the Carnegie and Rockefeller Foundations, which institutionalized strategic giving and fostered a philanthropic culture.[33] As philanthropic tools advanced, so did donor expectations. The shift from traditional charity to donor-directed giving enabled more structured and personalized approaches. This transition reflected a broader movement toward strategic, long-term philanthropy, one that empowered individuals to take an active role in shaping their charitable impact.

UNITED WAY AND COMMUNITY-FOCUSED MOVEMENTS

On October 16, 1887, in Denver, Colorado, a group of concerned citizens established the Charity Organization Society to improve their community through cooperative action. They coordinated services and launched a single fundraising campaign to support more than 20 local health and welfare agencies, an approach that laid the foundation for what would become the modern United Way movement.[34] The first Community Chest, widely recognized as the precursor to the United Way movement, was established in 1913 in Cleveland, Ohio.[35] This milestone in coordinated philanthropy was influenced by earlier federated giving models from the Jewish philanthropic community. Notable examples include the Associated Jewish Philanthropies of Boston, founded in 1895, and the United Jewish Social Agencies of Cincinnati, founded in 1896.[36] These early models laid a strong foundation for organized, community-based fundraising and grantmaking structures that continue to shape modern philanthropic practices.

---

[31] Lester K. Little, Religious Poverty and the Profit Economy in Medieval Europe. (Cornell University Press, February 28, 1983.)

[32] Maarten Prak, Citizens Without Nations: Urban Citizenship in Europe and the World, c.1000–1789 Cambridge University Press, 2018.

[33] Oliver Zunz, Philanthropy in America: A History. Princeton University Press, 2014.

[34] By the People: A History of Americans as Volunteers. (Lexington, MA: Lexington Books, 1978.)

[35] National Museum of American History, Smithsonian Institution, "Community Chest Collection," accessed April 21, 2025. https://americanhistory.si.edu/collections/object/nmah_1317530.

[36] Fifty Years of Jewish Philanthropy in Greater Boston: 1895–1945. Associated Jewish Philanthropies. (Boston: The Combined Jewish Appeal, 1945.)

Unlike the mutual aid societies that preceded them, often reliant on informal, peer-driven support networks, the Community Chest introduced a centralized approach to fundraising and resource distribution. By streamlining donor contributions and allocating funds across a network of service providers, this model significantly enhanced efficiency and coordination among charitable organizations.

The success and replication of the Community Chest model ultimately gave rise to the United Way movement, which formalized these principles on a national and eventually global scale.[37] As a bridge between grassroots mutual aid traditions and institutional philanthropy, United Way embodied the power of collective action while embracing strategic coordination. Its structure foreshadowed the scalable and donor-centric approaches that define modern philanthropic tools like DAFs.

By fostering cross-sector collaboration among nonprofits, businesses, faith and mission-based communities, and individuals, the United Way helped pioneer a new era of community-focused philanthropy. This evolution not only strengthened local support systems but also inspired broader innovations in structured giving, demonstrating that efficiency, inclusivity, and shared responsibility can coexist in modern charitable models.

AMERICA'S PHILANTHROPIC TRADITION

America is revered worldwide for its strong philanthropic tradition and leadership. The nation's commitment to charitable giving can be traced back to the early colonial period when mutual aid and religious charity laid a solid foundation.[38] By the 20th century, the establishment of major charitable foundations showcased America's pioneering role in strategic philanthropy. These institutions tackled global issues such as healthcare, education, and poverty, setting a precedent for international philanthropic engagement.

This era of strategic giving also inspired local philanthropic initiatives, one example being the creation of the Roswell P. Flower Memorial Library in my hometown of Watertown, New York. The library was built through the generosity of Emma Flower Taylor (and many local citizens) in memo-

[37] United Way Worldwide. A Brief History of United Way. Accessed October 2024. https://www.unitedway.org/about/history

[38] Generosity Commission. Philanthropy and the American People: The Generosity Commission 2024 Full Report. 2024.

ry of her father, Roswell P. Flower, a Watertown native who served as both a U.S. Congressman and the 30th Governor of New York.[39] It was dedicated in 1904 and quickly heralded as "the most beautiful library in the United States."[40] In 1980, it was added to the National Register of Historic Places, solidifying its status as a cherished cultural and architectural landmark.[41] While Andrew Carnegie was funding libraries across the nation during this period, Watertown's library stood out as the product of local philanthropy, made possible by Emma's transformative gift of $250,000, equivalent to over $9 million today.[42]

This story, deeply rooted in the values of local generosity, is a personal source of inspiration in my own work. As a child growing up in Watertown, I could walk to the library from my grandmother's house after school and during summer breaks. There, the world opened up to me. I spent countless hours exploring its reading rooms, researching school projects and reading about faraway places, planting the seeds for a lifelong journey beyond New York's North Country. That early exposure to knowledge, beauty, and civic generosity helped shape my understanding of philanthropy not just as an act of giving, but as an enduring investment in our community.

Predating the library and standing just blocks away is another local landmark that captures the spirit of civic pride, the monumental bronze statue of Governor Roswell P. Flower. Sculpted by Augustus Saint-Gaudens and unveiled on Labor Day in 1902, the 18-foot-tall monument was funded entirely through local donations.[43]

---

[39] "Roswell P. Flower, Wikipedia: The Free Encyclopedia, Wikimedia Foundation. Accessed February 7, 2025. https://en.wikipedia.org/wiki/Roswell_P._Flower

[40] Library Tour Guide: Roswell P. Flower Memorial Library, Flower Memorial Library, accessed May 2025, https://www.flowerlibrary.org or print brochure (2020s).

[41] Roswell P. Flower Memorial Library, National Register of Historic Places, Ref# 80002632, listed June 19, 1980. U.S. Department of the Interior, National Park Service.

[42] Flower Memorial Library Tour Guide, Flower Memorial Library, Watertown, NY, accessed May 2025. This brochure confirms the gift amount of $250,000. Present-day value calculated using historical CPI data from OfficialData.org: $250,000 in 1904 is equivalent to $9,029,916 in 2025 dollars. https://www.officialdata.org/us/inflation/1904?amount=250000

[43] Governor Roswell P. Flower Monument (1902–Present)," MemoryLn.net, accessed May 2025. https://www.memoryln.net/places/new-york/watertown/monuments/governor-roswell-p-flower-monument-1902-present/

It remains one of the most iconic features of downtown Watertown, standing at the foot of Washington Street near Public Square. Like the library, the monument was not imposed from afar but built by the people of Watertown themselves, reaffirming a community-wide commitment to generosity, beauty, and remembrance. Together, these landmarks shaped my early understanding of how philanthropy, local and strategic, can leave a legacy that enriches generations to come.

Today, the U.S. leads global charitable efforts, with Americans donating over half a trillion dollars annually.[44] This tradition of innovation and generosity underscores America's enduring influence in shaping modern philanthropy. In the 21st century, digital tools have further transformed the philanthropic landscape, expanding access, accelerating donor engagement, and enabling real-time giving through online platforms. These technologies have empowered grassroots campaigns while also enhancing the reach and responsiveness of large philanthropic institutions. Together, they represent a convergence of individual empowerment and institutional capacity, reshaping how charitable dollars flow in today's interconnected world.

THE RISE OF FOUNDATIONS

As industrialization transformed society in the late 19th century, philanthropy evolved from informal charity into a formalized system of strategic giving. The unprecedented wealth generated during this period, coupled with rapid urbanization and stark social inequalities, created a new philanthropic class. Industrial magnates sought to address systemic challenges through structured, large-scale giving, giving rise to the modern foundation. Yet this model did not emerge in a vacuum. Its roots stretch back to medieval European guilds, which pooled resources to support artisans and communities, and to the Islamic waqf system, centuries-old endowment structure funding public goods like schools and hospitals. These early innovations demonstrated the enduring power of organized philanthropy to tackle societal needs. The foundations of the Industrial Revolution built upon these traditions, but with a new emphasis on scalability, professionalization, and measurable impact, setting the stage for today's philanthropic landscape.

---

[44] Lilly Family School of Philanthropy. "Giving USA: U.S. Charitable Giving Totaled $557.16 Billion in 2023." Indiana University–Purdue University Indianapolis, June 25, 2024. Accessed August 21, 2024. https://philanthropy.indianapolis.iu.edu/news-events/news/_news/2024/giving-usa-us-charitable-giving-totaled-557.16-billion-in-2023.html

The emergence of vast fortunes and a heightened awareness of societal issues created fertile ground for philanthropic endeavors. A growing desire for greater involvement in charitable giving led to more sophisticated philanthropic vehicles, allowing donors to play an advisory role in their giving strategies. DAFs emerged as one such tool, designed to offer the benefits of structure and tax efficiency while restoring donor influence and adaptability.

Hillel Korin, President of Korin Development Associates, observes,

> When we talk about DAFs, we're really talking about a tool that has transformed the landscape of charitable giving, bridging gaps between donors and causes worldwide.[45]

> # DAFs have transformed the landscape of charitable giving.
> ## - Hillel Korin

This insight highlights a fundamental shift in modern philanthropy, where giving has moved beyond traditional channels to encourage direct engagement. It reflects the growing demand for more personalized approaches to charitable activities, emphasizing the transformative role of DAFs.

To truly make an impact, we need to ensure that philanthropy is inclusive. DAFs can be a vehicle for that if we allow them to be.[46]

adds Donna Callejon, former Chief Executive Officer at GlobalGiving, emphasizing the importance of inclusivity in modern philanthropy and highlighting how DAFs, as an evolving philanthropic tool, can provide broader access and create more equitable opportunities for individuals to engage with charitable giving.

Federal tax policy also played a defining role in modern philanthropy. After the Civil War–era income tax was repealed in 1872, Congress reestablished a federal income tax in 1913. By excluding charities from taxation, the Revenue Act of 1913 implicitly confirmed their tax-exempt status. Four years later, amidst the financial strains of World War I, the Revenue Act of 1917 introduced the first federal deduction for charitable contributions. That new incentive encouraged wealthy donors to give more generously, and more strategically, paving the way for the formation of major private foundations.

[45] Korin, H. Interview by Ted Hart, September 11, 2024.
[46] Callejon, D. Interview by Ted Hart, September 16, 2024.

The Tax Reform Act of 1969 reshaped modern philanthropy by imposing new accountability measures on private foundations, including prohibitions on self-dealing, limitations on business holdings, and the introduction of a mandated payout requirement. While the Act itself did not specify a precise percentage, subsequent IRS regulations finalized in 1973 established the now-familiar 5% minimum payout rule, requiring private foundations to distribute at least 5% of their investment assets annually for charitable purposes. As Thomas Troyer explains in his retrospective on the 1969 reforms, the payout requirement was part of a broader effort to curb the accumulation of passive assets and ensure foundations were actively fulfilling their charitable missions.[47]

This rule was intended to discourage the indefinite accumulation of assets without corresponding public benefit. It ensured more money reached nonprofits, though some critics argue that it has become a de facto ceiling rather than a floor, with many foundations giving little more than the minimum required. These regulations also reinforced the appeal of DAFs, which provide similar long-term philanthropic benefits but with fewer administrative constraints.

This growing interest in greater donor involvement has fueled the rise of alternative philanthropic vehicles. DAFs, in particular, offer a compelling solution by combining the tax advantages and structure of foundations with streamlined administration and enhanced donor engagement. They empower individuals and families to make strategic philanthropic decisions on their own terms. As Jay Grab, CEO at RealtyGiftFund.Org, explains:

> What I love about donor-advised funds is that they offer individuals and families, especially future generations, the opportunity to get involved in philanthropy. It's not just about giving money; it's about making philanthropy a family conversation and helping the next generation think about who they want to support and why.[48]

DAFs help make philanthropy a family conversation.

- Jay Grab

---

[47] Thomas A. Troyer, "The 1969 Private Foundation Law: Historical Perspective on Its Origins and Underpinnings." The Exempt Organization Tax Review 27, no. 1 (2000): 52–65. National Center on Philanthropy and the Law, NYU School of Law.
[48] Grab, J. Interview by Ted Hart, November 8, 2024.

Rather than replacing foundations, DAFs represent a broader shift in the philanthropic landscape, one that emphasizes donor agency, flexibility, and alignment with personal values. Their accessibility has helped democratize structured giving, enabling more people to participate meaningfully participate meaningfully in charitable impact.

Giving Mirrors Societal Changes

The trajectory of philanthropic giving has always reflected broader societal changes. In early human societies, communal sharing was essential for survival, fostering mutual support and interdependence. As civilizations advanced, the Industrial Revolution brought rapid urbanization and unprecedented wealth concentration, creating complex social challenges that required innovative approaches to giving.

This era saw the emergence of a philanthropic class that recognized the need for more structured mechanisms to address these challenges. Foundations, trusts, and later vehicles like DAFs exemplified this shift, formalizing philanthropy as a strategic response to societal transformation. These innovations were driven by the same timeless principles of generosity and shared responsibility but adapted to meet the needs of an increasingly interconnected and industrialized world.

The rise of DAFs highlights how philanthropy continues to change in response to societal shifts. DAFs embody the modern era's approach to giving while maintaining deep roots in historical practices of community support and collective responsibility. This revolution reflects the enduring role of philanthropy in addressing societal complexities and advancing the common good.

From Industrial Foundations to Digital Frontiers

With the dawn of the 21st century, a new transformation unfolded. Building on the institutional models of the 20th century, technology redefined how donors connect, give, and mobilize. Online platforms, real-time transactions, and data-driven philanthropy marked a shift from centralized models to decentralized, user-directed giving.

The Rise of Digital Philanthropy and the Post-9/11 Shift

The early 2000s brought transformative change with the rise of online platforms and digital tools. These innovations began to democratize philanthropy, allowing individuals from all backgrounds to contribute with ease. Online giving, once novel, quickly became mainstream. However, early efforts required building trust in digital channels. One initiative that played an important role in establishing that trust was the ePhilanthropy Foundation.

In 2000, I co-founded the ePhilanthropy Foundation, one of the first global non-profits dedicated to secure, ethical, and transparent online giving. Our mission was to guide nonprofits in using digital tools responsibly and effectively. When the September 11 attacks occurred, digital giving became a national lifeline. Donations surged through online platforms, fundamentally shifting public perception. What was once experimental became essential.

Supported by partners such as AOL Time Warner Foundation, Yahoo!, Cisco Foundation, and Network for Good, we launched a global education initiative that trained thousands of nonprofit professionals through e-learning courses, in-person seminars, and the pioneering eTour series led by certified ePhilanthropy Master Trainers. Our programs reached cities across the United States, Canada, the United Kingdom, France, India, Italy, and South Africa and produced cornerstone publications, including Fundraising on the Internet (2001), Nonprofit Internet Strategies (2005), and Major Donors (2007), resources that shaped a generation of digital fundraisers.[49]

> # What was once experimental became essential.

What set the ePhilanthropy Foundation apart was its international, inclusive focus at a time when digital fundraising guidance was largely U.S.-centric. We emphasized cross-border collaboration, open-access education, and ethical standards to instill trust in the emerging digital charitable landscape.

Having met the goals, we set out for the foundation we concluded our work in 2008. Yet its legacy endures. Through partnerships with organizations such as NTEN, the Direct Marketing Association of Washington, the Association of Fundraising Professionals (AFP) and the Electronic Frontier Foundation, we

---

[49] The ePhilanthropy Foundation was co-founded by Mark Banbury, Matt Bauer, Vinay Bhagat, Jon Carson, Bob Carter, Michael Cervino, Fred Fournier, Gail Freeman, Ted Hart, Darian Rodriguez Heyman, Nancy Johnson, Mike Johnston, Philip King, Jay Love, Steve MacLaughlin, Bill McGinly, Andrew Mosawi, Bob Ottenhof, David Phillips, Jason Potts, Ric Pratte, AJ Robinson, Bo Rice, Charles Riess, Michael Schreiber, Charles Schultz, Shirley Sexton, Chris Sinton, Steve Sterba, Mark Sutton and Ken Weber.

laid the ethical and operational groundwork for today's vibrant online philanthropic ecosystem. The exponential growth of global digital giving stands as a
lasting tribute to the vision, collaboration, and commitment of the ePhilanthropy
Foundation's founders and contributors.[50]

Since then, digital tools have only expanded. AI-powered analytics help personalize engagement. Blockchain introduces real-time transparency. Fintech apps
enable frictionless micro-donation giving. These innovations build upon the
foundation laid by early pioneers and continue to reshape global philanthropy.

Data from Nonprofit Tech for Good shows that 63% of donors in Canada and
the United States now prefer to give online. Digital platforms not only simplify
giving; they also magnify underrepresented voices. Around the world, up to 41%
of donors say social media is the channel that most inspires their generosity.[51]

Technology has undoubtedly revolutionized giving, yet it builds upon a long
history of philanthropic innovation. The rise of online giving platforms is not
an isolated event but rather the latest chapter in philanthropy's continual adaptation to societal and economic change. Before digital platforms democratized
philanthropy, the 20th century witnessed another transformative shift, one that
placed large-scale institutions at the heart of structured giving. The expansion
of private foundations, the emergence of DAFs, and the integration of corporate
giving programs marked a pivotal moment in modern philanthropy. These shifts
provided the infrastructure that made digital philanthropy's rapid rise possible,
setting the stage for today's flexible and technology-driven giving landscape.

The rapid growth of online giving was made possible by the infrastructure built
in the 20th century. As donors demanded flexibility and real-time engagement,
structures like DAFs emerged to meet these expectations, combining the agility of
individual giving with the long-term strategy of institutional philanthropy.

DAFs are not just a refinement of existing models; they represent a revolution
in giving. They empower donors of all levels with foundation-like capabilities,
real-time adaptability, and global reach. Unlike previous models, DAFs decen-
tralize philanthropic decision-making, placing unprecedented tools in the hands
of donors who advise on grants, while preserving the benefits of structured

[50] "ePhilanthropy Foundation," Philanthropy News Digest, Candid. Accessed May 2025. https://philanthro-
pynewsdigest.org/features/on-the-web/ephilanthropy-foundation
[51] Nonprofit Tech for Good, Global Trends in Giving Report. (Sponsored by Fundraise; produced by Nonprofit
Tech for Good, September 14, 2020). https://www.nptechforgood.com/reports/

giving. As Sampriti Ganguli of Ganguli Associates LLC and former CEO of Arabella Advisors observes:

> Philanthropy has always been about moving hearts. But what's shifting now is the expectation for it to also move minds and resources efficiently. [52]

This shift underscores the transformative role of DAFs. They offer a modern answer to an ancient interest in giving generously and strategically, building a legacy of meaningful change.

THE JUGGERNAUT BEGINS

Centuries of philanthropic evolution set the stage for a true game-changer: DAFs. Unlike institution-led trusts or foundations, DAFs put donors in the driver's seat, offering simplicity, strategic options, and global reach, all from a single account. They adapt to each donor's needs, streamlining grant recommendation and distribution timelines into real-time and making thoughtful, impactful giving more accessible than ever.

Today, DAFs collectively hold over $250 billion in assets and distribute more than $54 billion in grants annually, reshaping how dollars flow into communities and how nonprofits sustain themselves.[53]

The spark for this revolution came in 1931, followed by decades of regulatory refinements, most notably the Tax Reform Act of 1969 and the Pension Protection Act of 2006, which transformed that early concept into today's modern DAF. By the 1990s, national sponsors and emerging digital platforms further broadened access, cementing DAFs as indispensable tools in the ever-evolving landscape of modern philanthropy.

KEY TAKEAWAYS

Philanthropy has always been a reflection of humanity's enduring desire to support others, from early communal sharing and religious obligation to structured civic duties and merchant-led giving. Across time and cultures, charitable practices evolved in response to changing societal needs, forming a rich global tradition that laid the groundwork for today's structured giving models. The rise of mutual aid societies, institutional foundations, and digital platforms all

---

[52] Ganguli, S. Interview by Ted Hart, September 11, 2024.
[53] National Philanthropic Trust. 2024 Donor-Advised Fund Report. Published November 2024. https://www.nptrust.org/reports/daf-report/

"Philanthropy has always been about moving hearts."

- Sampriti Ganguli

demonstrate how philanthropy continuously adapts to new challenges while preserving its fundamental aim: to strengthen communities and advance the common good.

Today's DAFs don't just extend philanthropy's legacy; they upend it. By marrying foundation-level rigor with individual agility, DAFs unleash generosity in real-time, empower donors to target impact with surgical precision, and tear down the barriers that once confined giving to the privileged few. Whether in response to an urgent crisis or through long-term strategic planning, donors now command unprecedented speed, flexibility, and scale. As this chapter has demonstrated, DAFs represent a true revolution, reshaping the flow of charitable capital and setting a bold new standard for generosity in our interconnected world.

In the next chapter, we move from history to practical applications, unpacking how DAFs operate and why they're reshaping the future of giving. From legal structures and sponsor responsibilities to strategic features that distinguish DAFs from other vehicles, *Chapter 2: DAFs: Redefining Modern Philanthropy* offers the essential knowledge donors, advisors, and nonprofit leaders need to engage with these tools effectively. Understanding how DAFs function is the first step toward using them with confidence, purpose, and impact.

DAFs: Redefining Modern Philanthropy

EXECUTIVE SUMMARY

This chapter examines how Donor-advised funds (DAFs) have democratized charitable giving, making it easier for individuals and families to participate in philanthropy with minimal barriers and impressive impact. By comparing DAFs with private foundations and charitable trusts, it highlights their simplicity, cost-effectiveness, and cross-generational appeal. This chapter also addresses common critiques while emphasizing how donor autonomy and technology continue to drive innovation, even as regulatory frameworks evolve. As a result, DAFs have become foundational to inclusive, adaptive, and impactful philanthropy, enabling both immediate action and enduring legacy. They offer donors flexible, efficient giving tools while preserving privacy and grant-advising privileges, a structure that reflects the implicit promise at the heart of the DAF model.

> # DAFs surpassed first $100 billion in assets in just 30 years, a milestone that took community foundations nearly 100 years to achieve.

WHAT IS A DAF? WHAT IS A DAF SPONSOR?

In simple terms, a DAF is a flexible and efficient way for donors of all types to engage in charitable giving. But what exactly is a DAF, and how does it work? According to the IRS regulations, a DAF is defined as a fund or account that meets three key criteria:

- **Donor-linked:** The fund is tied to contributions from a named individual, family, or entity.

- **Sponsor-controlled:** A qualified 501(c)(3) organization (the DAF sponsor) legally owns and manages the account.

- **Advisory privileges:** The donor (or their designee) may recommend grants to IRS-recognized charities or validated charitable causes and may recommend investments, though the DAF sponsor has final approval.[54]

---

[54] Internal Revenue Service, Revenue Procedure 2023-10, 2023-2 Internal Revenue Bulletin 123 (January 9, 2023).

This definition provides the legal framework for what has become one of the fastest-growing philanthropic tools in modern history, surpassing $100 billion in assets in just three decades[55], a milestone that, Lester Salamon notes, took community foundations nearly a century to achieve.[56]

DAFs are charitable accounts set up under the umbrella of a public charity with IRS designation 501(c)(3), which serves as the DAF sponsor. DAF sponsors generally fall into three categories: national, community, and faith/mission-based (single-issue charities), a framework explored in more detail in *Chapter 5: The Philanthropic Advisor: Maximizing Donor-Client Success.* In addition to grant-making flexibility, many DAF sponsors offer donors the ability to recommend investment strategies for their funds. This allows donors to align their philanthropic capital with their broader values. They support appropriate investments, ensure that grants go to eligible nonprofits or validated charitable causes, and honor donor philanthropic intentions. Importantly, many DAF sponsors also enable donors to designate successors, allowing for the management of the funds to be passed down to future generations. This feature supports the continuity of philanthropic efforts across multiple generations, enhancing the appeal of DAFs.

MISCONCEPTION:
DAFs hoard funds instead of granting them.

REALITY:
78% of accounts grant regularly, with mean payouts of 18% of assets.

Source: 2024 National Study on Donor-Advised Funds (DAFRC)

For donors, a DAF offers a combination of simplicity and flexibility. By making an irrevocable contribution, eligible for a tax receipt, they can recommend grants to their chosen charitable causes at a comfortable pace. This structure enables them to concentrate on their philanthropy without the burden of administrative

[55] National Philanthropic Trust. 2018 Donor-Advised Fund Report, November 13, 2018. https://www.nptrust.org/wp-content/uploads/2018/11/2018-DAF-Report.pdf

[56] Lester Salamon. America's Nonprofit Sector: A Primer, 4th ed. (New York: Foundation Center, 2021.)

complexities. The funds can also be invested, potentially growing over time and increasing their philanthropic impact, while remaining fully dedicated to charitable purposes. In this way, DAF sponsors act as professional administrators between the donor's financial resources and their charitable goals. Whether the aim is to support local initiatives, address global challenges, or build a multigenerational legacy of giving, DAFs offer a modern and highly adaptable solution.

How DAFs Are Transforming Philanthropy

Over the past decade, DAF assets have surged from approximately $57 billion to over $250 billion, as reported in *Barron's*, based on research from the National Philanthropic Trust.[57] This extraordinary growth underscores DAFs' increasing appeal as a philanthropic vehicle, offering donors greater flexibility, efficiency, and accessibility.

Critics have raised concerns that DAFs stockpile charitable contributions delaying or avoiding distributing charitable funds to operating nonprofits. However, the data tells a different and compelling story. Year after year, DAFs have distributed funds at rates four to five times higher than the rate granted by private foundations. Despite having no legally mandated distribution requirement, DAF donors regularly support nonprofits at a scale and speed that surpass many traditional philanthropic structures. Their giving reflects not stagnation, but active, sustained generosity.

Sampriti Ganguli, Ganguli Associates LLC and former CEO of Arabella Advisors, underscores the broader impact of this growth, emphasizing that DAFs are not just financial tools, but enablers of a more inclusive philanthropic landscape:

> DAFs are not just financial vehicles; they are gateways that democratize giving. They allow people who might not consider themselves philanthropists to engage meaningfully with causes they care about.[58]

By lowering barriers to entry and offering unparalleled flexibility, DAFs have transformed philanthropy, making charitable giving more accessible to a broader range of donors than ever before.

Although DAF contributions and grants fluctuate with economic conditions, their long-term trajectory remains strong. Even during profound crises, such as

---

[57] Schultz, Abby. "Donor-Advised Funds Are a Boon to Major Nonprofits, Study Finds." Barron's, July 23, 2024. Access date August 15, 2024. https://www.barrons.com/articles/donors-who-give-through-dafs-tend-to-be-generous-contributors-study-finds-83f0ac8f
[58] Ganguli, S. Interview by Ted Hart, September 11, 2024.

the COVID-19 pandemic, which disrupted financial markets, donor behavior, and nonprofit operations, DAFs continued to provide substantial funding to charities. This demonstrated their resilience as a stabilizing force in philanthropy when communities needed it most.

A TOOL FOR ALL DONORS

A persistent myth suggests DAFs are exclusively for high-net-worth individuals. Yet research from the Donor-Advised Fund Research Collaborative reveals that 49% of all DAF accounts hold less than $50,000 in assets demonstrating a broad appeal to everyday donors. This data directly challenges the perception of DAFs as tools only for the ultra-wealthy. Instead, it highlights their role in democratizing philanthropy: many require no minimum contribution, and all simplify complex giving processes. DAFs empower donors at all wealth levels to participate in strategic, long-term giving.[59]

What makes this finding particularly significant is how it reflects a fundamental shift in philanthropic access. While it's true that wealthy donors do contribute substantial assets to DAFs, and their large accounts often dominate aggregate dollar figures, the reality is that DAFs have quietly become one of the most democratic tools in modern philanthropy. Many DAF sponsors have eliminated minimum contribution requirements entirely.

MISCONCEPTION: DAFs are only for the ultra-wealthy.

REALITY: 49% of DAFs hold less than $50K in assets.

Source: 2024 National Study on Donor-Advised Funds (DAFRC)

Others keep thresholds deliberately low, opening the doors to middle-income donors who previously lacked access to structured giving vehicles.

---

[59] Donor-Advised Fund Research Collaborative. 2024 National Study on Donor-Advised Funds, February 2024. https://www.dafresearchcollaborative.org/national-study

This accessibility revolution has been supercharged by digital innovation. User-friendly platforms now allow donors of all means to establish funds, recommend grants, and track their charitable impact with unprecedented ease. The implications are profound. As DAFs shed their elitist image, they're emerging as perhaps the most scalable tool for disciplined, long-term charitable planning. John Brothers, President, T. Rowe Price Foundation and T. Rowe Price Charitable, reinforces this inclusivity:

> How do we ensure that DAFs, as a donor option, are as inclusive as they can be for all different segments of society...ensuring that donors of all different levels have the ability to get tax breaks and some of the utility that DAFs provide?[60]

This push for greater accessibility aligns with a key advantage of DAFs: donor empowerment. Reynolds Cafferata, Partner at Rodriguez, Horii, Choi & Cafferata, LLP, highlights this shift:

> The beauty of DAFs is they offer both a way to democratize philanthropy and a mechanism for strategic giving that wasn't available before. The flexibility they provide has the potential to elevate the impact of smaller donors in meaningful ways.[61]

As donor engagement increases across all income levels, advancements in technology are further enhancing accessibility and impact. Digital tools are transforming how donors interact with DAFs, providing seamless giving expriences and greater insight into philanthropic effectiveness.

MISCONCEPTION:
Most DAF grants are made anonymously.

REALITY:
Only 4% of DAF grants are made anonymously.

Source: 2024 National Study on Donor-Advised Funds (DAFRC)

---

[60] Brothers, J. Interview by Ted Hart, August 19, 2024.
[61] Cafferata, R. Interview by Ted Hart, September 11, 2024

A MORE INCLUSIVE GIVING EXPERIENCE

Beyond their tax efficiency and investment benefits, DAFs have redefined the philanthropic experience by making giving more accessible, engaging, and inclusive. With DAFs now at the forefront of charitable giving, it is essential to understand the factors fueling their growth. These include not only favorable tax treatment and cost efficiency but also an evolving donor landscape that demands flexibility, values alignment, and hands-on engagement. Increasingly, donors are choosing DAFs not just as financial vehicles but as platforms for deeper participation.

There is an implicit promise embedded in the design of donor-advised funds: by relinquishing legal control, donors receive immediate tax benefits and the right to remain anonymous. This promise protects freedom of speech and freedom of religion, cornerstones of American charitable life.

There is an implicit promise at the heart of every donor-advised fund: donors who relinquish legal control of their contribution receive immediate tax benefits, may preserve their anonymity, and retain the ability to advise grants. This structure empowers individuals to give with confidence, supporting causes aligned with their values while maintaining privacy and strategic flexibility.

The rapid rise of DAFs is driven not just by their structural advantages but by these deeper, human-centered dynamics. Fred Kaynor, Managing Director, Relationship Management, Marketing and Partnerships, DAFgiving360, informs us:

> Next-generation donors demand innovation, alternative grant mechanisms, collaborative philanthropy, and deeper engagement. They don't just want to give; they want to participate in how their giving creates change.[62]

The convergence of tax incentives, technology, cost efficiency, and donor engagement has positioned DAFs as a transformative force in modern philanthropy.

---

[62] Kaynor, F. Interview with Ted Hart, June 2, 2025.

MULTIGENERATIONAL ENGAGEMENT AND LEGACY GIVING

One of the most powerful yet often overlooked strengths of DAFs is their ability to foster intergenerational engagement. More than financial tools, DAFs serve as vehicles for transmitting values, nurturing a shared culture of philanthropy, and building lasting legacies. Families increasingly use DAFs to bring generations together, empowering younger members to participate meaningfully in charitable decisions while honoring the experiences and intentions of senior generations.

CASE STUDY: THE BRADBURY FAMILY

A compelling example from Fidelity Charitable highlights how one multigenerational family used a DAF to unify their philanthropic vision. After selling their business, David and Nancy Bradbury established a DAF and invited their sons and grandchildren to help recommend grants. Together, they supported causes that reflected both shared and individual passions, including food insecurity, healthcare, domestic violence prevention, and educational access.

By involving younger family members in these decisions, the Bradburys created a space for purpose-driven dialogue and aligned action. As David Bradbury reflected, "It's been very rewarding to see our children and our grandchildren become involved in this process." The experience not only deepened family bonds but also cultivated a philanthropic legacy that will endure across generations.[63]

A GENERATIONAL LENS ON PHILANTHROPY

Effectively engaging donors across generational lines means understanding the different motivations, values, and expectations each group brings to philanthropy. DAFs are uniquely suited to bridge these differences by offering flexible, personalized, and technology-enabled solutions that resonate with every age group.[64]

- **Baby Boomers (Born 1946–1964)**
  Often focused on legacy, Boomers are drawn to the efficiency and impact of DAFs. Their giving reflects long-standing commitments to causes like education, healthcare, and the arts. Many use DAFs to

---

[63] Fidelity Charitable. Growing the Family Philanthropy Tree. Fidelity Charitable, 2021. https://www.fidelitycharitable.org/content/dam/fc-public/docs/insights/growing-the-family-philanthropy-tree.pdf

[64] Adapted in part from insights in Generation Impact: How Next Gen Donors Are Revolutionizing Philanthropy (Goldseker & Moody, 2017) and "Engaging the Next Generation in Giving" (Philanthropy Focus, 2024), with additional framing on the use of DAFs across generations.

initiate family succession plans and value-sharing conversations, to aid
in carrying their philanthropic vision forward.

- **Generation X (Born 1965–1980)**
  Strategic and pragmatic, Gen X donors align their giving with long-
  term goals and often include their children in philanthropic decisions.
  DAFs enable them to lead by example, modeling shared values and
  cultivating a family-wide culture of engagement.

- **Millennials (Born 1981–1996)**
  Insights from the *Millennial Impact Report,* based on over 10 years of
  research with 150,000 young adults, confirm that Millennials are redefining the expectations of philanthropy. This generation favors causes
  over institutions, values real-time impact, and expects flexibility in
  how they give. They treat all their assets, money, time, social networks,
  as equally valuable contributions to a cause. Digital fluency and peer
  influence play critical roles in their engagement, with many motivated
  to donate or volunteer because of friend or co-worker participation.
  These values align directly with the strengths of DAFs, which offer the
  personalized, accessible, and collaborative tools Millennials increasingly demand.[65]

- **Generation Z (Born 1997–2012)**
  As digital natives, Gen Z donors are drawn to innovation, transparency, and participatory giving. They gravitate toward DAFs with
  intuitive, mission-aligned features that reflect their deep commitment
  to what they value most and community-based outcomes.

- **Generation Alpha (Born 2013–Present)**
  Still in their formative years, Generation Alpha represents the future
  of philanthropy. Raised in a hyper-digital, socially conscious world,
  they are poised to engage with philanthropy through gamified experiences, AI-driven tools, and immersive storytelling. Early involvement,
  through family grantmaking activities and value-based learning, can
  prepare them for future leadership in giving.

---

[65] Feldmann, D., & Thayer, A. Understanding how millennials engage with causes and social issues: Insights from 10 years of research working in partnership with young Americans on causes today and in the future (also known as 10 Years Looking Back) Millennial Impact Project, July 26, 2019. https://www.themillennialimpact.com

MOVING BEYOND TRANSACTIONAL GIVING

DAFs offer the structure and adaptability needed to unify philanthropic goals across generations. Whether Boomers are focused on legacy, Gen X on strategy, Millennials on measurable impact, or Gen Z and Alpha on innovation and transparency, DAFs provide the infrastructure to meet each where they are, while keeping family and values at the core.

This capacity to adapt makes DAFs powerful tools for fostering intergenerational dialogue and collaboration. Through shared decision-making, storytelling, and inclusive planning, DAFs help families move beyond transactional giving to cultivate a shared sense of purpose, helping families pass their philanthropic traditions on to future generations.

BUILDING A CULTURE OF PHILANTHROPY

By democratizing access to giving, encouraging inclusive family participation, and supporting innovative engagement, DAFs do more than enable individual generosity, they cultivate lasting cultures of philanthropy. Building on the intergenerational strategies just explored, DAFs provide tools that allow families, individuals, and communities to sustain meaningful philanthropic practices over time.

As barriers to entry fell, donors and sponsors alike began embracing digital and collaborative approaches to deepen impact and strengthen community bonds. Whether through family meetings, educational workshops, collaborative grant-making, or impact-focused investments, DAFs help donors of all ages engage in causes they care about. This reflects a broader transformation in the philanthropic landscape, from elite-driven institutions to dynamic, value-based ecosystems grounded in accessibility and long-term impact.

TECHNOLOGY AND INNOVATION

Technology has become a driving force behind the evolution of DAFs, enhancing the donor experience while expanding access, personalization, and transparency. Once limited to paper forms and manual grant cycles, many modern DAFs now offer seamless, digital-first experiences that meet the expectations of a new generation of donors.

Modern DAFs are developing ways to merge charitable giving with personal identity in ways unimaginable just a decade ago. No longer content with passive checkbook philanthropy, today's donors increasingly demand the same level of personalization from their charitable vehicles that they expect from their streaming services or investment accounts.

DAFs merge giving and identity in ways unimaginable just a decade ago.

At the heart of this transformation lies sophisticated digital architecture that allows donors to weave their deepest values into every aspect of their giving. Many sponsors now offer curated investment pools where charitable dollars can grow in alignment with specific principles, for example, faith-based portfolios screened according to religious guidelines, values-based funds that curate grantmaking in alignment with personal values, or mission-driven options laser-focused on areas of great need. This change represents a fundamental shift: the period between contribution and grant distribution is no longer a values-neutral holding pattern, but an extension of the donor's mission.

The personalization extends beyond investment choices. Machine learning algorithms now analyze past giving patterns to surface new causes a donor might support, automatically recommending disaster relief funds when hurricanes strike or highlighting local food banks during economic downturns. Custom dashboards transform abstract generosity into tangible impact, allowing donors to track exactly how their growing philanthropic "nest egg" translates into meals served, scholarships funded, or acres preserved.

This change perfectly mirrors the expectations of rising generations. Recent data reveals near-universal interest in values-aligned finance among younger donors. For example, 97 percent of Millennials and 99 percent of Gen Z investors actively seek sustainable options, with over 90 percent citing ESG offerings as decisive factors in platform selection. For these donors, the segregation of financial growth from social impact feels increasingly archaic. They expect their philanthropic dollars to work as intentionally as their personal investments, earning returns that are measured not just in percentages but in lives changed. The implications are profound. As DAF platforms evolve from transactional tools to holistic expressions of personal identity, they are creating new opportunities for donors to live their values at every stage of the giving process. This is not merely about convenience; it is about fundamentally reimagining what it means to be a philanthropist in the 21st century.[66]

REAL-TIME IMPACT AND DEEPER ENGAGEMENT

One of the most transformative outcomes of technology is the ability for donors to see and shape their impact. From real-time grant tracking to AI-powered insights into social outcomes, donors are now equipped with data and tools that encourage sustained involvement and strategic decision-making. As Jane Wales, Co-Chair, National Generosity Commission and Vice President, The Aspen Institute, observes:

> Donors today are not just writing checks; they want to be partners in change, to see how their contributions make a tangible impact.[67]

This deeper engagement fosters a sense of ownership and satisfaction, transforming donors into collaborators in social progress. The digital infrastructure of today's DAFs makes this level of involvement not only possible but expected.

"Donors today are being much more creative with their giving," explained Rebecca Moffett, President of Vanguard Charitable. "As a key partner in their philanthropy, we've needed to evolve and modernize right alongside them to help maximize their impact."

Moffett outlined four ways donor-advised funds are meeting, and in many cases exceeding, the needs of modern philanthropists:

1. **Personalization and Flexibility**
    "Donors are looking for tools that reflect their values, timelines, and impact goals," she noted.
    "The inherent structure of a DAF offers flexible granting — they can recommend grants at any time, 24/7. At Vanguard Charitable, in just a few clicks, they can even set up recurring giving, which amplifies

[66] Morgan Stanley Institute for Sustainable Investing. (2025). Sustainable Signals: Individual Investors 2025. April 30, 2025. https://www.morganstanley.com/sustainableinvesting
[67] Wales, J. Interview with Ted Hart, September 11, 2024.

their impact over time. And they can easily bring in multiple generations to pass down a legacy of giving."

2. **Agility in Crisis Response**
    "DAFs are incredibly responsive to urgent giving — what we often
    call 'unexpected giving.' Donors are leveraging their DAFs, as they
    absolutely should be, to respond quickly to crises and emerging needs.
    DAFs are becoming vehicles for agile philanthropy, which is
    so important."

3. **Impact Measurement Through Data**
    "To determine the outcomes of their giving, donors need robust
    reporting. They want access to dashboards and metrics that reflect how
    their philanthropy is making a difference."

4. **Technology-Enabled Decision Support**
    "Modern DAFs provide digital guidance and real-time access to data
    that help donors make enhanced, high-quality decisions with their
    grantmaking. That's why we invest so heavily in technology — to
    empower donors with the tools they need."[68]

A MORE DYNAMIC FUTURE

The integration of technology has not only streamlined administration but also
opened new avenues for donor expression, collaboration, and accountability.
With tools that adapt to donor goals and reflect real-time feedback from the
philanthropic landscape, DAFs are no longer passive funding vehicles; they are
dynamic platforms for action.

As technology transforms how donors interact with their charitable assets, it
also opens new opportunities to optimize those assets strategically. For many
donors, digital platforms not only enhance the giving experience but also make
it easier to align philanthropy with personal financial planning. This intersection
of innovation and financial strategy is especially clear in how DAFs are used
for tax optimization, a critical consideration for donors seeking both impact
and efficiency.

---

[68] Moffett, R. Interview with Ted Hart, August 4, 2025.

Cost-Effective Professional Management

DAFs unlock powerful tax-optimization tools to maximize both philanthropic impact and tax efficiency. As Amir Pasic, Eugene R. Tempel Dean at Indiana University Lilly Family School of Philanthropy, observes,

> By allowing donors to separate the timing of their tax benefits from their philanthropic decisions, DAFs give them more space to be deliberate in how they make distributions. This approach can lead to more targeted and impactful philanthropy, both for the recipients and for the donors' sense of fulfillment.[69]

For a full playbook of strategies, including IRS limits, carryforward rules, and worked examples, see *Chapter 5: The Philanthropic Advisor: Maximizing Donor-Client Success.*

> **DAFs lead to more targeted and impactful philanthropy.**
>
> - Amir Pasic

One of the key advantages of DAFs is the access they provide to professional management at a fraction of the cost of other structured giving options. DAF sponsors handle complex tasks such as investment management, grant distributions, and IRS reporting. These streamlined services allow donors to focus on their philanthropic goals while benefiting from expert oversight and increased efficiency.

DAF sponsors also simplify administrative tasks and provide donors with access to tailored investment options, managed under the sponsor's fiduciary oversight, enhancing their appeal to donors. As Elinor Carson Ramey, Partner at Lowenstein Sandler, explains,

> One reason DAFs have grown so quickly is the autonomy they offer donors. In a sense, they provide the freedom of a private foundation without the administrative burden.[70]

As Dan Heist, Assistant Professor at Brigham Young University observes,

> DAFs have shifted the power dynamics in philanthropy, enabling individuals at all income levels to participate meaningfully in giving.[71]

This combination of autonomy and inclusiveness illustrates how DAFs meet the needs of both new and seasoned donors. This shift underscores the transformative

---

[69] Pasic, A. Interview with Ted Hart. November 5, 2024.
[70] Ramey, E.C. Interview with Ted Hart. December 11, 2024.
[71] Heist, D. Interview with Ted Hart, September 17, 2024.

role of DAFs in democratizing access to charitable giving and fostering a culture in which philanthropy becomes a meaningful and integral part of more lives.

PHILANTHROPIC FLEXIBILITY

"DAFs give donors the ability to separate the timing of the gift from the application of the gift, explains John Bennett, Partner at Simpson Thacher & Bartlett LLP.

This flexibility allows people to make thoughtful, long-term philanthropic plans, even when wealth comes in a windfall, giving them time to decide how to best use charitable funds."[72]

This insight reflects a growing emphasis on donor strategy within modern philanthropy. DAFs enable individuals to engage with their giving through careful planning, aligning their charitable intentions with broader financial goals.

This strategic alignment might also be guided by trusted financial or legal advisors. These professionals provide critical expertise in areas such as tax optimization, regulatory compliance, impact investing, and legacy planning. They can help donors craft giving strategies that integrate with estate and wealth management.

As a result, DAFs have become more than just a convenient tool; they are a core component of modern philanthropic planning. Their flexibility allows advisors and donors to work together in designing customized approaches that respond not only to immediate opportunities but also to long-term impact goals.

DAFs have also been at the forefront of innovation in charitable investment. Many sponsors now offer mission-aligned or impact investment portfolios, enabling donors to grow their funds while supporting nonprofit, social or community goals. In some cases, charitable capital can be deployed into affordable housing, re-

> # DAFs give donors time to decide how to best use charitable funds.
> — John Bennett

---

[72] Bennett, J. Interview by Ted Hart, November 13, 2024.

newable energy, or community development initiatives, generating both social returns and financial performance. This alignment of values and impact is especially important to younger donors, who are increasingly shaping the future of philanthropy.

As Megan Hyman, President and CEO, Dallas Jewish Community Foundation, observes,

> The next generation of philanthropists is looking for tools that are flexible, transparent, and impactful, DAFs meet those demands perfectly.[73]

As younger donors embrace DAFs for their flexibility and alignment with values, the cumulative effect is profound. These accounts collectively represent a growing force for targeted impact. Sir John Low, former Group Chief Executive of Charities Aid Foundation (CAF), adds,

> Philanthropy, when done thoughtfully, can be a powerful catalyst for social change. DAFs have a unique role in this as they allow for flexible, targeted impact.[74]

Together, these insights show how combining structural simplicity with innovative deployment tools enables DAFs to reshape the mobilization of charitable capital, offering donors a streamlined yet powerful way to align purpose with performance.

Building on this flexibility, DAFs enable donors to adapt their giving strategies in real-time by responding to urgent needs, pursuing multi-year initiatives, and aligning grants with long-term goals.

DAFs also empower donors to diversify their philanthropic efforts, supporting multiple causes or shifting focus as their priorities change. Shannon Scott, SVP and Chief Financial Officer at NCTA, The Internet & Television Association, offers this vivid description:

> Donor-advised funds are like the Swiss Army knives of philanthropy; they offer donors' flexibility, efficiency, and the ability to respond quickly to societal needs.[75]

DAFs are uniquely positioned to bridge the gap between traditional philanthropy and modern donor expectations. They offer unparalleled flexibility and adaptability, which is essential in today's dynamic giving environment.

---

[73] Hyman, M. Interview by Ted Hart, September 25, 2024.
[74] Low, Sir John. Interview by Ted Hart, September 12, 2024.
[75] Scott, S. Interview with Ted Hart, October 7, 2024.

Karen Heald, Vice President at Fidelity Charitable®, adds:

> DAFs offer donors the flexibility to be generalists, allowing them to be dynamic in their giving and integrate philanthropy into a broader portfolio approach.[76]

DAFs allow for dynamic giving.

- Karen Heald

Beyond flexibility in grantmaking, DAFs can accept a wide variety of assets, including cash, stocks, and more complex contributions, like real estate. This versatility allows donors to optimize their tax benefits while retaining advisory rights over how and when their contributions are distributed. Together, these features make DAFs a powerful tool for donors seeking dynamic and responsive ways to achieve their philanthropic goals.

SCALABILITY AND GLOBAL REACH

DAFs stand out for their remarkable ability to scale. Whether a donor is contributing a few hundred dollars or managing a complex, multimillion-dollar philanthropic portfolio, DAFs offer a flexible platform that accommodates all levels of giving. This adaptability makes them uniquely suited for individuals, families, foundations, and corporations seeking a streamlined approach to charitable impact.

As the philanthropic landscape becomes increasingly global, many DAF sponsors have evolved to meet the needs of donors who wish to support causes beyond U.S. borders. From disaster relief in Southeast Asia to educational initiatives in sub-Saharan Africa, cross-border giving is now a routine part of many DAF strategies. To enable this, sponsors navigate the complex regulatory environment that governs international philanthropy.

Although DAF sponsors are classified as 501(c)(3) public charities and are not subject to the same stringent international grantmaking rules as private foundations, many voluntarily adopt Expenditure Responsibility (ER), which involves tracking how grant funds are used, and Equivalency Determination (ED), a process to confirm that a foreign nonprofit operates similarly to a U.S. public charity as their international grantmaking protocols.

---

[76] Heald, K. Interview with Ted Hart, August 27, 2024.

These safeguards do more than follow best practices. They align with IRS guidance, including Revenue Procedure 2017-53 (which superseded Revenue Procedure 92-94) and related Treasury regulations, which require grants to further charitable purposes. Failure to comply can result in excise taxes on improper distributions under Internal Revenue Code §4966, and in extreme cases, could jeopardize the organization's tax-exempt status. The risks are serious, and responsible sponsors act accordingly.

For donors, this means they can support global causes with ease and compliance. Whether addressing climate change, global poverty, or access to education, DAFs provide the infrastructure and confidence needed to make a meaningful difference across borders. As Donna Callejon, former CEO of GlobalGiving, aptly noted:

> DAFs have transformed from simple giving accounts into strategic tools for long-term philanthropic impact.[77]

That journey, from local giving tools to global philanthropic engines, underscores why DAFs are increasingly viewed not just as convenient financial instruments but as vital components of a connected and compassionate world. For a comprehensive guide to international grantmaking, see *Chapter 7: International Grantmaking: A Worldwide Blueprint.*

Evolving Donor Expectations

As the DAF revolution continues, donor expectations are shifting across all generations, reflecting broader societal changes in how philanthropy is approached. Fundraisers increasingly view DAF donors not just as generous, but as thoughtful, strategic participants in long-term impact. As reported by the Donor Advised Fund Research Collaborative:

> Fundraisers viewed DAFs as a sign that the donor was philanthropically savvy, ready for more complex conversations.[78]

This insight reinforces how DAFs are not just giving tools, but signals of philanthropic intent, making them especially relevant for multigenerational, values-aligned giving strategies.

---

[77] Callejon, D. Interview with Ted Hart, September 16, 2024.
[78] Reinventing the Cycle: Adapting Relationship Fundraising for Donors Who Use DAFs, Donor Advised Fund Research Collaborative. May 5, 2025. https://www.dafresearchcollaborative.org/dafrc-research

DAFs have become vital components of a connected and compassionate world.

DAFs foster this deeper engagement by enabling families to define shared priorities, pass down philanthropic values, and involve younger generations in meaningful, strategic giving. This multigenerational approach not only strengthens family bonds but also sustains a culture of philanthropy across time.

TRANSPARENCY AND ACCOUNTABILITY

Transparency in grant distributions remains a contentious issue. Unlike private foundations, which must publicly disclose their donors, DAFs can allow donors to remain anonymous when making charitable gifts. Supporters argue that this protects donor privacy and prevents unsolicited funding requests from nonprofits. However, critics contend that such limited disclosure makes it more challenging to track philanthropic funding flows and assess how quickly and effectively DAF funds are distributed to working charities.[79] Jacqui Valouch, Head of Wealth Planning and Philanthropy at Deutsche Bank Wealth Management, underscores a key tension in the DAF transparency debate:

> The biggest challenge with DAFs is transparency. How do you ensure that the funds are being used effectively without putting too much burden on the donor or the charity?[80]

This concern reflects a broader discussion in philanthropy: how to balance donor autonomy with accountability in charitable distributions without placing undue burden on donors or charities.

DAF sponsors are required to report aggregate financial data, including total assets, contributions, and grants made, on Schedule D of IRS Form 990. However, individual grant details remain confidential, offering only a broad overview of DAF activity without full disclosure. While this structure helps preserve donor privacy, some policymakers worry it reduces transparency regarding the flow of charitable dollars.

---

[79] WINGS. (2015). Transparency and Accountability in Philanthropy and Private Social Investment: Toolkit. Worldwide Initiatives for Grantmaker Support. Accessed March 25, 2025. https://wingsweb.org
[80] Valouch, J. Interview with Ted Hart, August 8, 2024.

Beyond transparency, some critics also raise concerns about delayed distributions. However, they often overlook the benefit of DAF flexibility in responding to emergencies or structuring multi-year commitments. IRS rules count transfers from private foundations into DAFs as qualifying distributions, and inactivity policies adopted by nearly all sponsors ensure that funds do not sit idle.[81]

Ray Madoff, Professor at Boston College Law School, has called this a regulatory loophole, noting:

> Private foundations can meet their 5% payout requirement by giving to donor-advised funds. This undermines the very division between private foundations and public charities.[82]

As DAFs continue to evolve, the conversation around regulation will remain dynamic. Balancing donor flexibility with public accountability is essential to maintaining the integrity and effectiveness of this powerful philanthropic tool. Thoughtful donors may choose to retain funds for strategic reasons, whether to respond to future crises, support long-term initiatives, planning for grantmaking during retirement or engage in multigenerational planning. Honoring that autonomy, while upholding clear standards of compliance, is vital to preserving the trust and impact DAFs bring to modern philanthropy.

PSYCHOLOGICAL AND EMOTIONAL BENEFITS

DAFs not only provide financial and logistical advantages but also offer psychological and emotional rewards. A key benefit is the sense of fulfillment and purpose that donors experience when supporting causes, they deeply care about. Engaging in philanthropy through DAFs allows donors to align their charitable contributions with personal values and passions, fostering a stronger emotional connection to the act of giving.

Dr. Russell James, Professor of Charitable Financial Planning at Texas Tech University, explains in his book *The Storytelling Fundraiser* that breaking apart the giving process into multiple steps, such as the initial fund contribution, fund management, and eventual grant distribution, can enhance the donor's experience of generosity. Each phase provides an opportunity for the donor to feel charitable, making DAFs more appealing than one-time gifts. This multi-step process heightens the emotional satisfaction donors derive from their philanthropy,

[81] Donor-Advised Funds: Payout Trends, Inactivity Policies, and Accessibility (Philanthropy Roundtable, 2025).
[82] Madoff, R. Interview with Ted Hart, December 11, 2024.

encouraging ongoing engagement and reinforcing their sense of purpose."[83]

For many donors, the ability to give anonymously is not simply a preference, it is rooted in deeply held values. Some seek to avoid public attention, while others are guided by religious teachings that emphasize humility or discretion in giving. For example, within Judaism, anonymous giving is considered a higher form of charity; in other traditions, protecting one's identity is essential to avoid undue praise or pressure. Still others may wish to shield their giving choices from political, familial, or professional

> # The structure of DAFs makes them more appealing for donors than one-time gifts.
>
> - Dr. Russell James

scrutiny. DAFs provide a safe, legal, and respectful mechanism for such donors to honor their convictions. This protection is not only ethical but constitutional: the U.S. Supreme Court, in *NAACP v. Alabama* (1958), affirmed that anonymity in association and expression, including philanthropy, is a fundamental element of freedom of speech.[84] Together, freedom of religion and freedom of speech underscore why anonymous giving must be preserved.[85] Howard Husock, a senior fellow in Domestic Policy Studies at the American Enterprise Institute (AEI), reminds us,

> Anonymity represents the pinnacle of charitable giving, embodying humility and focusing solely on the impact rather than recognition.[86]

This deeper connection is further enhanced by the donor's ability to track and understand the impact of their giving through DAFs. Real-time grant tracking gives donors a tangible link between their contributions and the difference they make, reinforcing their emotional satisfaction. With greater involvement in their charitable grantmaking, donors experience a heightened sense of joy, pride, and accomplishment.

---

[83] James, R. N., The Storytelling Fundraiser: The Brain, Behavioral Economics, and Fundraising Story. (August 26, 2021).

[84] NAACP v. Alabama, 357 U.S. 449 (1958). The Court held that compelled disclosure of membership in advocacy groups could infringe upon the freedom of association protected by the First Amendment. For additional context, see *Chapter 3: The History of the DAF Revolution.*

[85] Maimonides, Mishneh Torah, Laws of Charity 10:7–14. In Jewish tradition, anonymous giving ranks among the highest forms of charity because it protects both the giver's humility and the recipient's dignity.

[86] Husock, H. Interview with Ted Hart, November 22, 2024.

A national study on DAFs confirms that a significant share of DAF grants is structured as general operating support, enabling nonprofits to allocate resources where they are most needed. This flexible funding model can enhance the effectiveness of donations and may foster greater donor engagement by reinforcing the sense that contributions are making a meaningful, unrestricted impact.[87]

Together, freedom of religion and freedom of speech affirm that anonymous giving is not merely a preference, it is a protected form of expression that enables donors to honor their convictions, uphold their privacy, and experience the emotional and spiritual fulfillment that philanthropy can bring.

DAFs are becoming mainstream tools for generosity.

PROMOTING COMMUNITY AND SHARED PURPOSE

DAFs facilitate collaborative philanthropy by encouraging collective action through giving circles and donor collaboratives. Jay Weisman, Principal at the Legacy Philanthropy Group, emphasizes this collaborative power:

> DAFs are a great way to foster collaborative giving, whether it's within a family or through corporate philanthropy and employee engagement.[88]

These platforms enable individuals to pool resources and make joint decisions about grant distributions, amplifying the impact of individual contributions and strengthening bonds within communities. As documented by the Collective Giving Research Group, giving circles, one of the most common forms of collaborative philanthropy, have tripled in number over the past decade, engaging more than 150,000 donors and granting over $1 billion.[89]

Advances in technology have further enhanced these efforts, enabling donors to connect across geographic boundaries. Online platforms offer real-time tracking of donations and their impact, deepening donor engagement and reinforcing the shared sense of purpose that defines modern philanthropy.

---

[87] Donor Advised Fund Research Collaborative (DAFRC). National Study on Donor Advised Funds. February 5, 2024. https://www.dafresearchcollaborative.org/dafrc-research
[88] Weisman, J. Interview with Ted Hart, August 29, 2024
[89] Collective Giving Research Group. The State of Giving Circles Today: Overview of New Research Findings. (2017). Accessed February 12, 2025. https://philanthropy.iupui.edu/gendergiving

Many DAF sponsors also provide opportunities for donors to engage beyond financial contributions. Educational workshops, volunteer events, and networking sessions connect donors with nonprofit organizations and fellow philanthropists, fostering a deeper understanding of the causes they support. These initiatives enhance donors' sense of fulfillment and promote a vibrant, interconnected philanthropic ecosystem.

INSPIRING INNOVATIVE APPROACHES TO PHILANTHROPY

The inherent flexibility of DAFs has catalyzed groundbreaking approaches to charitable giving, fostering creativity and collaboration among donors and organizations. Specialized funds, often managed by DAF sponsors, tackle pressing social challenges, such as climate change, public health, and social justice. These funds leverage collective donor expertise and pooled resources to address these issues more effectively and at scale.

DAFs have also fueled the growth of innovative philanthropic models, including venture philanthropy and impact investing. Venture philanthropy applies the principles of venture capital to philanthropy, where donors provide strategic funding and guidance to social enterprises or nonprofits aiming for scalable impact. For instance, a DAF might support a startup developing affordable clean energy solutions, while donors contribute non-financial expertise, such as mentoring founders, sharing technical resources, or connecting them to relevant networks. These engagements can enhance impact without conferring control or personal benefit. DAF sponsors increasingly offer investment portfolios aligned with causes like renewable energy or sustainable agriculture, allowing donors to grow their charitable assets while advancing their values.[90] Fidelity Charitable has committed to doubling its impact-investing support to nonprofits, from $500 million to $1 billion by 2028, through a combination of recoverable grants and grants to impact-focused organizations. This commitment reflects the rising demand for philanthropic strategies that generate both social and financial returns, positioning DAFs as increasingly central to mission-aligned philanthropy.[91]

A growing trend in DAF use is fostering multigenerational philanthropy. Families are increasingly involving younger members in decision-making, using

---

[90] Amouyel, A., & van der Stricht, C. Using donor-advised funds to invest in early-stage entrepreneurs. Stanford Social Innovation Review. (September 13, 2019.) https://ssir.org/articles/entry/using_donor_advised_funds_to_invest_in_early_stage_entrepreneurs
[91] Fidelity Charitable, 2025 Giving Report (Boston, MA: Fidelity Investments Charitable Gift Fund, 2025), Accessed April 21, 2025. https://www.fidelitycharitable.org.

DAFs as a practical tool to instill charitable values and create enduring legacies. This approach not only strengthens family bonds but also supports a sustained commitment to philanthropy across generations.

Anne Hennessy, Director at Foundation Source, highlights how younger donors are reshaping philanthropy with a heightened sense of intentionality and accountability:

> I think donor-advised funds will continue to grow... Younger donors are much more thoughtful about who they're giving to, why they're giving to them, how much they're giving, and how do I know that those funds are being used again in a timely basis for the purpose for which it's given.[92]

For example, a family may hold annual meetings to collectively determine grant recipients, giving younger members a platform to voice their priorities and actively shape the family's philanthropic vision. This deliberate engagement moves charitable giving beyond the financial transaction toward a strategic and value-driven process that spans generations.

By encouraging collaboration, strategic innovation, and intergenerational engagement, DAFs have become an essential instrument in today's philanthropy. They empower donors to think beyond traditional giving models, fostering a dynamic culture of generosity that responds flexibly to evolving social challenges.[93]

KEY TAKEAWAYS

By lowering barriers to entry, DAFs empower individuals across income levels to give strategically, meaningfully, and in alignment with their values. Their accessibility, cost-effectiveness, and flexibility have positioned DAFs as compelling alternatives to more complex giving vehicles such as private foundations.

DAFs resonate across generations. They offer transparency and tech-enabled engagement for Gen Z, flexible purpose-driven tools for Gen X and Millennials, and legacy planning opportunities for Baby Boomers. Technology is driving their adoption, as digital platforms and real-time insights enhance the donor experience and enable measurable, mission-aligned giving.

---

[92] Hennessy, A. Interview with Ted Hart, August 19, 2024.
[93] Adapted from The Next Generation of Philanthropy (2025), Indiana University Lilly Family School of Philanthropy.

At their core, DAFs offer a unique promise: donors receive immediate tax benefits, retain the ability to recommend grants over time, and may preserve anonymity. This combination of trust, autonomy, and impact continues to drive their widespread appeal.

As DAFs grow in influence, questions around transparency, distribution pacing, and regulatory oversight have sparked healthy debate. These discussions reflect a maturing field responding to evolving public expectations. As the chapters ahead explore, DAFs are not only adapting to these challenges but actively shaping what inclusive, scalable, and collaborative philanthropy looks like in the 21st century.

THE HISTORY OF THE DAF REVOLUTION

Note to the Reader: *This chapter is intentionally designed as a comprehensive reference on the historical development of donor-advised funds (DAFs). For those seeking a high-level overview before diving deeper, the Executive Summary below provides a concise introduction. Readers interested in current applications and strategic best practices may wish to continue with Chapter 4: Making a Difference: Best Practices for DAFs.*

EXECUTIVE SUMMARY

The history of DAFs is one of continuous innovation, legal refinement, and growing accessibility. Beginning with the first DAF at the New York Community Trust in 1931, this chapter explores how legislative developments defined DAFs and distinguished them from private foundations. The rise of national sponsors in the 1990s expanded participation and helped mainstream structured philanthropy. Technological innovations and impact investing further streamlined giving and aligned donor values with strategic philanthropic tools. By tracing the intersection of tax policy, donor behavior, and regulatory oversight, this chapter illustrates how DAFs developed into a flexible, efficient, and widely used philanthropic vehicle.

SETTING THE STAGE FOR THE DAF REVOLUTION

Donor-advised funds did not emerge in isolation. Their rise was shaped by a century of evolving tax policy, cultural shifts in giving, and innovations that made philanthropy more accessible and strategic. From charitable tax deductions established in the early 20th century to modern digital platforms that simplify giving, a foundation was laid for an entirely new way to engage donors. As the Indiana University Lilly Family School of Philanthropy notes,

> While motivations for giving are diverse and personal, tax incentives significantly influence donation frequency and size.[94]

Yet policy alone didn't drive the DAF revolution. The real transformation came in the 1990s, when national sponsors like Fidelity Charitable, Vanguard Charitable, and Schwab Charitable opened structured giving to a broader population. For a deeper understanding of how DAFs function, see *Chapter 2: DAFs: Redefining Modern Philanthropy.* As Elinor Carson Ramey, Partner at Lowenstein Sandler LLP, observes:

---

[94] Hall, P. D. Inventing the Nonprofit Sector and Other Essays on Philanthropy, Voluntarism, and Nonprofit Organizations. Baltimore, MD: Johns Hopkins University Press, 1992.

The creation of national DAF sponsors like Fidelity and Schwab opened the door to a whole new set of philanthropists who had never been exposed to DAFs before.[95]

This development broadened structured giving from high-net-worth circles to donors of all financial backgrounds.

Digital tools and mission-aligned investments accelerated this shift, making it easier than ever to manage giving, pursue impact, and engage family members in long-term philanthropic planning. This infrastructure would prove essential during the COVID-19 pandemic, when DAFs served as vital reservoirs of ready-to-grant capital. For a deeper look at how DAFs continue to innovate with impact investing and digital tools, see Chapter 4: *Making a Difference: Best Practices for DAFs*. This chapter traces the key milestones of the DAF Revolution that have turned DAFs into a defining force in philanthropy.

> "The creation of national DAF sponsors ... opened the door to a whole new set of philanthropists.
>
> - Elinor Carson Ramey

THE OFFICIAL HISTORY OF THE DAF REVOLUTION

1931–1969: DAFs: The Early Years

The origins of DAFs trace back to 1931, when William Slocum Barstow and his wife Françoise Duclos Barstow established the first-known DAF at The New York Community Trust (NYCT). Their vision was to create a charitable vehicle that allowed them to both support their favorite charities during their lifetimes and leave a legacy to support those charities in perpetuity.[96]

The creation of the first DAF occurred during the economic downturn of the Great Depression, a time of widespread unemployment and heightened financial disparities, straining existing charitable institutions. Traditional charitable institutions struggled to meet the overwhelming demand for social services, while government programs were still in their infancy. In this context, the Barstows'

---

[95] Ramey, E.C. Interview with Ted Hart, December 11, 2024.
[96] The New York Community Trust. William and Françoise Barstow: Pioneers in Charitable Giving. The New York Community Trust. Accessed September 17, 2024. https://thenytrust.org/news/william-and-francoise-barstow/

innovation offered a new way for private individuals to contribute to public welfare, bridging the gap between personal philanthropy and community needs.

The creation of DAFs was more than a financial breakthrough; it sparked discussion about the balance between government regulation and private philanthropy in shaping social welfare. Lila Corwin Berman explains,

> ...The emergence of a specific financial structure called the Donor-Advised Fund (DAF) developed in tandem with postwar efforts to extend the private sector's reach into public welfare through new forms of charitable giving and voluntarism.[97]

This innovation reflected the continuation of a longstanding ideological tension in American life, one that weighed state-based regulation against the desire to preserve individual philanthropic freedoms. The 1931 NYCT model can be seen as an early example of how public charities provided donors with a vehicle that allowed for structured giving while avoiding some of the administrative burdens imposed on private foundations.

Despite this innovation, DAFs remained largely obscure and underutilized for decades, overshadowed by private foundations and the United Way's highly centralized workplace giving campaigns. Private foundations, typically established by high-net-worth individuals, became the dominant model for structured philanthropy, offering donors significant control over their giving. Meanwhile, United Way campaigns gained widespread public trust by simplifying charitable giving for the broader public, primarily attracting payroll-deducted, unrestricted gifts from middle-income donors through employer-sponsored programs. This consolidation of philanthropic dollars into a single community fund model further marginalized the visibility and growth of early DAFs.

Throughout the mid-20th century, DAFs primarily operated within community foundations and religious federations offering donors a structured yet flexible approach to charitable giving. However, without clear regulatory oversight, skepticism persisted among financial professionals and donors, who questioned the legitimacy and governance of DAFs. Meanwhile, charitable tax deductions incentivized philanthropic contributions but largely benefited private foundations.[98] By the 1960s, concerns over self-dealing and tax avoidance within

---

[97] Berman, L. C. Donor advised funds in historical perspective. In The Rise of Donor-Advised Funds: Should Congress Respond? 2015.
[98] Collins, C., and Flannery, H. "The Rise of the Monster DAFs." Institute for Policy Studies, (August 2, 2022.) https://ips-dc.org/the-rise-of-the-monster-dafs/

private foundations sparked calls for reform. The lack of regulatory guidance around DAFs contributed to their slow adoption, as potential donors hesitated to engage with a philanthropic model that lacked formal recognition in tax law. This period set the stage for pivotal legislative reforms, beginning with the Tax Reform Act of 1969.[99]

1958: NAACP v. Alabama

The U.S. Supreme Court ruled in *NAACP v. Alabama* that compelled disclosure of donor identities could deter civic engagement and expose individuals to intimidation and harassment. This decision established a foundational legal precedent affirming the constitutional right to anonymous association and giving, a principle that would later influence the design of modern philanthropic tools.

This landmark ruling reinforced a truth that transcends law: the right to give anonymously is not only constitutional, but also moral and, for many, sacred. Religious traditions across faiths have long recognized the spiritual and ethical value of discreet giving. In *Mishneh Torah* (Laws of Charity 10:7–14), Maimonides ranks anonymous giving as the second-highest form of *tzedakah*, surpassed only by empowering the poor toward self-sufficiency.[100] Christian teachings often cite Matthew 6:3 as a call to humility in generosity: "Do not let your left hand know what your right hand is doing."[101] Islamic teachings on sadaqah (charity) also encourage anonymous giving to protect the dignity of the recipient and the sincerity of the donor's intention.[102] When considered alongside *NAACP v. Alabama*, these

> # The right to give anonymously is not only constitutional, but also moral and, for many, sacred.

traditions form a cross-cultural and constitutional affirmation of the donor's right to discretion, an ideal now embedded in the very framework of DAFs.

---

[99] Wadsworth, Homer C. "Private Foundations and the Tax Reform Act of 1969." Law and Contemporary Problems, vol. 39, no. 4, 1975, pp. 255–274.

[100] Maimonides, Mishneh Torah, Laws of Charity 10:7–14. In this ranking of eight levels of giving, anonymous donations are ranked second only to empowering the recipient to become self-sufficient.

[101] Matthew 6:3, Holy Bible, New Testament. This verse encourages discreet giving as a form of spiritual humility.

[102] Qur'an 2:271 and Hadith sources in Sahih al-Bukhari. Islamic charity (sadaqah) is encouraged to be given privately to preserve the dignity of the recipient and sincerity of the donor.

1969: THE TAX REFORM ACT OF 1969

The Tax Reform Act of 1969 marked a pivotal moment in philanthropy by formalizing and expanding the regulatory framework for private foundations. Although the distinction between public charities and private foundations existed prior to the Act, the 1969 reforms introduced significantly stricter oversight of private foundations. These included prohibitions on self-dealing, limitations on business holdings, and a requirement for annual charitable distributions. While the legislation did not specify a payout percentage, subsequent IRS regulations finalized in 1973 established the 5% minimum distribution rule, a standard that continues to shape philanthropic practice today. These reforms were designed to enhance transparency, discourage the accumulation of idle charitable assets, and ensure consistent support for public benefit.

Although DAFs were not explicitly addressed in the Act, the increased regulatory scrutiny on private foundations helped pave the way for the growth of alternative giving structures. As components of public charities, DAFs were exempt from many of the burdens imposed on private foundations, including the 5% payout mandate. This distinction, combined with greater administrative simplicity and donor flexibility, made DAFs an increasingly appealing option for individuals and families seeking to engage in strategic philanthropy without the complexity of foundation management.[103]

Ray Madoff, Professor at Boston College Law School provides insight into the congressional intent behind these regulations, stating:

> In 1969, when private foundation rules were established, Congress recognized that donor control over charitable funds delayed the public benefit. Donor-Advised Funds reintroduce that delay.[104]

These restrictions increased oversight and accountability for private foundations but also inadvertently positioned DAFs as a more flexible and administratively simple alternative, free from similar payout obligations. While proponents view this flexibility as a strength, critics argue it can delay the flow of funds to active charitable use.

---

[103] John G. Simon, The Regulation of Private Foundations: A Reconsideration. Paper presented at the Conference on Philanthropy, National Center on Philanthropy and the Law, New York University School of Law, October 28–29, 1999. https://www.nyu.edu/philanthropy/pdf/Conf1999_Simon_Final.pdf
[104] Madoff, R. Interview with Ted Hart, December 11, 2024.

The Emergence of DAFs as an Alternative

The Tax Reform Act's stricter oversight of private foundations prompted some donors to explore DAFs as a more streamlined charitable vehicle. Unlike private foundations, which require complex legal structures, annual IRS Form 990-PF filings, and compliance with a mandatory 5% payout and excise tax rules, DAFs offer an efficient, professionally managed alternative with significantly lower administrative costs.

Ron Ransom, CEO of the American Endowment Foundation observes,

> Contrary to the misconception that DAF sponsors hoard assets, national DAFs consistently distribute grants at a rate three times higher than private foundations.[105]

This statement underscores a critical yet often overlooked point: while DAFs are sometimes criticized for stockpiling philanthropic capital, data and practitioner insight alike suggest a pattern of active, high-volume grantmaking that surpasses the legal minimums required of private foundations. This sponsor-level behavior reinforces DAFs' reputation as nimble and responsive philanthropic vehicles, offering donors a streamlined and impactful alternative to the more adminis-tratively complex and slower-moving private foundation model.[106]

This flexibility makes DAFs especially attractive to individuals and families seek-ing strategic philanthropy without the overhead. Donors are not required to manage investment portfolios or hire advisors themselves; instead, most DAF sponsors offer professionally managed investment pools, along with the option to recommend customized strategies aligned with the donor's values. This en-ables donors to engage in long-term philanthropic planning while maintaining advisory privileges over the timing and direction of their grants.

1972: Treasury Department Regulations on Pooled Accounts

In 1972, the U.S. Treasury Department introduced new rules that clarified how community foundations and other public charities could manage pooled funds, accounts that combine contributions from multiple donors. These regulations, part of the broader framework established by the Tax Reform Act of 1969, were a key step in the evolution of DAFs.

---

[105] Ransom, R. Interview with Ted Hart, December 5, 2024.
[106] National Philanthropic Trust. 2024 Donor-Advised Fund Report. Jenkintown, PA: National Philanthropic Trust, 2024, https://www.nptrust.org/reports/daf-report

At the time, community foundations were growing in popularity, but there was uncertainty about how they could structure their funds without losing their status as public charities. The 1972 regulations addressed this by allowing community foundations to create component funds, separate accounts within a larger pool of charitable assets, without violating IRS rules. This was important because it ensured that these foundations could continue to receive broad public support while offering donors more flexibility in how their contributions were used.

One of the most significant aspects of these regulations was that they allowed private foundations, charitable organizations typically funded by a single donor or family, to transfer their assets into a community foundation's component fund. This transfer was permitted as long as the donor did not impose overly restrictive conditions on how the funds were used. This flexibility made community foundations more attractive to donors and helped them grow their resources, laying the groundwork for the future expansion of structured philanthropic giving.

The 1972 regulations did not explicitly mention DAFs, but they recognized the concept of pooled charitable accounts managed by charitable organizations. They also hinted at the idea of donor influence in charitable distributions, which would later become a defining feature of DAFs.

In essence, these regulations were a turning point for community foundations, enabling them to operate more effectively and attract more donors. Over time, this framework became essential in shaping the growth of DAFs, both within local community foundations and national charitable institutions. Though DAFs were not formally defined until much later, the 1972 regulations marked an important step in recognizing donor-advised structures as a legitimate and tax-compliant way to support charitable causes.

In retrospect, these rules helped establish the functional DNA of what would become DAFs, allowing public charities to accept donor-contributed assets while maintaining donor involvement and IRS compliance.[107]

The Evolving Role of DAF-Like Structures (1970s–1980s)

Throughout the 1970s and early 1980s, community foundations and religious federations, such as Jewish federations, continued to develop pooled charitable giving models. The 1972 Treasury guidance, codified in Treasury Regulation §1.170A-9(f)(11)(v)(B), clarified how public charities, including community

---

[107] U.S. Department of the Treasury, Treasury Regulations §1.170A-9(e) (1972), clarifying pooled fund rules for public charities under the Tax Reform Act of 1969.

foundations, could maintain pooled charitable funds while still qualifying as publicly supported organizations under IRS rules.

As early as the mid-20th century, Jewish federations pioneered innovative philanthropic models that allowed donors to contribute assets to communal funds while retaining advisory privileges over grant distributions. These community-based funds not only provided a practical framework for structured giving within public charities but also influenced future regulatory decisions regarding DAFs.

Norman Sugarman, a prominent tax attorney, played a crucial role in securing IRS rulings that clarified the tax treatment of philanthropic funds housed within public charities, paving the way for the eventual formalization of DAFs.[108] Sugarman's legal arguments, particularly in the case of the Cleveland Jewish Federation, helped establish a framework that allowed donor-advised structures to operate as public charities, a model that national DAF sponsors would later adopt in the 1990s.

By demonstrating how pooled charitable funds could align with IRS public charity requirements while still enabling donor influence, Jewish federations set a legal and operational precedent that shaped national DAF sponsors in later decades.

However, despite these innovations, DAFs remained a relatively small segment of the philanthropic landscape throughout the late 20th century. Most high-net-worth donors still favored private foundations, which, despite their increased regulatory burdens, offered greater donor control over charitable assets.

At the same time, growing concerns over tax avoidance and philanthropic transparency led to heightened government scrutiny of private foundation activities. These concerns culminated in major policy reports, such as those by the Filer and Peterson Commissions, which examined nonprofit sector oversight.[109]

1986: The Tax Reform Act of 1986

The Tax Reform Act of 1986 (TRA86) introduced sweeping changes to the U.S. tax code, aiming to simplify the system, broaden the tax base, and eliminate loopholes.[110] It reduced the top marginal income tax rate from 50% to 28%, con-

---

[108] Berman, Lila Corwin. Donor Advised Funds in Historical Perspective. The Rise of Donor-Advised Funds: Should Congress Respond? Urban Institute, 2015. https://lira.bc.edu/files/pdf?fileid=b66abca8-4fad-4040-afb6-c87a575280bf

[109] Brilliant, E. L. Private charity and public inquiry: A history of the Filer and Peterson commissions. Indiana University Press, January 22, 2001.

[110] Tax Reform Act of 1986, Public Law No. 99-514, 100 Stat. 2085.

solidated tax brackets, and raised the lowest tax rate from 11% to 15%. To offset the rate reductions, the Act eliminated numerous deductions and tax shelters and required a larger number of people to pay taxes.[111]

A significant consequence of the Act was its impact on charitable giving. Although the itemized deduction for charitable contributions remained intact, the increased standard deduction led to fewer taxpayers itemizing. According to the Joint Committee on Taxation, the percentage of taxpayers itemizing deductions dropped from 30% in 1986 to 21% in 1988.[112] This resulted in a 3.2% decline in total charitable donations in 1987.[113] Middle-income donors, particularly those earning between $50,000 and $100,000, reduced their contributions by 5–10%.[114]

For smaller donors who no longer benefited from itemizing, the Act inadvertently diminished their incentive to give, creating challenges for nonprofits that traditionally relied on broad-based, smaller contributions. However, for wealthier donors, who continued to itemize, the charitable deduction remained a valuable tool.

TRA86 did not directly address DAFs. It did imposed stricter reporting obligations and payment deadlines on private foundations, increasing their administrative burdens. This shift made DAFs, which are typically easier to manage and not subject to the same stringent regulations, a somewhat more attractive option for donors seeking flexibility, lower cost and reduced regulatory concerns. Additionally, TRA86's reduction of the top marginal income tax rate led to a decrease in the tax incentives associated with charitable giving. In response, some donors may have sought more efficient giving vehicles, such as DAFs, to maximize their philanthropic impact under the new tax laws.

The TRA86 accelerated the adoption of DAFs as a tax-efficient and flexible vehicle for charitable giving.[115] By preserving the charitable deduction but reducing the number of itemizers, the Act encouraged an early shift toward DAFs, which offered professional asset management, administrative simplicity, and a powerful alternative to private foundations.

[111] C. Eugene Steuerle, The Tax Decade: How Taxes Came to Dominate the Public Agenda (Washington, DC: Urban Institute Press, 1992), Chapter 6.

[112] Joint Committee on Taxation, Estimates of Federal Tax Expenditures for Fiscal Years 1988–1992, JCS-7-88 (Washington, DC: Government Printing Office, 1988).

[113] Giving USA Foundation, Giving USA 1988: The Annual Report on Philanthropy for the Year 1987 (Chicago, IL: American Association of Fundraising Counsel, 1988).

[114] William C. Randolph, "Dynamic Income, Progressive Taxes, and the Timing of Charitable Contributions," The Journal of Political Economy 103, no. 4 (1995): 709–738.

[115] David Joulfaian, The Behavioral Responses of Donors to the Tax Reform Act of 1986 (Washington, DC: U.S. Department of Treasury, 1990), 14–17.

1987: National Foundation Court Case

The National Foundation, Inc. v. United States case (U.S. Court of Claims, 1987) set a critical legal precedent that helped shape the future of DAFs. The court ruled that an organization engaged primarily in raising and distributing funds to other charities could qualify as a public charity rather than a private foundation, provided it met the public support requirements under IRC §509(a)(1) or IRC §509(a)(2). This decision clarified that grantmaking organizations could maintain public charity status even if their primary function was funding other nonprofits, rather than operating direct charitable programs.

The ruling reduced regulatory burdens for such organizations, allowing them to avoid the excise taxes, mandatory distribution requirements, and self-dealing restrictions imposed on private foundations. For DAF sponsors, this ruling was a turning point. It solidified the legal framework for community foundations and emerging national DAF sponsors by reinforcing their ability to function as public charities while administering DAFs. This distinction provided greater flexibility for donors, who could receive higher charitable deduction limits than those available for private foundations, further incentivizing philanthropy.

Although the ruling did not explicitly address DAFs, its principles were later applied to DAF sponsors. This reassured financial institutions and nonprofit leaders that DAFs could be structured as public charities and provided the legal clarity that set the stage for the industry's rapid expansion in the coming years.[116]

1991–1999: Establishment of National DAFs

Note: Many national DAF sponsors are affiliated with major financial firms but operate as independent public charities. These DAF sponsors, not the financial institutions themselves, administer DAFs and hold full fiduciary responsibility for their management.

The early 1990s marked a pivotal era for DAFs, driven by the creation of the national DAF Sponsor model. A critical turning point came in 1991 with the establishment of the Fidelity Charitable Gift Fund, which received a public charity designation from the IRS. This was the first national DAF program created

---

[116] National Foundation, Inc. v. United States. U.S. Court of Claims, 1987. 13 Cl. Ct. 486.

with the support of a prominent financial institution. Turney P. Berry, Partner at Wyatt, Tarrant & Combs, LLP, explains,

> The real growth of Donor-Advised Funds began after the 1991 IRS ruling for Fidelity. Before that, DAFs were primarily used by large foundations, but when everyday donors realized they could create their own funds with minimal complexity, the floodgates opened.[117]

The IRS ruling was pivotal in confirming that DAFs could qualify as public charities under Section 501(c)(3) of the Internal Revenue Code. Community foundations had long been recognized as public charities, allowing contributions to their DAFs to receive tax benefits; the Fidelity Charitable Gift Fund ruling extended this framework to the national DAF sponsor model not tied to a specific geographic community. This provided regulatory clarity that such organizations could qualify as public charities, provided they met requirements such as broad public support, a charitable purpose, and operational compliance. As Elaine Martyn, Vice President at Fidelity Charitable® reflects:

> Fidelity Charitable's goal of democratizing philanthropy, which began in 1991, has led to extraordinary growth over the years.[118]

This perspective underscores how Fidelity's innovation opened the doors to more inclusive and accessible philanthropy, ultimately transforming DAFs from a niche product into a scalable feature of modern giving.

This assurance boosted donor confidence and fueled the growth of DAFs as flexible, tax-efficient giving vehicles. Fidelity Charitable's success marked a broader industry shift, positioning DAFs as cost-effective, user-friendly alternatives to private foundations through professional fund management and the eventual introduction of intuitive digital platforms. These advantages, such as the absence of startup costs and lower operational expenses compared to private foundations, contributed to the democratization of structured philanthropy by enabling donors to prioritize strategic impact.

The creation of additional national DAF sponsors in the following years further accelerated this transformation. Russell James, Professor of Charitable Financial Planning at Texas Tech University, observed,

---

[117] Berry, T. Interview with Ted Hart. November 15, 2024.
[118] Martyn, E. Interview with Ted Hart, August 27, 2024.

The real inflection point in the growth of DAFs came when national financial institutions got involved. They created an army of financial advisors who could benefit from having DAF conversations, making DAFs a mainstream option for donors.[119]

National DAF sponsors introduced a new model of structured philanthropy during the 1990s, and their partnerships with major financial institutions helped accelerate growth and legitimacy. These DAF sponsors were supported by robust investment infrastructures, helping donors preserve and grow charitable assets through diversified portfolios. This collaboration improved the donor experience, enabling individuals to align investment strategies with their financial goals, philanthropic values, and mission-aligned objectives. These national DAF Sponsors also benefited from technological sophistication and administrative efficiency in their DAF operations, streamlining processes and reducing costs. These enhancements made DAFs more attractive to a broader donor base.

2000s: Advances in Digital Philanthropy and Online Giving Platforms

The 2000s brought transformative changes to philanthropy, driven by the rapid expansion of the internet and digital technologies. These advancements simplified how donors connected with and supported charitable organizations, removing traditional barriers to giving. Online platforms like Network for Good and GlobalGiving enabled donors to make direct contributions with just a few clicks, revolutionizing the philanthropic landscape.

This digital revolution also significantly impacted DAFs. DAF sponsors capitalized on emerging technologies by developing intuitive online interfaces that offered features such as real-time account oversight, automated financial reporting, and personalized grant suggestions. These tools streamlined the giving process, attracting tech-savvy donors who valued convenience, speed, and involvement in their philanthropic decisions.

Beyond enhancing the donor experience, digital tools improved operational efficiency for DAF sponsors. They reduced administrative costs and provided donors with real-time updates on fund balances, grant statuses, and the impact of their contributions. The combination of these efficiencies and the tax advantages of DAFs further boosted their popularity, enabling donors to manage their giving remotely and quickly adapt their strategies to address urgent needs.

---

[119] James, R. Interview with Ted Hart, October 24, 2024.

The shift toward digital philanthropy in the 2000s played a pivotal role in expanding the reach and appeal of DAFs. Advancements in technology and digital platforms facilitated the expansion of DAF accessibility, enabling a broader demographic of donors to engage in structured philanthropy. These technological advancements not only scaled DAF operations but also set new standards for transparency, efficiency, and donor empowerment, laying the groundwork for continued innovation in charitable giving.

2006: PENSION PROTECTION ACT OF 2006

The Pension Protection Act of 2006 (PPA) marked a transformative moment, particularly for DAFs. This landmark legislation provided the first formal definition of DAFs under Internal Revenue Code §4966(d)(2), establishing a robust legal framework for their operation. According to the PPA, a DAF is defined as:

- A Fund or Account: The DAF must be a separately identified fund or account maintained and operated by a DAF sponsor, such as a public charity or community foundation.

- Donor Advisory Privileges: The donor (or a person designated by the donor) must have, or reasonably expect to have, advisory privileges regarding the distribution of funds or the investment of assets in the account. However, the DAF sponsor retains ultimate control over the distribution of funds.

- Exclusions from Certain Fund Types: The definition explicitly excludes certain types of funds, such as designated funds benefiting a single organization, funds established for specific individuals, and employer-sponsored disaster relief funds under certain conditions.

Key Provisions of the PPA

The PPA introduced several critical provisions to secure the integrity and transparency of DAFs:

- To safeguard charitable integrity, the Pension Protection Act reinforced prohibitions on self-dealing and personal benefit. Donors and related parties cannot use DAF funds to secure more than incidental benefits, such as gala tickets, membership perks, or satisfaction of personal pledges. These restrictions reflect existing rules under IRC §§4941 and 4958 and are further clarified in IRS Notice 2017–73. Even indirect benefits or informal arrangements can trigger excise taxes if they confer private advantage. Advisors and donors must remain attentive to ensure all DAF activity supports only legitimate charitable purposes.[120]

- Increased Transparency: The PPA did not mandate public disclosures but required DAF sponsors to report certain information to the IRS (e.g., on Form 990), enhancing accountability.

- Restrictions on Distributions: The PPA explicitly prohibited grants to individuals and restricted distributions to only charitable purposes, directing that DAFs cannot be used for personal or non-charitable benefits.

Robert Collins, Global Managing Director at TrustBridge Global Foundation, explained:

> The Pension Protection Act legitimized DAFs. Before then, you could not find the word Donor-Advised fund in any IRS regulations. It just didn't exist in the eyes of the regulators as a legal concept. The first time we had what a Donor-Advised Fund is, and here's what it does, or here's how it works, and here's what it's not.[121]

The PPA provided regulatory clarity, legitimizing DAFs and addressing concerns about potential misuse. This legal framework boosted donor confidence and encouraged broader participation in charitable giving. The combination of tax efficiency, flexibility, and donor influence over grantmaking further solidified DAFs as an appealing philanthropic vehicle.

Clarification of Tax Treatment for DAF Contributions

The PPA also addressed critical aspects of the tax treatment of DAF contributions. Contributions to DAFs are treated as irrevocable gifts to a public charity, offering donors immediate tax benefits while placing legal control of the funds with the DAF sponsor. This framework aligns DAF contributions with other donations to 501(c)(3) organizations, granting donors the flexibility to give anonymously if desired. By relinquishing control over the funds, donors maintain advisory privileges, but the DAF sponsor retains full discretion and fiduciary responsibility over the assets, providing proper management and compliance with tax regulations. Sara C. DeRose, Director, Development and Philanthropic

---

[120] IRC §§4941, 4958; IRS Notice 2017-73, 2017-51 I.R.B. 562; IRS Pub. 526 (2023); IRS Pub. 561 (2023).
[121] Collins, R. Interview with Ted Hart, September 16, 2024.

Services at Fairfield County's Community Foundation, clarifies:

> One major misconception is that donors use DAFs solely for tax benefits, but by law, every dollar in a DAF must ultimately support charitable causes.[122]

This underscores the fundamental principle that DAFs exist to facilitate philanthropy, not to serve as indefinite holding accounts for tax-advantaged assets. This clarification not only strengthened donor confidence but also positioned DAFs as vital tools in philanthropy. By reinforcing the irrevocable nature of contributions and the obligation for charitable distribution, these regulations dispel misconceptions and affirm the role of DAFs in advancing meaningful philanthropic impact.

The PPA not only catalyzed the rapid growth of DAFs but also elevated the standards of transparency and accountability across the philanthropic sector. By providing clear operational guidelines, the Act encouraged innovation and growth while fostering trust and credibility. It remains a cornerstone of modern philanthropic practices, so that DAFs can continue to serve as a dynamic and impactful tool for charitable giving.[123]

2006: The New Dynamics Foundation Case

Just weeks after the Pension Protection Act became law, the judiciary echoed these priorities in *New Dynamics Foundation v. United States* (2006), a pivotal case that reinforced the new standards by denying tax-exempt status to a foundation abusing charitable status for private gain. The abuses revealed in the New Dynamics Foundation case (449 F. Supp. 2d 90, D.D.C. 2006) contributed to growing public and legislative concern about DAF misuse. The case centered on the New Dynamics Foundation (NDF), a nonprofit organization that sought 501(c)(3) tax-exempt status while allowing donors to use charitable assets for personal expenses and wealth preservation strategies. The U.S. District Court for the District of Columbia ruled against NDF, denying its tax-exempt status and upholding the IRS's determination that the foundation violated the private benefit doctrine.

The court found that NDF permitted donors to improperly benefit from foundation assets, including using funds for personal travel, research into investment opportunities, scholarships for family members, and compensating donors' chil-

---

[122] DeRose, S. Interview with Ted Hart, December 12, 2024.
[123] Internal Revenue Service. (n.d.). Donor-Advised Funds. https://www.irs.gov and Pension Protection Act of 2006, Pub. L. No. 109-280, 120 Stat. 780 (2006).

dren for charitable work. The ruling emphasized that charitable organizations must operate exclusively for charitable purposes and cannot provide undue private benefit to donors. This decision reinforced the principles earlier codified in the PPA, which prohibit DAFs from being used for personal expenses. The court described NDF's practices as a blatant attempt to warehouse wealth while securing tax advantages, contradicting the fundamental principles of nonprofit organizations.

The New Dynamics Foundation ruling served as an early example of the regulatory framework that the PPA formalized in the same year. It signaled to DAF sponsors and donors that the IRS and courts were actively scrutinizing the misuse of DAFs and would take action against organizations failing to comply with charitable giving requirements. This case reinforced the legal foundation so that DAF assets remain dedicated to legitimate philanthropic purposes, paving the way for stronger compliance measures across the sector.[124]

2006: The Uniform Prudent Management of Institutional Funds Act (UPMIFA)

The adoption of the Uniform Prudent Management of Institutional Funds Act (UPMIFA) modernized nonprofit fund management standards, impacting how DAF sponsors approached the stewardship of charitable assets. UPMIFA applied broadly to all institutional funds and reinforced public expectations for responsible investment, sustainability, and alignment with donor intent. This development contributed to the broader professionalization and accountability of DAF operations in the 21st century.

This legal clarity not only strengthened donor confidence but also aligned fund management with donor intent, solidifying UPMIFA's role as a critical milestone in DAF history. The act's focus on prudent investment and spending practices helps DAF sponsors remain effective stewards of philanthropic capital, maintaining trust and credibility within the broader nonprofit sector.[125]

---

[124] New Dynamics Foundation v. United States. U.S. District Court for the District of Columbia, 2006. 449 F. Supp. 2d 90.
[125] Carnegie Investment Counsel. "What Every Nonprofit Should Know About UPMIFA." Carnegie Investment Counsel Blog, n.d. Accessed May 15, 2025. https://blog.carnegieinvest.com/nonprofit-investment-services-blog/what-every-nonprofit-should-know-about-the-uniform-prudent-management-of-institutional-funds-act.

2006: Fidelity Charitable Introduces the Charitable Investment Advisor Program

On June 28, 2006, Fidelity Charitable launched the Charitable Investment Advisor Program, enabling independent investment advisors to manage DAF assets on behalf of individual donors. This innovation significantly expanded both the accessibility and appeal of DAFs by allowing donors to incorporate professional investment management into their philanthropic strategies. The program democratized access to sophisticated financial planning tools, making DAFs more attractive to a broader range of donors and contributing to the sector's rapid growth. As DAFs evolved into professionally managed philanthropic platforms, donors gained not only the ability to recommend grants but also to shape investment strategies, aligning both their giving and asset management with personal values. [126]

2007: First National Philanthropic Trust (NPT) DAF Report

Under the leadership of Eileen Heisman, President and CEO (retired) of the National Philanthropic Trust (NPT), NPT began publishing its annual Donor-Advised Fund Report in 2007. The first report was two pages in length and tracked 10 DAF sponsors with $31.5 billion in assets and $6.27 billion in total grants made.[127] Since its inception, the report has become a benchmark for tracking DAF trends, providing valuable insights into the growth and impact of DAFs.

2008: IRS Redesign of Form 990 and DAF Transparency Milestones

The 2008 redesign of IRS Form 990[128] represented a major regulatory shift for public charities, including DAF sponsors. For the first time, the IRS required enhanced disclosure around DAF activities through Schedule D, which collected data on the number of funds, total assets, contributions received, and grants made.[129] This created a new baseline for DAF transparency and allowed for consistent data reporting across the sector.

Simultaneously, the introduction of Schedule F marked a turning point in international grantmaking disclosure.[130] It required nonprofits, including DAF

---

[126] Fidelity Investments. Fidelity Charitable introduces program allowing independent investment advisors to manage Donor-Advised Fund assets (Press release), June 28, 2006. Accessed October 15, 2024. https://www.fidelity.com/products/funds/fnx/press_releases/release2.html

[127] National Philanthropic Trust.. DAF Spotlight: Economic Uncertainty. National Philanthropic Trust. (2025.) https://www.nptrust.org/annual-reports/daf-spotlight-economic-uncertainty/

[128] IRS, Notice 2008-117, 2008-2 C.B. 1227.

[129] Instructions for IRS Form 990 (2008), Internal Revenue Service.

[130] IRS, 2008 Schedule D Instructions and Schedule F Instructions, Form 990.

sponsors, to report foreign expenditures, regions of activity, and due diligence processes. For DAF sponsors facilitating cross-border grants, this raised the compliance bar and signaled growing IRS interest in global philanthropy oversight.

Together, these reporting schedules signaled a broader regulatory expectation: that DAFs should operate not only efficiently and flexibly, but also transparently, particularly as they expanded in scope and scale.

2012: International Grantmaking Comes of Age

The U.S. Department of the Treasury and the IRS introduced proposed rules under the Reliance Standards for Making Good Faith Determinations, aimed at simplifying international grantmaking for U.S.-based DAFs and other grantmakers.[131] These rules allowed U.S. grantors to determine whether a foreign organization was equivalent to a U.S. public charity by thoroughly reviewing the organization's financial records, governance documents, and other relevant information.

This clarification provided DAF sponsors and other grantmakers with a structured process to attain compliance with U.S. tax laws while confidently supporting international charitable initiatives.

During the early 2010s, U.S. foreign policy began to recognize philanthropy as a tool for global engagement, prompting new conversations around international grantmaking.[132]

2013: Launch of the NGOsource Equivalency Determination Repository

On March 18, 2013, NGOsource, a joint initiative of the Council on Foundations and TechSoup Global, introduced its Equivalency Determination (ED) service. This created the first centralized repository to streamline and standardize the process for DAF sponsors, foundations, and other grantmakers to obtain equivalency determinations for foreign organizations. According to NGOsource's official announcement, the service simplified verifying foreign organizations' compliance with U.S. public charity standards, enabling grantmakers to rely on pre-validated charities.[133]

---

[131] U.S. Department of the Treasury and Internal Revenue Service. Reliance Standards for Making Good Faith Determinations. Federal Register, vol. 80, no. 186, 25 Sept. 2015, pp. 57709–57714, https://www.federalregister.gov/documents/2015/09/25/2015-24346/reliance-standards-for-making-good-faith-determinations.

[132] NGOsource. Changing the Landscape of International Philanthropy: 10-Year Retrospective. TechSoup, 2024. https://www.ngosource.org

[133] NGOsource. NGOSource Launches Online Equivalency Determination Service That Streamlines International Grantmaking, May 18, 2013. https://www.ngosource.org/blog/ngosource-launches-online-equivalency-determination-service-that-streamlines-international-grantmaking

By reducing the time, cost, and administrative burdens associated with individual equivalency determinations, NGOsource's repository aligned with the IRS's 2012 proposed rules (Reliance Standards for Making Good Faith Determinations). This innovation made international grantmaking more efficient and accessible, fostering greater participation in cross-border philanthropy.

2015: Final IRS Rules on Equivalency Determinations

The U.S. Department of the Treasury and IRS issued final regulations titled "Reliance Standards for Making Good Faith Determinations" (T.D. 9740, September 25, 2015).[134] These rules created a safe harbor for all U.S. grantmakers, including DAFs, private foundations, and public charities, allowing them to rely on centralized repositories for equivalency determinations. The regulations aligned with the model pioneered by NGOsource by expanding the pool of qualified practitioners, CPAs, enrolled agents, and attorneys, who may provide written opinions verifying that foreign organizations meet U.S. public charity criteria (for full IRS requirements on ED, see *Chapter 7: International Grantmaking: A Worldwide Blueprint*).

Before these rules, grantmakers depended on affidavits or case-by-case legal reviews for each foreign grantee. By clarifying that reliance on a qualified ED constitutes good faith, the 2015 safe harbor rules reduced administrative burden and cost and made cross-border philanthropy more efficient for all U.S. grantmakers.

Along with the 2012 proposed rules and NGOsource's 2013 launch, these final regulations broadened the capacity of DAFs and other charities to support global causes, streamlining compliance and reinforcing DAFs as a powerful globally oriented vehicle for strategic charitable giving.

2017: The Tax Cuts and Jobs Act (TCJA)

The Tax Cuts and Jobs Act (TCJA) of 2017 introduced significant changes to the U.S. tax code, profoundly impacting charitable giving. Among the most notable changes was the near-doubling of the standard deduction, from $6,350 to $12,000 for individual filers and from $12,700 to $24,000 for married couples

---

[134] Adler & Colvin. Final Regulations on Foreign Public Charity Equivalency Determinations. Adler & Colvin, December 2017. https://www.adlercolvin.com/wp-content/uploads/2017/12/Final-Regulations-on-Foreign-Public-Charity-Equivalency-Determinations-00834838xA3536.pdf.

filing jointly. This simplified tax filing for many Americans; it also reduced the number of taxpayers who found it advantageous to itemize their deductions, directly influencing charitable giving patterns.[135]

Before the TCJA, many taxpayers itemized their deductions, including those for charitable contributions. The higher standard deduction, however, made itemization unnecessary for many middle-income donors, raising concerns about a potential decline in overall charitable donations. In response, financial advisors increasingly recommended DAFs as a tax-efficient solution. By "bunching" multiple years' worth of charitable donations into a single tax year, donors could surpass the itemization threshold, maximize their deductions, and retain the flexibility to distribute grants over time.

In response, high-net-worth individuals and other committed donors turned to DAFs as a solution. Using a strategy known as "bunching" or "stacking," donors could consolidate multiple years of anticipated charitable contributions into a single year, enabling them to surpass the standard deduction threshold and continue itemizing. This approach allowed donors to maximize their tax benefits while maintaining consistent charitable giving.

Beyond timing adjustments, DAFs offered additional advantages, such as accepting appreciated assets like securities. These assets could be liquidated within the fund without incurring capital gains taxes, allowing donors to grow their charitable assets tax-free.

The Tax Cuts and Jobs Act (TCJA) of 2017 introduced significant modifications to charitable deduction limits, further increasing the appeal of DAFs, particularly among high-net-worth donors.

One of the key changes was the increase in the deduction limit for cash contributions to public charities, including DAFs. Previously set at 50% of Adjusted Gross Income (AGI), the limit was raised to 60% AGI, allowing donors making large cash contributions to claim a higher tax deduction than before. Additionally, donors who exceeded this new limit could carry forward any unused deduction for up to five years, further enhancing the tax benefits associated with charitable giving.

[135] Tax Policy Center. How Did the TCJA Affect Incentives for Charitable Giving? Tax Policy Center, Urban Institute & Brookings Institution, https://www.taxpolicycenter.org/briefing-book/how-did-tcja-affect-incentives-charitable-giving.
[136] Joint Economic Committee. Economic Impact on Charities of the 2017 Tax Act. U.S. Congress, 2019. Accessed December 10, 2024. https://www.jec.senate.gov/public/_cache/files/06846810-f7dc-4789-a3c1-2c22c7b95a4c/economic-impact-on-charities-of-the-2017-tax-act-final.pdf.

For non-cash donations, such as appreciated securities, real estate, or business interests, the TCJA did not change the existing 30% AGI deduction limit. However, many high-net-worth individuals continued to prioritize non-cash giving due to the double tax benefit it provides. Donors could avoid capital gains tax on the asset's appreciation while still receiving a charitable deduction at fair market value, maximizing both their tax efficiency and philanthropic impact.[136]

More than 60% of contributions to Fidelity Charitable were in the form of non-cash assets like stocks.[137] It is clear that the TCJA spurred increased contributions to DAFs beyond just cash donations. By allowing donors to leverage both cash and non-cash assets strategically, the TCJA reinforced the role of DAFs as an essential tool for modern philanthropy, enabling donors to optimize tax savings while continuing to support charitable causes. Reynolds Cafferata, Partner at Rodriguez, Horii, Choi & Cafferata, LLP observes,

> The tax incentives are undoubtedly a big part of why DAFs have grown, but we can't ignore the intrinsic motivation of many donors. This is a tool for real change in their communities, not just a financial strategy.[138]

As a result, the TCJA spurred a marked increase in the creation and funding of DAFs. The Act's provisions, including an increase in the deductible limit for charitable contributions, further enhanced the appeal of DAFs, particularly for wealthier donors, contributing to a growing concentration of charitable assets in these funds.

The TCJA reshaped charitable giving by altering standard deduction and itemization rules, prompting new donor strategies and driving the continued growth of DAFs. Although the 60% AGI deduction increase applied only to cash gifts, the surge in DAF contributions extended beyond cash donations. High-net-worth donors continued to contribute appreciated securities, real estate, and other complex assets, reinforcing the role of DAFs as a powerful tool for philanthropy. These legislative changes highlight the evolving role of DAFs in contemporary philanthropy and invite further exploration of broader trends in charitable giving.

2017 IRS Notice Clarifying DAF Rules

In 2017, the IRS issued Notice 2017–73 to address growing concerns about the use of DAFs in areas such as donor pledges, public support rules, and donor

---

[137] Fidelity Charitable. 2024 Giving Report, p. 4. https://www.fidelitycharitable.org
[138] Cafferata, R. Interview with Ted Hart, September 11, 2024.

benefits. Though framed as proposed regulations, the notice marked a turning point in federal attention to DAF oversight. It reflected the government's evolving interest in promoting transparency and maintaining the charitable integrity of these funds, while foreshadowing potential future regulatory developments.

The 2017 proposed regulations laid the groundwork for future refinements in DAF oversight. They highlighted critical areas, such as donor benefits, fund distribution practices, and public support calculations, which could shape subsequent regulatory developments. Anne Hennessy, Director at Foundation Source, observed,

> I definitely think there will be additional restrictions, similar to restrictions on private foundations... I think at some point in time, there will be a minimum required distribution from Donor-Advised Funds.[139]

This period of regulatory evolution underscored the IRS's intent to enhance the clarity and accountability of DAF operations. By addressing these areas of concern, the proposed regulations reinforced the proper administration of DAFs, helping to maintain public trust in this increasingly popular philanthropic tool.

2015–2019: Expansion of Corporate DAF Programs

The late 2010s witnessed a notable expansion of corporate DAF programs, reflecting a broader trend in the philanthropic landscape. Companies began integrating DAFs into their corporate social responsibility (CSR) initiatives, offering employees structured and tax-efficient avenues for charitable engagement. This integration fostered a culture of giving within organizations and extended the reach of DAFs beyond high-net-worth individuals to a more diverse audience.

By incorporating DAFs into workplace giving programs, companies normalized their use as versatile tools for both personal and corporate philanthropy. Employees were empowered to support causes they cared about while benefiting from tax advantages and simplified administration. This corporate involvement positioned DAFs as integral components of modern philanthropic strategies, enhancing their influence across various sectors.

A case study during this period is the collaboration I fostered with Mark Layden, then CEO of Cybergrants (later Bonterra), to bring to life a shared vision for

---

[139] Hennessy, A. Interview with Ted Hart, August 19, 2024.

transforming corporate giving, at scale. Together, our two organizations launched a streamlined system that empowered hundreds of thousands of employees to support causes worldwide, extending DAF grantmaking domestically and internationally across a broad range of corporate clients. This partnership not only helped channel billions of dollars to tens of thousands of charities but also established a model that CAF America and Bonterra continue to value today as a milestone in the expansion of corporate DAF programs.

The rise of corporate DAF programs has helped democratize access to structured charitable giving. Many companies now use their philanthropic infrastructure to empower employees at all income levels to participate in giving, often through workplace DAF benefits, matching gift programs, and charitable workshops. Fidelity Charitable has reported administering over 500 corporate DAFs, which collectively granted $256 million, averaging 65 grants per account This growing adoption of corporate DAFs highlights their role in streamlining charitable giving and supporting broad-based causes such as disaster relief, education, and health services.[140]

By integrating DAFs into their CSR strategies, corporations are providing greater flexibility and long-term philanthropic engagement, making DAFs an essential component of modern corporate philanthropy.

2017: NPT DAF Report: DAF Assets Surpass $100 Billion for the First Time[141]

In 2017, total assets in DAFs grew to $110.01 billion, a 27.3% increase from 2016, according to the National Philanthropic Trust.

2020: CARES Act: Coronavirus Aid, Relief, and Economic Security Act

Enacted in 2020 in response to the COVID-19 pandemic, the CARES Act introduced measures to stimulate charitable giving during an unprecedented time of need. A key provision temporarily increased the limit on cash contributions to public charities from 60% to 100% of a donor's adjusted gross income (AGI) for 2020, enabling some donors to offset their taxable income entirely through charitable giving. This 100% AGI limit did not apply to contributions to DAFs. This indirectly encouraged strategic use of DAFs. Donors could continue to

---

[140] Fidelity Charitable, 2024 Giving Report (Boston, MA: Fidelity Investments Charitable Gift Fund, 2024), 16–17, https://www.fidelitycharitable.org
[141] National Philanthropic Trust. 2017 Donor-Advised Fund Report, (2017), https://www.nptrust.org/philanthropic-resources/philanthropist/npt-releases-2017-donor-advised-fund-report/

contribute up to 60% of their AGI to DAFs, claim immediate tax benefits, and distribute grants over time, maintaining flexibility while maximizing impact.

The CARES Act also introduced a $300 universal charitable deduction for non-itemizers, marking a significant policy shift. Although modest, this deduction broadened the base of taxpayers eligible for charitable tax benefits, potentially increasing overall donations. DAFs, though not directly eligible for the deduction, remained a favored tool for efficiently channeling contributions, particularly during a crisis.[142]

The COVID-19 pandemic revealed the strategic value of DAFs as donors accelerated grantmaking to support urgent needs such as COVID-19 relief and racial justice. A 2025 peer-reviewed study published in Administrative Sciences introduced the concept of "donative slack," referring to the latent philanthropic capacity held in DAFs that donors can activate in times of crisis. The study found that DAF sponsors reported substantial increases in grant activity during 2020, highlighting how these funds function as philanthropic reserves, essentially "rainy day funds" that enable rapid, high-impact charitable responses in times of emergency. This behavior is especially noteworthy considering that many donors were simultaneously navigating profound personal and financial challenges caused by the global pandemic. Without resources already allocated in DAFs, it might have proven too difficult for many to assess their financial situation and contribute meaningfully in the moment. In this light, DAFs played a vital role in bridging donor intent and timely action, buffering nonprofits during a period of widespread disruption.[143]

The CARES Act's incentives, combined with the unique flexibility and adaptability of DAFs, significantly influenced donor behavior during the crisis. These developments reinforced the critical role of tax policy in driving philanthropy, particularly during times of national and global emergencies, and demonstrated the power of DAFs to bridge the gap between immediate relief and sustained charitable impact.

2021: National Philanthropic Trust (NPT) DAF Report Shows Total Assets of DAFs surpass $200 Billion for the First Time

The total assets of DAFs surpassed the $200 billion milestone for the first time,

---

[142] Independent Sector. Coronavirus Aid, Relief, and Economic Security Act (CARES Act): Summary for Nonprofits. Independent Sector, https://independentsector.org/resource/coronavirus-aid-relief-and-economic-security-act-cares-act-summary-for-nonprofits/
[143] Heist, H. D., Shaker, G. G., Sumsion, R. M., Tomlinson, J., & Minor, A. How Donor Advised Funds Change Fundraising. Administrative Sciences, 2025, 15(4), 137. https://doi.org/10.3390/admsci15040137

marking a significant moment in the growth of this philanthropic vehicle. This milestone reflected both the increasing popularity of DAFs among donors and their resilience as a charitable giving tool during times of economic uncertainty.

2021: Americans for Prosperity Foundation v. Bonta

The Supreme Court reaffirmed donor privacy protections in *Americans for Prosperity Foundation v. Bonta,* striking down California's donor disclosure law as unconstitutional. The decision reinforced *NAACP v. Alabama* and strengthened legal safeguards that allow donors to give anonymously. Although the ruling was not directly related to DAFs, it solidified the broader legal foundation for philanthropic confidentiality.

2023: IRS Proposed Regulations on DAFs

IRS-proposed regulations on DAFs represent a significant shift in the regulatory landscape. The proposed rules, titled Taxes on Taxable Distributions from Donor-Advised Funds Under Section 4966 if enacted would clarify and, in some cases, expand existing rules governing distributions, investments, and oversight. Note: These regulations are proposed and are not currently enforceable. They will not have legal effect unless and until they are finalized through the formal IRS and Treasury rulemaking process.[144]

One of the most notable areas of focus is the intersection of DAFs and impact investing. The IRS has proposed additional limitations on investments that could result in private benefit or fail to demonstrate a charitable purpose. Key provisions related to impact investing include:

- Expanded prohibitions on self-dealing, so that DAF-funded investments cannot benefit the donor, their family, or related entities (IRC §4941)
- Stronger compliance requirements for investments, reinforcing that DAF investments must prioritize charitable impact over financial return
- Tighter restrictions on DAF-to-DAF transfers for investment purposes, preventing funds from being moved between accounts to delay charitable distributions

The proposed regulations signal the IRS's intent to introduce stricter reporting requirements for DAF investments, so that all assets remain aligned with charitable purpose mandates. If enacted, these rules could reshape the future

---

[144] See IRS Proposed Regulations REG-142338-07, 88 Fed. Reg. 85500 (Dec. 8, 2023).

of impact investing through DAFs, requiring more rigorous due diligence and transparency from DAF sponsors.

These regulations, currently under review, would modify the governance framework for DAF sponsors and donor-advisors, aligning them more closely with broader federal tax compliance requirements applicable to other charitable vehicles. The proposed rules introduce several key provisions that could alter the administrative and fiduciary responsibilities of DAF sponsors.

Key Provisions of the 2023 IRS Proposed Regulations: Expanded Definition of DAFs

The proposed regulations seek to broaden the IRS definition of DAFs, potentially classifying a larger subset of charitable accounts under IRS oversight. The proposals clarify when a fund qualifies as a DAF, including accounts where donors retain advisory privileges over distributions. A new 'record of contributions' test may subject certain pooled funds (e.g., donor-restricted accounts at community foundations) to DAF rules if they function like traditional DAFs.

- Compliance Impact: The American College of Trust and Estate Counsel (ACTEC) has expressed concerns that this expanded definition could lead to a significant increase in compliance burdens, particularly for community foundations and fiscal sponsors.
- Regulatory Risks: Legal analysts from Loeb & Loeb, LLP caution that collaborative giving pools, scholarship funds, and donor-restricted accounts may be unintentionally subject to DAF-specific regulatory oversight.[145]

Regulation of Investment and Advisory Fees

The proposed rules impose stricter limitations on investment advisor fees tied to DAF accounts, reinforcing the requirement that funds must be used exclusively for charitable purposes. Financial advisors argue that such restrictions may diminish donors' ability to engage in strategic, long-term philanthropy by limiting asset growth within DAFs. According to the American College of Trust and Estate Counsel (ACTEC), balancing compliance with the ability to maximize investment returns remains a key issue for advisors working with high-net-worth donors. Under the IRS Proposed Regulations (2023), investment fees must be

---

[145] Loeb & Loeb LLP, Proposed Regulations on Donor-Advised FundsPart I of the Anticipated Guidance: What Qualifies and What Doesn't (December 20, 2023; updated January 12, 2024), https://www.loeb.com/en/insights/publications/2023/12/proposed-regulations-on-donor-advised-funds.

[146] American College of Trust and Estate Counsel. "Comments of the American College of Trust and Estate Counsel on Proposed Regulations under Code Section 4966." ACTEC, January 2024.

reasonable, necessary, and cannot benefit the donor, donor-advisor, or a related entity, as outlined under IRC §4941.[146]

- Stakeholder Concerns: The Jewish Federations of North America (JFNA) has raised objections, citing the potential negative impact on community-based organizations that may lack the internal financial expertise of national DAF sponsors.[147]
- Operational Impact: If enacted, these limitations could reduce contributions to smaller DAF sponsors and restrict donor flexibility in selecting financial advisors for DAF asset management.

Encouraging Charitable Distributions

The regulations do not mandate a minimum payout requirement but introduce recommendations for DAF sponsors to establish policies that promote regular grant distributions.

- **Support for Voluntary Guidelines:** Some DAF sponsors have endorsed these non-binding distribution recommendations, arguing that they align with donor intent and IRS expectations for DAFs to serve as active grant-making vehicles.
- **Opposition to Mandatory Payouts:** Several national DAF sponsors have opposed the introduction of any compulsory payout requirement, warning that such provisions could undermine the long-term flexibility of DAFs as philanthropic planning tools.

Enhanced Reporting and Public Transparency

The proposed regulations increase reporting requirements for DAF sponsors, mandating detailed disclosures on fund balances, grant activity, and expenditure allocations.

- **Administrative Burdens:** The New York Community Trust has indicated that the additional reporting requirements may place a disproportionate compliance burden on community foundations, increasing operational costs without yielding significant public benefit.[148]

---

[147] Jewish Federations of North America, Comment Letter on IRS Proposed Regulations on Donor-Advised Funds (February 15, 2024), https://www.regulations.gov/comment/IRS-2023-0053-3252

[148] The New York Community Trust, Comment Letter on IRS Proposed Regulations on Donor-Advised Funds (January 16, 2024), https://www.regulations.gov/comment/IRS-2023-0053-2313

Restrictions on Successive DAF-to-DAF Transfers

The IRS has proposed limitations on successive DAF-to-DAF grants to prevent donors from using multiple DAFs to delay charitable distributions.

- **Compliance Considerations:** The Silicon Valley Community Foundation has highlighted potential unintended consequences, cautioning that these restrictions could impact legitimate pooled charitable initiatives, including scholarship funds and multi-DAF grantmaking collaborations.[149]

Expenditure Responsibility Rules for Certain Grants

The proposed rules impose new restrictions on grants that could ultimately benefit individuals, such as scholarship distributions and vocational training grants.

- **Sector Response:** The National Philanthropic Trust (NPT) has submitted formal objections, stating that these restrictions could limit grantmaking flexibility without significantly improving oversight or accountability.[150]

Regulatory Implications and Stakeholder Reactions

The proposed IRS regulations aim to strengthen oversight while ensuring that DAFs remain effective charitable vehicles. As the regulatory review process continues, key stakeholders, including DAF sponsors, nonprofit organizations, tax professionals, and philanthropy advocates, are engaging with the IRS to promote practical implementation and balanced compliance measures.

Beth Shapiro Kaufman, Partner and National Chair of Private Client Services at Lowenstein Sandler, LLP and former Associate Tax Legislative Counsel at the U.S. Department of the Treasury, observes:

> People often ask me about this, and I tell them that the fact there is proposed legislation on the table is a strong indication that DAFs are here to stay. While there are still questions being raised, there's also significant effort to address and clarify those issues. The IRS has recognized the concerns and is actively working on them, which is a positive sign that DAFs remain a viable and beneficial tool for philanthropy.[151]

---

[149] Silicon Valley Community Foundation, Comment Letter on IRS Proposed Regulations on Donor-Advised Funds (January 12, 2024), https://www.regulations.gov/comment/IRS-2023-0053-0147.

[150] Eileen Heisman, President and CEO, National Philanthropic Trust, Testimony at IRS Public Hearing on Proposed Regulations: Taxes on Taxable Distributions from Donor-Advised Funds under Section 4966 (REG-142338-07), U.S. Department of the Treasury/Internal Revenue Service, May 6, 2024.

[151] Kaufman, B. Shapiro. Interview with Ted Hart, November 5, 2024.

The finalized version of these regulations will shape the extent of new compliance obligations for charitable organizations, DAF sponsors, and donor-advisors in grantmaking and fund management. Striking a balance between regulatory oversight and donor flexibility will be essential to preserving the effectiveness and appeal of DAFs as a philanthropic tool.

Significant but Unenacted DAF Reform Proposals

Several high-profile reform bills shaped debate without becoming law. In 2014, a proposal would have imposed an excise tax on DAFs that failed to distribute gifts within five years, an early signal of concern over fund accumulation.[152] More recently, the Accelerating Charitable Efforts (ACE) Act (2021; reintroduced 2023) sought a 15-year distribution mandate and changes to contribution tax treatment.[153] Although neither measure passed, both prompted DAF sponsors to adopt voluntary payout and transparency best practices that continue to influence sector norms.

2025: OBBBA (OB3)

The One Big Beautiful Bill Act (OBBBA), also referred to as OB3, reshaped the tax and estate planning landscape in ways that indirectly elevate the role of donor-advised funds (DAFs). While the act does not impose DAF-specific mandates, it introduces reforms such as a universal charitable deduction and a 1% corporate giving floor. These changes may broaden participation in charitable giving among middle-income donors and corporate philanthropists. As a result, this legislation highlights some core advantages of DAFs, including bunching contributions, support for multiyear grantmaking, and long-term philanthropic planning.[154] For more on the advantages of DAFs see *Chapter 4: Making a Difference: Best Practices for DAFs.*

Regulatory Outlook for DAFs

The rise of DAFs represents not merely an evolution in charitable vehicles but a revolution in how modern philanthropy is conceptualized, structured, and practiced. From their inception in the 1930s to their explosive growth in the

---

[152] Tax Reform Act of 2014, H.R. 1, 113th Cong. § 5201 (2014); Urban Institute, Discerning the True Policy Debate over Donor-Advised Funds (2015), https://www.urban.org/sites/default/files/publication/72241/2000481-Discerning-the-TruePolicy-Debate-over-Donor-Advised-Funds.pdf
[153] Accelerating Charitable EUorts (ACE) Act, S.1981, 117th Cong. (2021); reintroduced as S.566, 118th Cong. (2023). See also H.R.6595, 117th Cong. (2021); H.R.6595, 118th Cong. (2023).
[154] Fidelity Charitable. "What the One Big Beautiful Bill (OBBB) Means for Philanthropy and Tax Planning." Fidelity Charitable, 2025, https://www.fidelitycharitable.org/articles/obbb-tax-reform.html

21st century, DAFs have shifted the center of gravity in charitable giving. They have unlocked donor flexibility, accelerated strategic philanthropy, and catalyzed innovations in areas such as impact investing and international grantmaking.

Today, this revolution enters a new phase of scrutiny and refinement. The IRS's proposed regulations in 2023 point toward a future shaped by greater transparency, clearer definitions of fees and responsibilities, and possible rules regarding distributions and reporting. These developments reflect an increasing focus on aligning DAFs with public trust and regulatory expectations, while also preserving the features that make them a preferred tool for millions of donors.

Ken Berger, who formerly served as President and CEO of Charity Navigator and now leads the New Jersey-based nonprofit Spectrum360, highlights the significance of this evolving landscape:

> As more and more money is concentrated in donor-advised funds, interest groups are going to probably bear down and want to increase regulations... I personally would hope those are thoughtful.[155]

Berger's comments capture the ongoing challenge of balancing oversight with innovation, and accountability with donor autonomy.

History shows that charitable tools tend to thrive when regulation is paired with flexibility. In 1969, Congress imposed mandatory payout rules on private foundations to ensure that charitable assets did not remain under donor control indefinitely. DAFs emerged as a more accessible and administratively streamlined alternative. While their flexibility is often viewed as a strength, critics argue that it can delay the flow of funds to active charitable use.

From the rise of national sponsors in the 1990s to the donor response during the COVID-19 pandemic, DAFs have consistently demonstrated their resilience. Their structure has enabled donors to act quickly and strategically, even in times of widespread disruption.

KEY TAKEAWAYS

The history of donor-advised funds reveals a quiet but profound transformation in the structure of charitable giving. What began as a modest innovation in charitable planning has grown into a powerful force that now shapes the philanthropic landscape in significant ways.

---

[155] Berger, K. Interview with Ted Hart, August 19, 2024

Over the decades, key policy milestones have defined how DAFs are governed and understood. The Tax Reform Act of 1969 imposed stricter oversight on private foundations, which in turn made donor-advised funds more attractive due to their simpler structure and fewer administrative burdens. The Pension Protection Act of 2006 provided further definition and legitimacy, codifying many of the rules that continue to guide the operation of DAFs today.

In the 1990s, the entrance of commercial DAF sponsors expanded access to these vehicles, introducing operational models that increased efficiency and appealed to a broader range of donors. This shift challenged traditional philanthropic institutions and contributed to the rapid rise of DAFs as a mainstream giving option.

Although academic and policy critiques have drawn attention to concerns such as transparency, payout practices, and donor control, these issues have not weakened the use or effectiveness of DAFs. Instead, they have helped to elevate important discussions about accountability and the role of charitable capital.

The COVID-19 pandemic brought these themes into sharp focus. Donors across the country turned to their DAFs to respond to urgent needs at a time when many were also facing personal uncertainty and financial stress. The concept of "donative slack" emerged from this moment, describing the philanthropic reserves that DAFs make possible. These reserves allowed donors to act quickly and meaningfully when the world needed it most.

From early experiments in community foundations to today's diverse and technology-enabled giving platforms, DAFs have become a central feature of philanthropic strategy. What started as a flexible tool for charitable contributions has matured into a system that supports intentional, values-aligned, and impactful giving.

The next chapter explores how donor-advised funds are used in practice and outlines the principles that ensure this revolutionary tool continues to deliver meaningful results for society.

Making a Difference: Best Practices for DAFs

EXECUTIVE SUMMARY

Donor-advised funds (DAFs) have become indispensable tools in modern philanthropy, offering individuals, families, corporations, and foundations a flexible, efficient, and strategic vehicle for giving. As DAFs grow in prominence, so too does the responsibility of sponsors to uphold the highest standards of transparency, accountability, and stewardship. This chapter presents **the 10 Best Practice Guidelines for DAF Sponsors** as a practical framework for responsible self-regulation. Leading DAF sponsors have developed and adopted policies that promote professional integrity, regulatory compliance, donor trust, and meaningful charitable impact. Through thoughtful governance, donor engagement strategies, and strong compliance practices, DAF sponsors can align charitable intent with community needs, encourage active grantmaking, and support nonprofit collaboration.

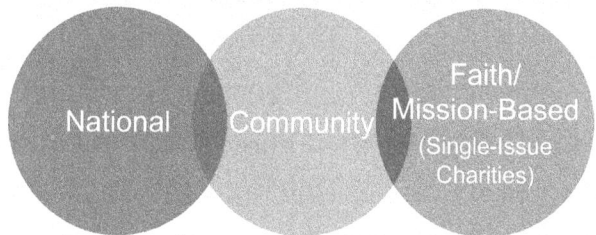

Three Types of DAF Sponsors

National Community Faith/ Mission-Based (Single-Issue Charities)

These standards apply across all types of sponsors, including national sponsors, community foundations, and faith/mission-based organizations. Regardless of sponsor type, these best practices help ensure responsible stewardship, operational transparency, and alignment with donor intent.

MAKING A DIFFERENCE: DAFS IN MODERN PHILANTHROPY

DAFs enable individuals to contribute a wide range of assets, such as cash, illiquid and complex assets, receive immediate tax benefits, and recommend grants over time. Unlike direct charitable donations, which are often made spontaneously, DAFs offer the flexibility to time grants strategically in response to evolving priorities or urgent needs. Erinn Andrews, Founder and CEO of Give-Team, underscores this point:

> I think it's so critically important that we don't only focus on getting money into DAFs. That is one half of the equation. We have to focus on how that money is going to get back out the door, not in order to hit some payout rate minimum, but because it's the right thing to do.[156]

By offering tax-free investment growth, DAFs help donors expand their philanthropic capacity over time. They also serve as a tool for legacy planning, allowing charitable giving to continue beyond the donor's lifetime. Engaging donors throughout their lifecycle requires a multi-faceted approach that begins with education at the initial contribution stage, continues with proactive engagement during active grantmaking years, and extends into legacy planning.

Kirk Hoopingarner, Partner at Quarles & Brady, LLP, and Chair of the Evanston, Illinois Community Foundation, emphasizes the need for balancing donor planning with the charitable purpose of DAFs:

> The debate over imposing minimum payout requirements on DAFs, akin to those for private foundations, raises critical questions about how to balance flexibility for donors with the need for timely charitable distributions.[157]

Beyond their efficiency, DAFs have made structured charitable giving accessible to a broader range of donors. DAF sponsors offer a professionally managed shared services approach to charitable gift management.[158]

SHARED SERVICES MODEL EXPANDS ACCESS

One of the key advantages of DAFs is their ability to make structured philanthropy accessible to a broad range of donors, not just the ultra-wealthy. DAFs operate through a Shared Services Model, allowing donors to benefit from professional charitable giving services without the complexity of managing a private foundation.

---

[156] Andrews, E. Interview with Ted Hart, August 22, 2024.
[157] Hoopingarner, K. Interview with Ted Hart, December 4, 2024.
[158] DAFgiving360™. Advisors: Charitable Giving Support. Accessed March 2025. https://www.dafgiving360.org/advisors

WHAT A SHARED SERVICES MODEL OFFERS

- **Access to professional investment and philanthropic services:** Historically, only the wealthiest families had access to tax-efficient giving vehicles managed by financial professionals and philanthropic advisors. The DAF shared services model allows donors of more modest means to benefit from the same high-level expertise once reserved for private foundations.
- **Streamlined grantmaking and regulatory compliance:** Private foundations must manage legal filings, investments, board meetings, and extensive due diligence for every grant. In contrast, DAF sponsors handle all compliance, tax reporting, and fund administration, freeing donors to focus entirely on their charitable goals.
- **Support for sustained, strategic philanthropy:** DAFs help ensure that giving is not just reactive or transactional. Through donor education and grant planning tools, DAF sponsors enable multi-year giving, legacy planning, and values-aligned philanthropy that can extend beyond a single moment of crisis.

DAF SPONSOR RESPONSIBILITIES

DAFs offer a powerful and flexible way to expand charitable giving, but their impact depends on how responsibly they are managed. When guided by best practices, these vehicles can effectively connect donor intent with community needs. With this influence comes a clear responsibility to ensure that DAFs remain effective, transparent, and accountable tools for philanthropy.

Transparency is a central element of responsible DAF management. Sponsors should provide donors with clear communication about fund balances, fee structures, and grant activity, while also preserving the privacy protections that make DAFs appealing to many donors. This balance between openness and donor autonomy reinforces public trust in donor-advised philanthropy.

Stewardship is equally critical. Sponsors must manage philanthropic assets prudently, ensure that donor-advised accounts remain active, and encourage ongoing charitable engagement. Building strong collaborations with nonprofit organizations further enhances the value of DAFs by directing funds to mission-driven initiatives that generate lasting impact.

By operating within a framework of best practices, DAF sponsors demonstrate that donor-advised funds are not only effective and flexible, giving vehicles, but also vital contributors to a strong and ethical philanthropic ecosystem.

WHY BEST PRACTICE DAF MANAGEMENT MATTERS

As DAFs continue to expand in influence, their management must be guided by principles that honor donor intent, promote public trust, and support regulatory compliance. Adopting best practices in transparency, timely grantmaking, and nonprofit collaboration allows DAF sponsors to strengthen the philanthropic sector and foster lasting relationships between donors and the organizations they support. Best practice management is not simply about meeting regulatory requirements. It is about embracing a higher standard of responsibility that advances the effectiveness and credibility of donor-advised giving.

BACKGROUND: 10 BEST PRACTICE GUIDELINES

The 10 Best Practice Guidelines for DAF sponsors outline core principles for responsible management, emphasizing transparency, compliance, accountability, and meaningful philanthropic impact. They serve as a flexible but reliable framework that accommodates different organizational models while upholding donor trust and effective grantmaking. Far more than theory, these guidelines represent a practical roadmap that DAF sponsors can adopt to demonstrate integrity, encourage active charitable engagement, and strengthen the charitable sector.

Note on Terminology

To avoid confusion, the term "sponsor" refers to the charitable entity and its governing board of directors responsible for the DAF. In the United States, "sponsor" specifically refers to the 501(c)(3) organization that hosts and administers the DAF. The sponsor's board holds ultimate responsibility for oversight, compliance, and fiduciary management. In other countries, such as Canada and the UK, the term "sponsor" is not commonly used. However, regardless of terminology, in each jurisdiction the responsibility lies with the charity and its governing body.

The Purpose of the Guidelines

These guidelines highlight the multifaceted responsibilities of DAF sponsors and emphasize their role as stewards of philanthropy. Offered as a voluntary resource, they are intended as a starting point for sponsors to reflect on and define their own best practices. Designed to be adaptable, the guidelines allow for tailoring based on mission, structure, and stakeholder needs.

For donors, the principles provide insight into how contributions are managed responsibly. For advisors, they offer a framework for aligning philanthropic goals with practical strategies. For nonprofits, they demonstrate the operational integrity and collaborative potential of DAFs as a funding partner. By addressing the core functions of effective DAF management, these guidelines help sponsors communicate their commitments with clarity, reinforcing public trust and sector-wide impact.

THE 10 BEST PRACTICE GUIDELINES FOR DAF SPONSORS

Best Practice #1. Compliance and Continuous Evaluation

DAF sponsors are responsible for ensuring full compliance with all applicable legal and regulatory requirements in the jurisdictions where they operate, and for fostering governance practices that sustain ongoing compliance, continuous evaluation, and operational excellence.

Description: Sponsors comply with all relevant legal and regulatory requirements to preserve their tax-exempt status and maintain public trust. This compliance extends to country-specific standards, such as IRS rules in the United States, CRA guidelines in Canada, and HMRC regulations in the United Kingdom.

Beyond meeting these standards, sponsors establish documented compliance policies, conduct regular legal and procedural audits, and provide training for staff and board members to ensure ongoing adherence. Strong governance systems, supported by clear accountability structures, help embed a culture of integrity, ethical stewardship, and operational excellence.

Sponsors should implement continuous evaluation processes to assess and improve policies, procedures, and systems in response to changes in law, regulatory guidance, and philanthropic best practices. This proactive approach ensures that compliance is not treated as a static requirement but as part of a broader commitment to high performance and responsible management.

When participating in international grantmaking (see *Chapter 7: International Grantmaking: A Worldwide Blueprint*), sponsors follow best practices to comply with recipient-country laws, sanctions regimes, and reporting requirements, using risk-based due diligence to guide grant approvals. By combining rigorous systems, continuous improvement, and a commitment to transparency, sponsors can protect their legal status, reinforce public trust, and ensure charitable resources are deployed effectively and responsibly across borders.

Best Practice #2. Avoiding Conflicts of Interest

DAF sponsors must establish, document, and actively enforce clear policies and oversight measures to prevent conflicts of interest in both grantmaking and asset management.

Description: DAF sponsors are responsible for ensuring that all DAF resources are used exclusively for charitable purposes, avoiding any transactions or arrangements that could create the appearance or reality of personal benefit for donors, donor-advisors, or related individuals. IRS regulations prohibit grants that result in personal gain, such as those covering tuition, membership dues, or event tickets that benefit the donor or their family. Comparable restrictions exist in other jurisdictions where sponsors may operate, and these must be observed in all cases. Robust conflict-of-interest policies, annual disclosure requirements, recusal procedures, and independent oversight help maintain impartiality and protect the integrity of the grantmaking process. These safeguards reinforce public trust and ensure that all DAF funds support charitable missions rather than personal interests.

Best Practice #3. Trust Through Transparency and Community Reporting

DAF sponsors prioritize transparency by providing donors, stakeholders, and the public with clear, accurate, and timely information on finances, operations, and impact.

Description: Transparency should extend beyond financial metrics to include operational policies, donor services accessibility, and meaningful community reporting. This can be accomplished through donor portals, annual reports, public filings, community summaries, or other accessible formats.

Preserving donor privacy remains an essential component of trusted philanthropic relationships, allowing donors to support causes without external pressures while safeguarding the integrity of their intent.

As DAFs become more central to philanthropic planning, transparency is critical to maintaining donor confidence. A Morningstar article titled "5 Questions to Ask When Choosing a Donor-Advised Fund" encourages donors to evaluate how sponsors report on performance and operational practices. Sponsors should proactively address questions such as:

- What fees are charged and how are they calculated?
- How frequently are grants recommended and fulfilled?

- Are inactive funds monitored, and what policies govern their use?
- Does the sponsor publicly share impact or grantmaking data?
- How accessible are donor services and reporting tools?

Regular, grounded, human-scale reporting builds public trust, helps address concerns about DAF visibility and accountability, and demonstrates that strong accountability can be advanced by sponsors of all sizes in ways that reflect their mission, capacity, and connection to the communities they serve. Examples of effective national and local reporting practices can be found in the case studies later in this chapter.[159]

Best Practice #4. Prudent Stewardship of Assets

DAF sponsors are responsible for managing philanthropic assets with integrity through prudent investment practices, robust oversight, risk management, and alignment with donor intent.

Description: Asset management within DAFs must reflect both fiduciary duty and philanthropic purpose. In the United States, the Uniform Prudent Management of Institutional Funds Act (UPMIFA) provides a legal framework for investment stewardship, emphasizing prudence, diversification, and alignment with mission and donor intent. Comparable principles exist in other jurisdictions, and sponsors should be familiar with the applicable standards where they operate.

Some sponsors offer socially responsible or mission-aligned investment options, enabling donors to incorporate values such as environmental sustainability or social equity into their investment strategy. While not required, these options can help meet donor expectations while maintaining the liquidity and performance necessary for effective grantmaking.

Prudent stewardship includes clear oversight structures, documented investment policies, regular performance and risk reviews, and transparent reporting on fees and results. These practices ensure that charitable assets are managed with a focus on long-term impact, timely grantmaking capacity, and public trust. UPMIFA, as introduced in *Chapter 3: The History of the DAF Revolution*, remains a foundational legal standard guiding responsible investment strategies across the nonprofit sector.

---

[159] Norton, Leslie P. "5 Questions to Ask When Choosing a Donor-Advised Fund." Morningstar, July 12, 2023. https://www.morningstar.com/funds/5-questions-ask-when-choosing-donor-advised-fund.

Best Practice #5. Purposeful Grant Distributions

Best practices for DAF sponsors encourage and facilitate the active, strategic use of charitable assets in ways that reflect both donor intent and community need.

Description: DAF sponsors can promote meaningful grantmaking by supporting a range of donor strategies, from immediate response to crises to long-term, strategic planning for future impact. While avoiding indefinite fund inactivity is essential to maintaining public trust, sponsors should also recognize that many donors intentionally build balances to support large, mission-driven grants, plan for retirement philanthropy, or create enduring, endowed-style giving.

Effective DAF management includes educating donors about grantmaking opportunities, providing tools such as donor dashboards and impact reports to support philanthropic planning, and implementing clear policies that prompt activity when appropriate. These policies might include periodic outreach to inactive accounts, setting reasonable distribution expectations, and highlighting time-sensitive opportunities for impact. The goal is not to rush distributions, but to ensure that charitable assets are ultimately put to work in service of the public good and in alignment with donor values and philanthropic purpose, while adhering to any applicable jurisdiction-specific requirements.

Best Practice #6. Transparent Grantmaking Policies

Best practices for DAF sponsors include making grantmaking criteria and review processes readily accessible and clearly communicating the reasons why certain recommendations may not be approved.

Description: Transparency in grantmaking policies promotes trust, fairness, and integrity. Sponsors should ensure that all grant recommendations are reviewed consistently and in accordance with legal, regulatory, and fiduciary standards. Criteria must be applied without bias or favoritism and should align with the sponsor's mission and published guidelines. Policies should be readily accessible to donors, such as through a sponsor's website, donor handbook, or onboarding materials, and should include clear explanations of review timelines.

Clear communication, both before and after a grant recommendation, helps manage donor and nonprofit expectations and strengthen relationships. This includes providing constructive reasons for declined recommendations and, where appropriate, guidance for resubmission or alternative approaches. Such practices help prevent confusion, reduce frustration, and reinforce confidence in the grantmaking process. Transparent policies strengthen accountability and build lasting relationships among donors, sponsors, and the nonprofit community.

Best Practice #7. Supporting Nonprofits and Charitable Activities

DAF sponsors recognize the essential role of nonprofits and other qualified charitable activities, making grants that comply with all regulatory requirements and that respect the operational realities and strategic needs of the organizations and initiatives they support.

Description: All grant recommendations must support qualified charitable purposes and comply with applicable regulations. While most DAF grants are made to compliant nonprofit organizations, sponsors may also approve grants to other qualified entities or projects that carry out charitable activities, such as fiscally sponsored initiatives, programs with charitable functions, hybrid or social enterprises with a charitable arm, or international organizations. These grants must be permitted under the sponsor's internal policies and supported by thorough due diligence that confirms charitable use of funds. Due diligence should review the recipient's governance, financial health, mission alignment, and capacity to use the funds effectively.

The outcome of any grantmaking decision is governed by the sponsor's policies within the applicable regulatory framework. These policies define what qualifies as a charitable activity, what documentation is required, and whether specific types of grants are allowed. For some grants, especially those to nontraditional or international recipients, additional compliance processes such as Expenditure Responsibility or Equivalency Determination may be required.

Beyond approving grants, DAF sponsors can strengthen the charitable sector by encouraging support for nonprofit capacity building, strategic planning, leadership development, technology upgrades, and operational improvements. Sponsors may also provide educational tools and advisory services to help donors make informed decisions that promote nonprofit sustainability and the long-term success of other qualified charitable activities.

By establishing clear policies, applying thorough due diligence, and offering guidance within regulatory parameters, DAF sponsors help ensure that charitable resources are used effectively and responsibly, regardless of whether the recipient is a traditional nonprofit or another qualified charitable entity.

Best Practice #8. Ensuring Data Security and Privacy Protection

DAF sponsors safeguard donor and grantee information through effective technology practices, strong data security protocols, and compliance with applicable privacy regulations.

Description: DAF sponsors are entrusted with sensitive personal, financial, and grantmaking information that must be protected against unauthorized access, loss, or misuse. While technology capacity may vary by sponsor, the obligation to protect this information is not negotiable. At a minimum, sponsors should ensure that data is stored securely, access is restricted to authorized personnel, and transmissions of sensitive information are encrypted.

Compliance with applicable privacy laws, such as GDPR in the European Union, CCPA in California, or PIPEDA in Canada, should be built into internal policies and procedures. Sponsors should periodically assess their security measures, maintain a clear plan for responding to data breaches, and work with vendors who meet reasonable standards for data protection. By combining sound technology practices with a culture of privacy awareness, DAF sponsors protect the integrity of their operations, maintain donor and grantee trust, and ensure that philanthropic resources are managed in a secure and responsible manner.

Best Practice #9. Balancing Donor Guidance with Sponsor Oversight

DAF sponsor best practices respect donor advice and provide guidance to help align it with outcomes that comply with all applicable legal, regulatory, and policy standards relevant to the sponsor's country of operation.

Description: Best practices require DAF sponsors to balance thoughtful donor input with their responsibility to ensure all grant recommendations adhere to applicable laws, regulations, and internal policies. While donor-advisors play an important role in shaping philanthropic intent, sponsors retain exclusive authority over final grant decisions. Maintaining this balance is supported by clear, accessible grant guidelines, proactive donor education, and the availability of staff to answer questions before a recommendation is submitted.

When a grant recommendation cannot be approved, sponsors should communicate the reasons clearly, reference the relevant policy or regulation, and, where possible, suggest compliant alternatives that align with the donor's intent. Jurisdictional differences may influence how donor advice is managed, and sponsors should be prepared to adapt their processes to meet the legal requirements of the countries in which they operate. Open communication, consistent policy application, and constructive guidance help donors align their giving strategies with outcomes that are both compliant and impactful.

Best Practice #10. Clear and Timely Donor Communication

DAF sponsors are encouraged to maintain open, proactive communication with donors that keeps them informed, engaged, and educated about their philanthropic opportunities.

Description: Best practices include providing donors with timely updates on fund performance, grant activity, and new opportunities for impact. Communication should be clear, consistent, and accessible through multiple channels, including phone, email, secure portals, and in-person or virtual meetings. Regular check-ins, such as quarterly reports or annual planning calls, help donors remain engaged and confident in their philanthropic strategy. As Ron Ransom, CEO of the American Endowment Foundation, notes:

> Educating advisors, donors, and the broader philanthropic community about the multifaceted benefits of donor-advised funds will amplify their impact and strengthen the sector.[160]

By blending proactive communication with ongoing education, sponsors can help donors make informed, strategic decisions that reflect both their values and the needs of the communities they support.

PUTTING BEST PRACTICES INTO ACTION

DAF sponsors are well positioned to elevate the field by actively implementing the principles outlined in this chapter. Whether national, community-based, or mission-driven, sponsors that embrace innovation and transparency can deepen donor trust and amplify social impact. Practical steps may include:

- Publishing annual reports that highlight aggregate grant payout rates and community impact
- Hosting donor education events that go beyond compliance and into strategic giving
- Offering personalized philanthropic advising and successor planning tools, either in-house or through trusted partners

---

[160] Ransom, R. Interview with Ted Hart, December 5, 2024.

- Creating stewardship programs with regular check-ins, reporting, and values-aligned resources

By leading in these areas, DAF sponsors do more than administer funds. They become philanthropic partners, helping donors move capital with intention and clarity. In doing so, they ensure that DAFs remain a powerful force for good in the evolving giving landscape.

These best practices are not theoretical ideals. They are actionable principles already embraced by DAF sponsors of all sizes and missions. By continuing to lead in transparency, donor engagement, and community responsiveness, sponsors can position DAFs as a cornerstone of modern philanthropy, one that addresses today's needs while preparing for the opportunities of tomorrow.

CASE STUDIES: COMMUNITY REPORTING

One example of national community reporting is Fidelity Charitable's annual *Giving Report*. In a recent edition, the organization shared that more than 322,000 donors recommended $11.8 billion in grants to qualified charities, its most impactful year to date. The report provides detailed insights into donor behavior, grant distribution patterns, and overall philanthropic outcomes. By publicly sharing this level of comprehensive data, Fidelity Charitable helps demystify DAF activity, reinforces public confidence, and responds to concerns about the visibility and accountability of DAF distributions.[161]

An example of community foundation community reporting comes from the Community Foundation of Southern New Mexico, which offers a model of accessible, community-centered reporting. A recent *Impact Report* includes county-level financial breakdowns, scholarship and grantmaking totals, and personal stories from both grantees and beneficiaries. The foundation documented more than 2,000 grants totaling $2.1 million in emergency relief, along with $192,090 in scholarships awarded to 328 students. Testimonials from local families and nonprofits appear alongside clearly presented data on DAF activity and endowment performance.[162]

---

[161] Fidelity Charitable. 2024 Giving Report. February 13, 2024. https://www.fidelitycharitable.org/insights/2024-giving-report.html
[162] CFSNM 2024 Impact Report. Community Foundation of Southern New Mexico. Accessed July 25, 2025. https://www.communityfoundationofsouthernnewmexico.org/impact-report/

CASE STUDY: PROACTIVE ENGAGEMENT

Many community foundations and DAF sponsors are adopting a proactive, education-first model to ensure that donors remain informed and engaged throughout their philanthropic journey. Rather than spotlighting a single fund or individual, this approach emphasizes strategic tools and timely guidance to drive charitable impact.

The San Diego Foundation offers a strong example of this model in action. Through publicly available educational materials such as donor guides and FAQs, the foundation helps demystify DAFs and explain key benefits, including tax deductions, the ability to contribute appreciated assets, and flexible grant timing. For instance, donors who contribute securities or real estate may eliminate capital gains taxes while receiving a charitable deduction for the full fair-market value of the asset, up to 30% of their adjusted gross income. These strategies can significantly increase the amount ultimately available for grantmaking.

DAF sponsors also play a critical role in aligning investment strategies with donor intent. Many, including the San Diego Foundation, offer multiple investment pools, such as non-endowed and endowed options. These allow donors to select an investment approach based on their grantmaking timeline and risk tolerance, while enabling philanthropic capital to grow tax-free and remain available for current or future giving.

Legacy planning is another area where proactive support matters. Donors are encouraged to appoint successors, designate final charitable recipients, or explore planned giving tools such as bequests or IRA rollovers. These services help ensure that philanthropic intent continues across generations.

Publicly reported data affirms the effectiveness of this model. According to the 2023 National Philanthropic Trust DAF Report, average payout rates from DAFs have exceeded 20% every year on record. In 2023, the San Diego Foundation reported a payout rate of 29%, far above the 5% minimum required of private foundations. This illustrates how donor education and active stewardship can translate into meaningful charitable activity.

Rather than relying on mandates, this model promotes voluntary participation through donor support, clear policies, and consistent communication. It reflects a growing trend in the DAF sector to prioritize mission, flexibility, and long-term charitable engagement.[163]

ENCOURAGING STRATEGIC GRANTMAKING AND INVESTING

One of the key benefits of DAFs is the flexibility they offer donors. Donors retain the ability to recommend grants at their own pace and to causes of their choice, subject to the review and policies of the DAF sponsor. Some sponsors place restrictions on eligible recipients or impose additional reviews to ensure compliance with legal requirements and alignment with charitable purpose.

In addition to recommending grants, donors may also be able to advise on how their contributed assets are invested prior to distribution. Increasingly, DAF donors are using this privilege to align their investment strategies with philanthropic values through impact investing, an approach that seeks to generate measurable social or environmental outcomes alongside financial returns.

This dual flexibility, strategic grant timing, and mission-aligned investing allows donors to play a more active role in driving meaningful impact. When combined thoughtfully, these practices enable DAFs to respond to urgent needs while supporting long-term solutions. John Bennett, a partner at Simpson Thacher & Bartlett, LLP, shares,

> The next generation of philanthropy, especially among younger donors, is moving beyond traditional grants to explore impact investments and mission-related investments. This shift is something DAF sponsors will need to address to remain relevant.[164]

This evolution in donor priorities signals the rising importance of mission-aligned investing as a core DAF strategy rather than a peripheral feature.

For readers interested in advanced philanthropic tools such as recoverable grants and investment-aligned giving, see *Chapter 5: The Philanthropic Advisor: Maximizing Donor-Client Success*, which explores how donors and sponsors can collaborate to enhance long-term impact.

[163] San Diego Foundation. Understanding Donor-Advised Funds: Your top 12 Questions Answered. May 8, 2024. https://www.sdfoundation.org/news-events/sdf-news/understanding-donor-advised-funds-your-top-12-questions-answered/
[164] Bennett, J. Interview with Ted Hart, October 20, 2024.

FRAMEWORKS FROM COF AND NPT

As DAFs continue to shape modern philanthropy, leading organizations such as the Council on Foundations (COF) and the National Philanthropic Trust (NPT) have introduced frameworks to strengthen transparency, accountability, and impact across DAF operations. These voluntary standards provide essential guidance for sponsors, helping to ensure that donor contributions align with both philanthropic best practices and evolving community needs.

The Council on Foundations' *Strengthening Community Philanthropy* Ad Hoc Working Group has issued key recommendations, including a 5% annual distribution benchmark for DAFs held by community foundations and the establishment of policies to address inactive funds. By encouraging consistent grantmaking, these principles help balance donor flexibility with the urgency of social impact.[165]

Similarly, the National Philanthropic Trust has advanced a range of voluntary policies that promote ethical fund management and proactive grantmaking. Its Minimum Account Activity Policy (MAAP) outlines thresholds and timelines for identifying and addressing inactive DAFs, reinforcing responsible stewardship and timely use of charitable assets. In addition, NPT offers impact investing strategies that allow donors to align their philanthropic capital with social and environmental priorities, including ESG portfolios and socially responsible investment pools.[166]

Together, these frameworks reinforce the integrity and effectiveness of DAFs, ensuring that the sector remains responsive to societal challenges while honoring donor intent. By adopting these principles, DAF sponsors can enhance public trust, promote responsible fund distribution, and maximize the transformative potential of donor-advised giving.

COMMUNITY FOUNDATIONS NATIONAL SERVICE BOARD

Community foundations have long played a vital role in advancing philanthropy and managing donor-advised funds with integrity and local insight. In the United States, the Community Foundations National Standards Board (CFNSB)

---

[165] Council on Foundations. Strengthening Community Philanthropy: Ad Hoc Working Group on DAFs. February 4, 2022. Accessed March 2025. https://cof.org/content/strengthening-community-philanthropy

[166] National Philanthropic Trust, Minimum Account Activity Policy (MAAP), updated February 25, 2020, https://www.nptrust.org/wp-content/uploads/2020/05/Minimum-Account-Activity-Policy-MAAP-NPT.pdf; and "Impact Investing," accessed March 6, 2025, https://www.nptrust.org/impact-investing/

has established a robust framework to support operational excellence and public accountability in this sector.

While the CFNSB standards provide a strong foundation for community foundations, the 10 Best Practice Guidelines for DAF Sponsors are designed to apply broadly to all DAF sponsor, regardless of size, geographic location, or charitable mission. These guidelines promote relevance and adaptability across the full spectrum of DAF providers worldwide.

Together, these principles articulate the core practices that define responsible DAF operations. By providing a clear and unified framework, they help demystify DAF management and make the sector's operations more transparent and accessible. They also reinforce the sector's critical role in fostering trust, collaboration, and meaningful social impact.

To further understand DAFs as a philanthropic vehicle, it is useful to compare them directly with private foundations.

KEY DIFFERENCES: DAFs AND PRIVATE FOUNDATIONS

DAFs and private foundations are two of the most popular charitable giving vehicles. Both provide donors with tax benefits and a structured approach to philanthropy, but they differ significantly in governance, payout requirements, operational complexity, and transparency. The following table outlines their key similarities and differences.

FEATURE	DAF	PRIVATE FOUNDATION
Legal Structure	A giving account held by a 501(c)(3) public charity (DAF sponsor)	A separate legal entity, typically a 501(c) (3) nonprofit organization
Payout	No legal requirement for annual payouts	Legally required to distribute at least 5% of assets annually
Control	Donor provides grant recommendations, but final decisions rest with the DAF sponsor.	Donors (or board members) have full control over investments, grantmaking, and administration
Tax Deduction Limits	Up to 60% of AGI for cash; up to 30% for appreciated assets	Up to 30% of AGI for cash donations; 20% of AGI for appreciated assets

FEATURE	DAF	PRIVATE FOUNDATION
Administrative Burden	Low; managed by the DAF sponsor, reducing legal and administrative complexities	High; requires board governance, IRS compliance (Form 990-PF), and legal oversight
Startup Costs	Low; usually no cost to open, though minimum contributions vary by sponsor	High; requires legal setup, incorporation fees, and initial funding, typically $1 million+
Ongoing Management	Funded and managed by the DAF sponsor; donor recommends grants but does not oversee investments	Donors or board members must manage assets, grant distributions, and compliance requirements
Privacy	Donor identity can remain anonymous when making grants	Must disclose Form 990-PF, detailing finances, grants, and donor information
Investment Control	Limited; investment management handled by the DAF sponsor	Full control over investment strategy and asset allocation

WHICH OPTION IS BEST?

- *DAFs* are ideal for donors who want a simplified giving vehicle, lower administrative burdens, and the flexibility to give anonymously.
- *Private foundations* are ideal for donors who want full control over grant-making, investment strategies, and the ability to hire staff or engage in direct charitable activities.

Both vehicles have their advantages. Some philanthropists use a hybrid strategy by leveraging DAFs for flexibility and private foundations for more customized, long-term philanthropic initiatives.

WHY DAFS SHOULD NOT BE CONFUSED WITH PRIVATE FOUNDATIONS

While both DAFs and private foundations allow donors to engage in structured philanthropy, they differ in how they are managed, the level of regulatory oversight, and their cost structures.

A *private foundation* is a standalone legal entity that requires a board of directors, dedicated staff, and annual filings with the IRS (Form 990-PF). Foundations must follow strict regulations, including a requirement to distribute at least 5 percent of their assets annually to charitable causes. Administrative costs, including legal, accounting, and staffing expenses, can significantly reduce the amount available for grants.

A *DAF*, by contrast, is a component fund of a public charity. Donors benefit from immediate tax deductions while avoiding the legal and tax compliance burdens associated with private foundations. Although there is no federally mandated payout requirement for DAFs, many sponsors voluntarily exceed expectations and typically distribute more than 20 percent of their assets each year. This average is significantly higher than the minimum required for private foundations. DAFs also do not require the donor to directly manage governance or administration. This makes them a lower-maintenance and cost-effective alternative for those who wish to give strategically without ongoing administrative responsibility.

> # I think the future of DAFs is continued growth because very few people need a private foundation these days.
> — Beth Shapiro Kaufman

Beth Shapiro Kaufman, Partner and National Chair of Private Client Services at Lowenstein Sandler, LLP and former Associate Tax Legislative Counsel at the U.S. Department of the Treasury, reinforces this view:

> I think the future of DAFs is continued growth because very few people need a private foundation these days. DAFs provide a simpler, more flexible alternative that allows donors to maintain control over their giving while avoiding the administrative burden and cost of running a private foundation. Some donors choose to use both vehicles strategically. They may use DAFs for flexible, immediate giving while maintaining a private foundation for long-term grantmaking and legacy philanthropy.[167]

FUTURE DIRECTIONS FOR DAF MANAGEMENT: ADDRESSING EMERGING CHALLENGES AND STRENGTHENING PUBLIC TRUST

As donor-advised funds (DAFs) continue to expand, the sector faces a range of important challenges that also present opportunities to reinforce transparency, equity, and effectiveness. Stakeholders, including regulators, sponsors, donors,

---

[167] Kaufman, Beth S. Interview with Ted Hart, November 5, 2024.

and nonprofits, are encouraged to collaborate in advancing best practices while preserving the flexibility that makes DAFs an attractive tool for strategic giving.

- *Regulatory Oversight*: Heightened scrutiny of payout expectations, fund activity disclosures, and nonprofit engagement may shape future policy proposals that affect DAF operations.
- *Technology and AI Integration:* New tools such as AI-driven grant recommendations and predictive analytics are expected to support more data-informed giving decisions. These advancements raise important considerations related to both efficiency and ethical use.
- *Shifting Donor Expectations:* Next-generation philanthropists emphasize measurable impact and support for unrestricted giving. This shift is prompting DAF sponsors to evolve their engagement strategies

Dan Heist, Assistant Professor at Brigham Young University, notes,

> The data shows that younger generations are more focused on impact and transparency, and DAFs provide a platform that aligns perfectly with these priorities.[168]

- *Global Expansion and Compliance:* As DAFs expand internationally, sponsors must navigate evolving cross-border regulations, anti-money laundering (AML) standards, and due diligence requirements for foreign nonprofit recipients.

LEGAL REFERENCES

For reference to legal definitions and compliance requirements relevant to DAF investments and grantmaking practices, see:

Internal Revenue Code §4944 - Jeopardizing Investments
Internal Revenue Code §4945 - Expenditure Responsibility
Internal Revenue Code §4958 - Excess Benefit
Transactions (Private Benefit Doctrine)
IRS Notice 2017-73 - Request for Comments on Donor-Advised Funds and Related Issues

---

[168] Heist, D. Interview with Ted Hart, September 17, 2024.

By proactively addressing these emerging issues, the DAF sector can reinforce public trust, deepen donor engagement, and strengthen the long-term effectiveness of donor-advised philanthropy.

SPONSOR OVERSIGHT AND DONOR FLEXIBILITY

DAF sponsors typically conduct due diligence on impact investments to ensure compliance and uphold donor intent. Strong investment review policies help mitigate regulatory risks while enabling donors to pursue their philanthropic goals.

Unlike private foundations, which require donors to manage investments directly, DAFs offer professional fund management that reduces administrative burdens. This structure allows donors to concentrate on strategic grantmaking while benefiting from diversified and professionally managed portfolios. The result is that more charitable dollars reach nonprofits, and donors retain the flexibility to support their long-term vision.

As DAF sponsors continue to evolve to meet donor expectations, those that actively provide guidance on estate planning, successor advisorship, and local impact positioning are setting a new standard for long-term stewardship. The following case study from a regional community foundation offers a compelling example of how these best practices are implemented in practice.

CASE STUDY: TESTAMENTARY DAFS, LEGACY PLANNING, AND COMMUNITY EXPERTISE

Contributed by Frances Sheehan, President, The Foundation for Delaware County

To illustrate how these principles work in practice, The Foundation for Delaware County offers a compelling example of how a regional DAF sponsor can support effective legacy planning strategies.

At The Foundation for Delaware County, donors are adopting creative approaches that align estate planning with long-term charitable goals. One donor, for example, seeded a DAF with a modest initial contribution during her lifetime, while arranging for the majority of her estate to be directed into the fund upon her passing. Her plan ensures continued support for four specific charities she cherished, demonstrating how testamentary DAFs can serve as powerful legacy tools, combining tax efficiency with sustained mission alignment.

Other donors have partnered with the foundation through charitable gift annuities (CGAs), securing lifetime income while ensuring that remaining funds support the endowment of a local retirement community. In another case, an attorney managing a bequest turned to the foundation to establish a DAF that could faithfully steward the donor's intent. With annual guidance from the foundation's team, grants continue to reflect the values originally expressed.

Some donors also maintain DAFs at national sponsors such as Fidelity, Vanguard, or Schwab, while creating complementary DAFs at the foundation to benefit from its deep local expertise. In several cases, they designate the foundation-managed DAF as the successor beneficiary of their national DAF. This structure ensures that long-term wishes are honored and often enables children to serve as successor advisors.

Together, these examples highlight the role a community foundation can play as a trusted steward of philanthropic intent. The foundation supports estate planning, facilitates intergenerational engagement, and aligns donor priorities with evolving community needs. These practices also underscore the importance of keeping philanthropic capital active and aligned with mission, a theme further explored in the next section on addressing fund warehousing.

For DAF sponsors, the Delaware County model reflects best practices in action. It offers testamentary DAF options, educates donors and advisors on legacy planning tools, partners with financial institutions, and supports successors in continuing a donor's vision. These strategies help preserve donor intent and empower DAF sponsors to amplify long-term community impact on both local and national levels.[169]

ENCOURAGING ACTIVE GRANTMAKING

One of the most debated issues surrounding DAFs is the absence of a legally mandated payout requirement. This has raised concerns about the potential accumulation of assets within DAFs without timely grant distributions.

Critics argue that without a required payout, some DAFs may function as indefinite, tax-advantaged holding vehicles, delaying charitable dollars from reaching nonprofits in need. To address this concern, many DAF sponsors have adopted best practices that include voluntary payout benchmarks and minimum distribu-

---

[169] Frances Sheehan, President, The Foundation for Delaware County. Email to author, October 14, 2024.

tion recommendations. By proactively engaging donors whose accounts remain inactive for extended periods, sponsors can encourage regular grantmaking. Outreach strategies such as impact storytelling, suggested grant opportunities, and distribution reminders help prompt action and ensure that charitable funds are effectively deployed. A key strength of DAFs is their ability to create space for more thoughtful, strategic giving. Joe Fisher, President and CEO at REN, puts a focus on this point:

> Decoupling the tax benefit from strategic giving was a game-changer. It gave donors the breathing room to think about their philanthropic goals rather than rushing to find a recipient.[170]

This flexibility supports practices that prioritize donor engagement, mission alignment, and sustained grantmaking over time.

As Holly Welch Stubbing, Chief Executive Officer of National Philanthropic Trust, emphasizes,

> DAFs are a unique philanthropic tool because they allow donors to be both strategic and flexible in their giving, while also encouraging thoughtful, ongoing engagement with the causes they care about.[171]

DAFs are not passive giving vehicles. DAF sponsors help activate grantmaking.

In response to concerns about payout rates and the pace of giving, many DAF sponsors have adopted additional strategies to encourage active use of charitable funds. Some recommend a minimum 5 percent annual distribution to ensure philanthropic capital remains in circulation. Others reach out to donors when a fund has seen no activity for two or more years, offering guidance and suggested grant opportunities. In some cases, these outreach efforts are combined with internal policies that require grantmaking after a certain period of inactivity.

Transparency has also improved. Many sponsors now publish annual payout reports that demonstrate their commitment to accountability while continuing to protect donor privacy.

---

[170] Fisher, J. Interview with Ted Hart, February 13, 2024.
[171] Stubbing, H.W. Interview with Ted Hart, May 6, 2025.

Sara C. DeRose, Director of Development at Fairfield County's Community Foundation, underscores this proactive approach:

> To prevent funds from sitting inactive, we actively engage donors. If there's no activity for two years, we initiate multiple outreach efforts before reallocating the fund to benefit the community.[172]

By integrating voluntary payout benchmarks, consistent donor outreach, and transparent reporting, DAF sponsors can preserve flexibility while ensuring that funds are actively deployed to strengthen communities.

FOREIGN INFLUENCE AND GOVERNANCE CONSIDERATIONS FOR DAFS

As DAFs expand globally and attract cross-border interest, U.S.-based sponsors must remain attentive to compliance risks associated with foreign involvement. While international philanthropy offers significant opportunities, it also introduces regulatory complexities that require careful management.

U.S. tax law does not explicitly prohibit foreign entities from influencing 501(c)(3) organizations, including DAFs. However, the Internal Revenue Service (IRS) mandates strict compliance to ensure these entities operate exclusively for charitable purposes as defined by U.S. law. Organizations with foreign governance ties may be subject to heightened scrutiny, particularly in three key areas:

1. Private Benefit Doctrine:
Tax-exempt organizations are prohibited from providing more than incidental private benefit to individuals or entities, whether domestic or foreign. For DAFs, this means advisory privileges and grant recommendations must not result in undue control or benefit, such as directing funds to foreign private interests or to entities affiliated with the donor. The IRS may review governance structures, grantmaking activity, and potential conflicts of interest to evaluate compliance

2. Public Support Test:
To maintain tax-exempt status, organizations must demonstrate that they serve public, not private, interests. Excessive reliance on foreign funding or influence could raise concerns about whether the organization meets the public support requirements under Section 501(c)(3).

---

[172] DeRose, S. Interview with Ted Hart, December 12, 2024.

3. Anti-Terrorism and Sanctions Compliance:
DAF sponsors must adhere to anti-terrorism laws and sanctions requirements, including screening for prohibited entities and avoiding diversion of resources. DAFs with foreign links must exercise rigorous due diligence to ensure compliance with the Office of Foreign Assets Control (OFAC) regulations and the USA PATRIOT Act. These concerns intersect with broader debates about transparency in philanthropy, such as those related to the Foreign Agents Registration Act (FARA). While FARA does not directly regulate nonprofits, its emphasis on transparency has contributed to ongoing discussions about foreign influence in the sector.[173]

Proactive governance, through clear policies on foreign advisory roles, grant restrictions, and independent oversight, can mitigate these risks and support regulatory compliance.

BEST PRACTICES FOR DAF SPONSORS: GOVERNANCE AND TRANSPARENCY

To manage the complexities of foreign involvement and maintain strong governance, DAF sponsors should implement key best practices. These include reviewing board composition to ensure independent oversight and minimizing the risk of foreign influence, particularly where affiliated individuals or entities may shape fund management or grantmaking decisions.

For organizations that are dual-qualified, recognized as tax-exempt in both the United States and another country, additional due diligence is necessary. This ensures alignment with U.S. charitable standards and prevents conflicts of interest. In international grantmaking, many sponsors voluntarily apply the standards of Equivalency Determination (ED) or Expenditure Responsibility (ER), even though these procedures are not legally required for DAFs. This approach reduces compliance risk and reinforces responsible giving.

DAFs are also governed by rules under Internal Revenue Code §4966, which prohibit grants to individuals or to organizations that are not qualified public charities, unless the grants meet strict expenditure responsibility requirements. This provision is essential to prevent charitable funds from being diverted for private benefit or used outside the nonprofit sector.

---

[173] Brian Wanko "The Foreign Agents Registration Act's NGO Impact," InterAction. March 20, 2019. https://www.interaction.org/blog/the-foreign-agents-registration-acts-ngo-impact

In addition to governance and grantmaking safeguards, transparency plays a vital role in reinforcing public trust. DAF sponsors with foreign governance involvement or management by foreign entities should clearly disclose these relationships. Transparency should be integrated into the organization's website, public governance documents, and DAF agreements where donors formally accept terms.

Disclosures should clearly identify any foreign-affiliated oversight or decision-making authority and outline the steps the sponsor takes to ensure regulatory compliance. Although not required by the IRS, this level of disclosure reflects emerging best practices and helps donors make fully informed decisions.

Proactive transparency fosters donor confidence, strengthens accountability, and aligns with the philanthropic sector's commitment to ethical governance. For DAF sponsors, adopting these practices supports responsible grantmaking, reinforces donor intent, and ensures that foreign partnerships meet both legal and mission-aligned standards.

For more detailed guidance on foreign entity validation, international compliance risks, and cross-border giving, see *Chapter 7: International Grantmaking: A Worldwide Blueprint. .*

ENSURING DAFs DRIVE MAXIMUM PHILANTHROPIC IMPACT

DAF sponsors play a critical role in promoting transparency, strengthening donor trust, and advancing meaningful philanthropic outcomes. By implementing a range of best practices, sponsors help ensure that charitable assets are actively mobilized to address pressing community needs.

In addition to the required Form 990 reporting, public communication of grantmaking performance is a valuable tool. Many sponsors already publish annual payout rates and grantmaking trends, which reinforces public confidence and encourages donors to remain actively engaged. When presented thoughtfully, these disclosures highlight the role of DAFs in driving timely and effective charitable giving.

Donor education is equally vital. Through workshops, webinars, and personalized guidance, sponsors can empower donors to pursue long-term, strategic philanthropy. Informed donors are more likely to support multi-year initiatives, invest in systemic change, and align their giving with evolving social and community priorities.

Encouraging active grantmaking over time is another key strategy for sustaining impact. Sponsors can monitor fund activity and engage donors when accounts remain inactive, helping ensure that charitable resources are consistently deployed to meet urgent needs. These efforts help preserve momentum, while also building long-term donor relationships rooted in accountability and mission alignment.

In contrast, the National Center for Family Philanthropy's *Trends in Family Philanthropy* report found that general operating support from family foundations declined from 72 percent in 2015 to just 66 percent in 2024. Only one in five foundations currently provide multi-year grants. Although nearly three-quarters report they are considering reforms such as streamlined reporting or increased flexibility, few have implemented those changes. DAF sponsors, by comparison, have the structural agility to adopt these practices now, offering a more responsive, collaborative, and values-driven model of philanthropy.[174]

Collaboration with nonprofit organizations and sector partners further amplifies this impact. By aligning DAF grants with high-priority initiatives and fostering strategic partnerships, sponsors contribute to a more coordinated and effective philanthropic ecosystem.

Together, these practices foster a culture of transparency, intentional giving, and active stewardship assuring that DAFs remain a dynamic force for community good.

THE FUTURE OF COLLABORATIVE PHILANTHROPY

In recent years, collaborative philanthropy has gained momentum as donors seek to amplify their impact by working together on large-scale initiatives. Unlike traditional grantmaking, which is often conducted independently, collaborative philanthropy brings together multiple donors, institutions, and funding networks to pursue shared goals. This approach leverages collective expertise, increases financial reach, and supports long-term, scalable solutions to complex societal challenges.

Donor-advised funds (DAFs) play a critical role in this space, serving as central funding vehicles for pooled philanthropic efforts. Many DAF sponsors have established dedicated funds for priority issues such as climate change, disaster relief, and global health. These structures allow donors to participate in coor-

---

[174] National Center for Family Philanthropy, Trends 2025: Results of the Third National Benchmark Survey of Family Foundations (Washington, DC: NCFP, 2024).

dinated giving efforts with streamlined administrative oversight and built-in strategic frameworks.

By promoting donor education, encouraging participation in shared initiatives, and enabling structured collaboration, DAF sponsors are helping to shape a more resilient and impactful charitable sector. Elaine Martyn, Vice President at Fidelity Charitable®, underscores this capacity:

> One of the key advantages of donor-advised funds is that they ensure funds are readily available to meet community needs when they arise.[175]

CASE STUDY: BLUE MERIDIAN PARTNERS

Blue Meridian Partners is a leading example of collaborative philanthropy focused on addressing systemic social challenges through large-scale funding initiatives. The model brings together contributions from DAFs, private foundations, and high-net-worth individuals to support high-impact solutions across the United States.

How It Works

Blue Meridian applies a structured investment approach, similar to venture philanthropy, to provide long-term, strategic funding to initiatives focused on economic mobility, poverty reduction, and educational equity. The organization collaborates with major philanthropists and institutions to mobilize pooled capital and deliver sustained operational support to scale proven solutions.

Impact
- More than $2 billion committed to initiatives that address social mobility and poverty
- $439.5 million in grants distributed in fiscal year 2023
- Key focus areas include early childhood development, workforce training, and criminal justice reform
- Sustained funding enables high-impact organizations to scale, innovate, and plan for long-term outcomes

By harnessing the power of collaborative philanthropy, Blue Meridian demonstrates how collaborative philanthropy can unlock significant and sustained resources for complex social challenges. DAFs play a critical role in this model by enabling donors to contribute flexibly and efficiently to shared missions. As

---

[175] Martyn, E. Interview with Ted Hart, August 27, 2024.

more donors seek to maximize their philanthropic impact, models like Blue Meridian highlight the importance of cross-sector collaboration and pooled giving strategies. These partnerships allow donors to participate in large-scale initiatives that might otherwise be out of reach individually.[176] The success of Blue Meridian underscores the evolving role of DAF sponsors in modern philanthropy. By facilitating donor participation in collaborative efforts, DAF sponsors can help shape a philanthropic sector that is more coordinated, more strategic, and more focused on long-term impact.

FINDING THE RIGHT BALANCE

For many donors, privacy is not about secrecy but discretion. They wish to support causes they care about without attracting unsolicited attention or external pressure. As Jack Salmon, Director of Policy Research at the Philanthropy Roundtable, notes:

> Transparency involves tracking where funds go and how they are spent, which DAFs handle effectively and continue to improve. However, concerns about transparency related to anonymous giving directly contradict the right to free association, a fundamental principle of civil society going back decades.[177]

DAF sponsors play a critical role in helping donors understand their options regarding privacy in giving. As part of broader donor education, sponsors can explain that anonymous grantmaking is available and may be especially valued by those whose philanthropy reflects deeply held personal, cultural, or religious convictions. In many religious traditions, discreet giving is seen as an expression of humility, integrity, and respect.

According to the National Study on Donor-Advised Funds, anonymous grantmaking represented less than 4 percent of all grants in the dataset. For those donors, the confidentiality provided by DAFs allows them to support causes without public scrutiny or unwanted solicitations.[178]

At the same time, many DAF sponsors have implemented voluntary best practices that enhance transparency while preserving donor privacy. These include

---

[176] Madison Community Foundation. Annual Report 2023: Adapting Philanthropy for the Future. Madison, WI, 2023. Accessed January 21, 2025. www.madisonfoundation.org.
[177] Salmon, J. Interview with Ted Hart, December 13, 2024.
[178] Donor-Advised Fund Research Collaborative. 2024 National Study on Donor-Advised Funds. February 5, 2024. https://www.dafresearchcollaborative.org/national-study

anonymized impact reports that detail annual grantmaking totals, payout rates, and areas of philanthropic focus. Such practices provide meaningful insight into giving trends without compromising donor identities.

By embracing these voluntary transparency measures, DAF sponsors can strengthen public confidence, demonstrate accountability, and uphold the

Anonymous grantmaking represented less than 4% of all grants.
-Donor-Advised Fund Research Collaborative

flexibility that makes DAFs a trusted and effective tool for modern philanthropy.

ADMINISTRATIVE FEES AND FUND MANAGEMENT COSTS

While DAFs offer tax advantages, simplified giving processes, and long-term charitable planning opportunities, some critics have raised concerns about the transparency of administrative fees. Although few donors enjoy paying fees, it is important to recognize that these costs support essential services, including fund management, regulatory compliance, and donor advising.

Supporters of DAFs emphasize that administrative expenses are typically much lower than the costs associated with managing a private foundation. Leading DAF sponsors publish clear and accessible fee structures, outlining administrative charges, investment management fees, and any advisory service costs. Transparent communication builds trust by helping donors understand how their contributions are allocated and what value they receive in return. According to the National Philanthropic Trust, most DAF sponsors charge administrative fees ranging from 0.15 percent to 1.00 percent, depending on account size and the level of services provided.[179]

Importantly, the flexibility offered by DAFs allows donors to be more strategic in their giving. With professional support and low overhead, donors can ensure that their charitable funds are deployed where and when they will have the greatest impact. As regulatory conversations continue, DAF sponsors have an

[179] National Philanthropic Trust. 2024 Donor-Advised Fund Report. Jenkintown, PA: NPT, November 12, 2024. https://www.nptrust.org/reports/daf-report

opportunity to lead by modeling transparency, communicating fee structures clearly, and ensuring that administrative costs remain reasonable and aligned with charitable outcomes.

THE ROAD AHEAD:

Growing attention on DAFs suggests that expectations for oversight and accountability will continue to evolve. This moment presents an opportunity for DAF sponsors, policymakers, nonprofit leaders, and donors to shape a thoughtful and balanced framework, one that ensures charitable resources are used effectively while preserving the flexibility that has made DAFs such a valuable philanthropic tool.

To demonstrate effective self-regulated leadership and reinforce public trust, DAF sponsors can:

- Promote active grantmaking through meaningful donor engagement.
- Embrace voluntary transparency practices that inform and inspire confidence.
- Support policies that uphold donor intent while strengthening nonprofit sustainability.

As discussions around regulation continue, it is essential that all stakeholders work together to preserve the integrity, effectiveness, and long-term viability of DAFs. The path forward requires collaboration, innovation, and a shared commitment to ensuring that philanthropic capital moves with purpose, equity, and impact.

KEY TAKEAWAYS

DAFs have transformed modern philanthropy by offering a flexible, tax-efficient, and professionally managed platform for charitable giving. Their continued success depends not only on favorable laws or financial structures, but on the leadership and integrity demonstrated by the institutions that sponsor them.

This chapter introduced ten best practices that define high-performing DAF sponsors. At the core of these practices is a voluntary commitment to transparency, regulatory alignment, donor education, and community impact. By adopting clear fee disclosures, strong governance policies, responsible investment strategies, and proactive donor engagement practices, DAF sponsors reinforce public trust and ensure that charitable dollars serve the public good.

The most effective sponsors provide much more than administrative processing. They serve as philanthropic partners, guiding donors through each stage of their giving journey, from onboarding and strategic grantmaking to legacy planning and multigenerational engagement. In doing so, they illustrate how voluntary standards, proactive payout benchmarks, and collaborative funding approaches can advance the philanthropic sector without the need for additional regulation.

The growing prominence of DAFs reflects more than tax advantages. It is a result of the trust they have earned through consistent, self-regulated leadership. As donors seek to align their giving with long-term values and engage the next generation, donor advisors play a pivotal role in guiding these conversations. Chapter 5 explores how thoughtful advising, strategic philanthropic planning, and family engagement can help donors use the DAF structure to preserve, expand, and fulfill their charitable legacies.

THE PHILANTHROPIC ADVISOR: MAXIMIZING DONOR-CLIENT SUCCESS

EXECUTIVE SUMMARY

Philanthropic advisors are vital partners in modern wealth planning, helping clients align charitable giving with financial, estate, and legacy goals. As donor-advised funds (DAFs) continue to expand in popularity and sophistication, this chapter equips advisors with practical tools to guide values-driven conversations, engage families across generations, and integrate DAFs into comprehensive strategies. Through best practices in sponsor selection, grantmaking, compliance, and long-term planning, the **Philanthropic Advisor's DAF Success Checklist** provides a step-by-step framework to transform philanthropy from one-time transactions into enduring impact and legacy.

STRUCTURING SUCCESS

Guidance for Advisors Maximizing Donor Impact through DAFs

Philanthropic advisors are at the core of strategic charitable planning, serving as partners in aligning donor intent with financial strategy, regulatory compliance, and nonprofit impact. As the use of DAFs continues to grow, these advisors, whether financial, legal, tax, or philanthropic professionals, play a vital role in helping clients make informed, values-driven decisions that harmonize their charitable goals with broader financial objectives.

The **Philanthropic Advisor's DAF Success Checklist** is a comprehensive and actionable roadmap designed to guide advisors in seamlessly integrating DAFs into client engagements. More than just a compilation of best practices, this checklist serves as a strategic framework, one that helps advisors navigate the evolving landscape of donor-driven philanthropy, ensure regulatory compliance, and support the long-term sustainability of the nonprofits their clients care about.

As DAFs have become a cornerstone of modern charitable giving, the advisor's role has expanded from facilitating one-time gifts to shaping long-term philanthropic strategies. With the right tools and insights, advisors can transform their approach, moving from transaction-focused planning to relationship-based, impact-driven guidance.

Used effectively, the checklist empowers advisors to:

- Master the art of engaging clients in meaningful philanthropic conversations, building trust and uncovering values.
- Develop strategies for tax-efficient giving and estate planning.

- Confidently evaluate and recommend the ideal DAF sponsor(s) to match each donor's needs.
- Understand compliance with regulatory frameworks and uphold professional integrity.
- Facilitate multigenerational giving fostering legacy planning.
- Enhance philanthropic impact by structuring grants that promote nonprofit sustainability.

This checklist is more than a static tool; it is a flexible framework, with each section of the chapter expanding on a key component through real-world examples, actionable insights, and expert perspectives to help advisors become indispensable partners in their clients' philanthropic journeys.

Using the Checklist to Navigate This Chapter

The following sections walk through the structure of the **Philanthropic Advisor's DAF Success Checklist**, a practical guide designed to equip advisors with the tools and insights needed to excel in DAF-related planning. Each component aligns with a key element of the checklist, offering actionable insights, real-world case studies, and expert recommendations that bring these strategies to life.

As advisors progress through the chapter, they will:

- Apply hands-on guidance for integrating DAFs into client strategies.
- Examine real-world examples that demonstrate these strategies in action.
- Use expert tools and insights to strengthen philanthropic planning.

By the end of the chapter, advisors will have a comprehensive toolkit to help deploy charitable dollars efficiently and with lasting impact. The checklist serves as a practical reference for client meetings, strategic planning, and ongoing philanthropic consultations.

ADVISOR'S DAF SUCCESS CHECKLIST

Advisor Checklist #1: The Role of Advisors

- Understand how advisors serve as strategic partners in charitable planning
- Define the distinct roles of financial advisors, legal professionals, and philanthropic consultants
- Recognize how advisors align donor intent with financial planning and nonprofit sustainability

Advisor Checklist #2: Proactive Conversations

- Clarify common donor misconceptions about DAFs
- Develop core competencies for effective philanthropic advising
- Deepen donor conversations to uncover values, legacy goals, and charitable intent

Advisor Checklist #3: Structuring a Giving Strategy

- Determine the donor's desired level of involvement in grantmaking
- Align the DAF strategy with broader financial, estate, and legacy plans
- Evaluate liquidity, timing, and charitable priorities when recommending contributions

By opening a donor-advised fund you get all the same great services a private foundation would hire, at a fraction of the cost as a shared services model with other philanthropists.

Advisor Checklist #4: Multigenerational

- Involve successor generations in grantmaking and philanthropic decision-making
- Facilitate structured family conversations to develop a shared giving philosophy
- Leverage DAFs to teach younger generations about philanthropy and financial responsibility

Advisor Checklist #5: Compliance

- Understand best practices for complying with IRS rules and regulatory guidelines
- Navigate grantmaking restrictions, including self-dealing, international compliance, and recommended philanthropic safeguards
- Structure compliant scholarship funding and grants to private foundations

Advisor Checklist #6: Strategic Grantmaking

- Collaborate effectively with DAF sponsors and nonprofit partners
- Encourage active grantmaking to prevent fund stagnation
- Balance donor intent with nonprofit needs to support sustainability

Advisor Checklist #7: Financial and Tax Planning

- Align DAF strategies with financial, tax, and estate planning to maximize impact
- Donate long-term appreciated assets to minimize capital gains and increase charitable deductions
- Coordinate contribution timing with high-income years, liquidity events, or major tax milestones

Advisor Checklist #8: Complement Private Foundations

- Distinguish the key differences between DAFs and private foundations
- Use DAFs to streamline administration, meet payout requirements, and support anonymous giving
- Design philanthropic strategies that effectively integrate both DAFs and private foundations

Advisor Checklist #9: Fexibility and Efficiency

- Facilitate complex asset contributions, including real estate, closely held business interests, and cryptocurrency, to unlock greater philanthropic capital
- Design and implement multi-year giving strategies that sustain long-term impact and align with donor priorities
- Review and adapt charitable plans regularly to reflect changes in market conditions, financial circumstances, and donor interests

Advisor Checklist #10: Long-Term Engagement

- Conduct regular check-ins to review donor goals and track grantmaking progress
- Measure philanthropic impact using nonprofit reports and independent evaluations
- Strengthen relationships with beneficiaries to build donor satisfaction and long-term commitment

By applying the **Philanthropic Advisor's DAF Success Checklist**, advisors can confidently guide their clients toward charitable giving that is impactful, compliant, efficient, and strategically aligned with their philanthropic goals.

CASE STUDY: SIMPLIFYING CHARITABLE GIVING

Jim Parks, a financial advisor from Parks Wealth Management, effectively demonstrated the benefits of DAFs through his experience with a client in Massachusetts. The client, a successful medical practitioner, was overwhelmed by the complexity of tracking and managing numerous charitable contributions each year. Recognizing the need for a more streamlined approach, Jim introduced him to the concept of a DAF.

By transferring appreciated assets from the client's investment portfolio into a DAF, they were able to centralize the management of his philanthropic activities. This strategic move not only simplified the giving process by reducing administrative burdens but also enhanced the client's tax benefits. The DAF enabled more substantial and strategic contributions, facilitating increased support not only for local community organizations but also for educational institutions, including the universities attended by the client's children.

This example clearly illustrates the practical application of the principles outlined in the **Philanthropic Advisor's DAF Success Checklist**, demonstrating how DAFs can significantly amplify the impact and efficiency of charitable giving. *Reprinted with permission from REN.*[180]

CHECKLIST OVERVIEW: STRATEGIC GUIDANCE FOR ADVISORS

The case study above illustrates how the principles in this checklist can streamline charitable giving and strengthen the advisor-client relationship. More than a process guide, the checklist empowers advisors to move beyond facilitation and become strategic partners in philanthropic planning.

ADVISOR CHECKLIST #1: THE ROLE OF ADVISORS

As philanthropy becomes increasingly integrated with wealth management and estate planning, advisors have become pivotal partners in shaping the future of charitable giving. No longer on the sidelines, they guide donors through the complexities and opportunities of modern philanthropy, helping them maximize financial efficiency, ensure legal compliance, and achieve meaningful social impact.

---

[180] Parks, J. (n.d.). Why integrate charitable giving into your practice. REN Inc. Accessed March 12, 2025, https://www.reninc.com/advisor-daf-resources/

Philanthropic advisors draw on expertise from fields such as financial planning, law, philanthropic consulting, and the nonprofit sector. Regardless of background, effective advisors serve as trusted strategists, aligning charitable intent with financial and legal considerations, identifying high-impact opportunities, and ensuring philanthropy remains both efficient and purposeful.

Their areas of expertise may include:

- **Structuring** contributions and optimizing tax-efficient giving strategies
- **Aligning** charitable goals with estate and financial planning
- **Managing** investments within DAFs to grow charitable assets
- **Ensuring** compliance with philanthropic regulation
- **Designing** strategic philanthropic plans that maximize impact
- **Navigating** the nonprofit landscape and identifying effective partners

Philanthropic advisors may work independently with donor-clients or as part of a multidisciplinary team, coordinating efforts across financial, tax, and estate advisors. Their role is multifaceted and mission-driven, balancing a donor's financial well-being with their philanthropic vision to create lasting, meaningful impact.

Depending on the type of DAF sponsor, philanthropic advisors bring different expertise to the table. For example, advisors at community foundations often provide deep consultative support rooted in local knowledge, helping donors align giving with the most pressing needs in their region. Their guidance is typically grounded in longstanding relationships with area nonprofits and a nuanced understanding of local priorities.

Advisors at national DAF sponsors emphasize scalability and efficiency. They support donors in structuring high-impact gifts across diverse geographies, navigating complex assets, and maximizing tax benefits through streamlined systems. These advisors often leverage technology and analytics to help donors align giving with broader financial strategies.

Advisors at faith- and mission-based DAF sponsors provide a values-driven approach, helping donors align their giving with religious convictions, ethical frameworks, or specific causes like education, environmental sustainability, or global justice. These advisors understand the donor's spiritual or ideological motivations and provide personalized support to ensure giving reflects deeply held values and advances mission-aligned goals.

All three models offer unique value: one through personalized, place-based insight; one through scale and technical sophistication; and one through mission-integrated guidance and ethical clarity. Advisors can help donors select the environment that best aligns with their giving style, whether geographic, strategic, or values driven.

The Expanding Role of DAFs in Philanthropy

DAFs have become a dominant force in modern philanthropy, outpacing private foundations in asset growth and grantmaking. As Michael P. Vito, Partner and Vice-Chair, Trusts and Estates, Lowenstein Sandler, LLP explains,

> In practice, donor-advised funds have largely supplanted private foundations for all but the most affluent clients seeking the added control and potential prestige offered by foundation structures.[181]

According to the latest report from National Philanthropic Trust (NPT), assets held in DAFs have surpassed $251 billion. Over a recent five-year period, DAFs maintained an impressive 14% compound annual growth rate and distributed more than 20% of their assets in grants annually.[182]

Estimates of the total number of DAF accounts vary depending on the source. While there is no universally agreed-upon count, recent analyses suggest the number likely falls between 1.4 million and nearly 2 million accounts.[183] By comparison, the IRS reports just over 105,000 private foundations in the U.S. While foundation assets exceed $1.2 trillion, their average annual growth rate has remained steady at 6–7%.[184]

This disparity underscores the unique advantages of DAFs: streamlined administration, increased flexibility, and faster deployment of charitable dollars.

By leveraging the infrastructure and oversight provided by DAF sponsors, donors can confidently pursue their philanthropic goals with a sophisticated, hassle-free giving vehicle. This combination of cost-effectiveness, professional

---

[181] Vito, M. Interview with Ted Hart, June 9, 2025.

[182] National Philanthropic Trust. 2024 Donor-Advised Fund Report. November 12, 2024. https://www.nptrust.org/reports/daf-report

[183] Collins, C., DeVaan, B., Flannery, H., and Petegorsky, D., The Independent Report on DAFs (Institute for Policy Studies, April 2025).

[184] Internal Revenue Service. (2023). SOI Tax StatsDomestic Private Foundation and Charitable Trust Statistics (Tax Year 2021). Accessed November 13, 2024. https://www.irs.gov/statistics/soi-tax-stats-domestic-private-foundation-and-charitable-trust-statistics

Donor-advised funds have largely supplanted private foundations.

- Michael P. Vito

support, and strategic flexibility continues to make DAFs an increasingly attractive option for donors seeking to amplify their charitable impact.

Advisors have a unique opportunity to move beyond donor support and become essential partners in nonprofit sustainability. Many nonprofits face chronic financial instability due to inconsistent funding, short-term grants, and restricted-use donations that limit operational flexibility. Advisors can help address these challenges by encouraging clients to consider:

- *Multi-year funding commitments*, which provide grantees with long-term stability and predictability
- *General operating support* to help nonprofits meet their most pressing needs and build organizational capacity
- *Endowed gifts or unrestricted grants* to sustain core programs and deliver long-term impact

While DAFs often allow for anonymity, multi-year commitments can signal a deeper alignment with a nonprofit's mission and long-term goals. This presents a unique challenge: how can donors preserve anonymity while still fostering learning, transparency, and strong grantee relationships?

Advisors can play a vital bridging role. Even when donors choose to remain anonymous, they may authorize the DAF sponsor or advisor to facilitate impact reporting, milestone updates, or anonymized feedback loops. By acting as relationship stewards, advisors help multi-year giving support nonprofit sustainability while enabling ongoing learning and deeper donor engagement, honoring donor privacy.

By aligning donor intent with nonprofit needs and facilitating communication, advisors enhance both nonprofit sustainability and the long-term impact of their clients' philanthropy.

ADVISOR CHECKLIST #2: PROACTIVE CONVERSATIONS

Initiating meaningful conversations is the first step in uncovering your client's philanthropic motivations, values, and long-term vision. At this stage, the advisor's role is to begin with curiosity, to listen, not prescribe. Advisors who create space for clients to explore their values lay the groundwork for trust, clarity, and action.

Many donors have a strong desire to give but hesitate due to uncertainty about where or how to focus their philanthropy. Advisors can address this hesitation with strategic guidance and empathy, building donor confidence and fostering lasting philanthropic relationships. Once clients gain clarity, advisors can guide them toward action, structuring their giving for maximum impact.

Best Practices for Philanthropic Conversations

- **Start with Personal Stories:** Ask clients about their earliest memory of giving or a cause that has personally shaped them. This sparks authentic dialogue and strengthens personal connection.
- Position Philanthropy as Part of Holistic Wealth Planning: Frame charitable giving as an integral component of their overall financial legacy, just like estate planning or investment strategy.
- **Use Open-Ended Questions to Explore Values:** Rather than asking, "Do you want to set up a DAF?" begin with broader discussions about what matters most to the client and what impact they hope to achieve.
- **Guide Clients Through Structured Reflection**: Help clients articulate their philanthropic values and legacy goals before introducing specific giving vehicles or tools.

Clarifying Information About DAFs

Many donors lack a complete understanding of how DAFs function, or how they can be used to achieve their philanthropic goals. Advisors play a critical role in dispelling misconceptions and educating clients about the flexibility and benefits of DAFs.

Myth 1: DAFs have mandatory minimum distribution requirements like private foundations.

Reality: Unlike private foundations, which must distribute at least 5% of their assets annually under IRC §4942, DAFs have no such federal requirement. Yet DAF donors consistently exceed that benchmark voluntarily. While the IRS does not mandate distributions, many DAF sponsors enforce their own "inactive account" policies, typically triggered after three to five years without grant activity, helping charitable assets to be actively deployed.

Myth 2: Assets contributed to a DAF are inaccessible for extended periods.
Reality Donors can recommend grants to qualified charities immediately after contributing to a DAF. This offers unmatched flexibility, allowing them to respond quickly to urgent needs or evolving philanthropic priorities.

Myth 3: DAFs can only support a limited set of charities.

Reality: Most DAF sponsors permit grants to any IRS-qualified public charity in good standing. However, some sponsors may restrict grants to specific causes or geographic areas. Advisors should help clients understand any limitations that may apply when selecting a DAF sponsor.

By proactively addressing these common myths, advisors empower clients to see DAFs not as passive holding accounts but as powerful tools for strategic, values-aligned philanthropy.

Common Barriers and How Advisors Can Address Them

Even the most generous clients may hesitate to act on their philanthropic intentions. By anticipating common concerns, advisors can offer empathetic, strategic solutions that move conversations forward.

Barrier 1: Clients feel uncertain about where to give.

Advisor Response: Emphasize the flexibility of DAFs. Clients can establish a DAF, contribute funds, and receive immediate tax benefits without needing to select specific grantees right away. This removes pressure and creates space for thoughtful exploration. Advisors can later introduce nonprofits aligned with the client's values and interests.

Barrier 2: Clients worry about balancing philanthropy with financial security.
Advisor Response: Demonstrate how giving strategies can be designed to support both generosity and financial well-being. Contributing appreciated assets, bundling donations during high-income years, or using a DAF to separate charitable and personal funds can make philanthropy tax-efficient and sustainable.

Barrier 3: Clients fear judgment or elevated expectations when discussing giving.
Advisor Response: Reinforce that philanthropy is deeply personal and should reflect the donor's own values and comfort level. Framing giving as an evolving journey, not a fixed commitment, helps clients engage on their own terms and timeline.

DAFs have emerged as a powerhouse in modern philanthropy.

By proactively addressing these barriers, advisors transform philanthropic conversations from moments of hesitation into action-oriented engagements that deepen donor confidence and impact.

Expanding Expertise in Philanthropic Strategies

To effectively guide clients in charitable planning, advisors will continually deepen their expertise. Specialized training programs offer a structured way to gain knowledge and credentials in philanthropy, helping advisors provide informed, strategic counsel.

Two programs, the Chartered Advisor in Philanthropy (CAP®) designation[185] or the DAF certification program, both offered by the American College of Financial Services, are options worth considering. These programs provide advanced education in philanthropic strategies. Advisors who pursue CAP® or similar continuing education courses can better help clients align their giving strategies with broader financial and legacy planning.

Beyond technical expertise, advisors play a critical role in shifting donor behavior from passive giving to active philanthropic planning. Beth Harper Briglia, IPA, CPA, CAP®, Philanthropic Advisor and fellow CAP® designee, underscores this challenge:

---

[185] The American College of Financial Services. (n.d.). Chartered Advisor in Philanthropy (CAP). Accessed April 21, 2025. https://www.theamericancollege.edu/learn/professional-designations-certifications/cap

One of the challenges we face is educating donors about the importance of being intentional with their giving. A donor-advised fund isn't just a holding account; it's a vehicle for change.[186]

However, this need for education extends beyond donors as Elaine Rasmussen, Founder and CEO, Social Impact Now and On-Air Host of Do.Different.Better, notes:

I think one of the big challenges with DAFs is the lack of education both for donors and their advisors. Many don't know how to leverage DAFs for greater impact, and there's no incentive for advisors to dig deeper into understanding the charitable landscape.[187]

Advisors who proactively seek training in DAF mechanics, grantmaking strategies, and nonprofit evaluation can bridge this gap, equipping clients with the insights needed to maximize their philanthropic impact. As Donna Callejon, former CEO of GlobalGiving, emphasizes:

Educating donors on how to maximize their giving is as important as the giving itself. DAFs are an opportunity to empower donors to make informed decisions.[188]

With the right expertise and guidance, advisors can enhance the donor experience, support more impactful grantmaking, and position themselves as trusted strategic partners. Once that foundation is established, advisors can help clients build a giving strategy that balances financial efficiency with lasting philanthropic impact.

Clients Want and Need: Assistance

According to Cerulli Associates, $124 trillion in wealth is expected to transfer through 2048, with $105 trillion flowing to heirs and $18 trillion projected for charitable giving. Nearly $100 trillion of this transfer will come from Baby Boomers and older generations, representing 81% of the total. This monumental shift in wealth presents both a significant opportunity and a profound responsibility for advisors. Those equipped to guide strategic charitable planning will be well positioned not only to capture assets in motion, but also to help shape the philanthropic legacy of the next generation.[189]

---

[186] Briglia, B.H. Interview with Ted Hart, October 2, 2024.
[187] Rasmussen, E. Interview with Ted Hart, August 19, 2024.
[188] Callejon, D. Interview with Ted Hart, September 16, 2024.
[189] Cerulli Associates, U.S. High-Net-Worth and Ultra-High-Net-Worth Markets 2024: The Great Wealth Transfer—Capturing Money in Motion. Boston: Cerulli Associates, December 2024.

Despite the clear advantages of integrating philanthropy into wealth planning, many advisors still overlook this critical opportunity. Research from Fidelity Charitable reveals that advisors who incorporate charitable planning into their client discussions achieve 1.5x higher Assets Under Management (AUM) and 20% higher organic growth compared to those who do not. Yet, only 57% of advisors proactively discuss philanthropy with their clients.[190] According to Schwab's 2025 RIA Benchmarking Study, 86% of RIAs now offer charitable planning services, reflecting a growing industry shift toward integrating philanthropy as a standard part of financial advice.[191] As John J. Bowen, Jr., and George Walper, Jr., highlight in *Bridging the Wealth Management Divide,*

> Almost nine in 10 (87.3%) wealthy clients want to make a meaningful impact through charitable giving. They seek advisors who can innovate in philanthropic planning, aligning charitable activities with broader financial goals and legacy aspirations.[192]

This data underscores a profound shift: philanthropy is no longer a peripheral concern for clients; it is becoming a central pillar of comprehensive wealth management. Advisors who consistently initiate philanthropic conversations, even before clients ask , are meeting a growing expectation while enhancing relationships, differentiating their practice, and unlocking new opportunities for growth.

Core Competencies for DAF Advisors

To effectively guide donors in maximizing the potential of DAFs, successful advisors develop a robust set of competencies. These skills extend beyond traditional financial expertise, encompassing an understanding of DAF mechanics, strategic philanthropic planning, and aligning donor goals with impactful giving strategies.

Aligning DAF Strategies with Donor Goals

Advisors can enhance client impact by integrating values-based philanthropy into financial planning discussions. This approach creates opportunities to align

---

[190] Fidelity Charitable, Looking Ahead: 2025 Market & Philanthropy Outlook webinar, February 4, 2025.
[191] Charles Schwab & Co., Inc. (2023). Schwab's 2023 RIA Benchmarking Study: Balancing Scale and Personalization. Schwab Advisor Services. July 2023. advisorservices.schwab.com
[192] John J. Bowen Jr. and George Walper Jr., Bridging the Wealth Management Divide: Advice for Advisory Professionals Who Want to Connect with High-Net-Worth Clients (Norwalk, CT: CEG Worldwide, 2006).

DAF strategies with donor priorities, harmonizing financial goals with philanthropic aspirations. Such conversations not only strengthen donor commitment but also foster mission-driven, strategic giving. Fred Kaynor, Managing Director of Relationship Management, Marketing, and Partnerships at DAFgiving360, explains,

> We have donors tell us, "I want my charitable dollars to go to work even before I grant them." That's a very powerful statement. It means they want their philanthropic capital to have an impact even while it's invested. So, they choose investment options aligned with their values, mission-aligned investments, so the money is doing good from the start, all the way through to grantmaking.[193]

Despite research showing that clients welcome discussions about philanthropy, many advisors hesitate to initiate them. Steve Mark, Head of Strategic Account Relationship Management at Fidelity Charitable, highlights this gap:

> The biggest competition or challenge to philanthropy is actually the lack of having the conversation... Advisors maybe don't feel comfortable, and they don't talk about it with their clients, even though lots of research would say that they would like to cover that topic with their advisor.[194]

Joe Fisher, President and CEO at REN, reinforces this point:

> Advisors don't need to be experts on DAFs; they just need to know the right questions to ask. Philanthropy is a bridge to multigenerational relationships and community engagement.[195]

Advisors who proactively guide clients through structured philanthropic discussions create meaningful opportunities for engagement. By embedding charitable planning into broader financial conversations, advisors help donors clarify their intentions, identify meaningful causes, and structure their DAF contributions strategically.

Connecting Wealth with Values

Beyond financial guidance, advisors play a vital role in helping donors connect their wealth with their values. As Reynolds Cafferata, Partner at Rodriguez, Horii, Choi & Cafferata, LLP, emphasizes,

---

193 Kaynor, F. Interview with Ted Hart, June 2, 2025.
194 Mark, S. Interview with Ted Hart, August 12, 2025.
195 Fisher, J. Interview with Ted Hart, February 13, 2025.

Advisors play a crucial role not just in financial guidance, but in helping donors connect their wealth to the causes they care deeply about. It's about aligning purpose with impact.[196]

DAFs can be transformed from passive financial vehicles into dynamic tools for mission-driven philanthropy. As donors gain confidence in their giving strategies, they are more likely to deepen engagement, embrace long-term planning, and maximize their charitable impact.

> # Advisors help donors connect their wealth to the causes they care deeply about.
> - Reynolds Cafferata

Enhancing Advisor-Client Conversations

At the heart of effective philanthropic planning lies the ability to have meaningful, client-centered conversations. Anne Hennessy, Director, Foundation Source underscores this point:

> The overwhelming majority of clients I have worked with have more than one philanthropic vehicle. Advisors are quick to jump to the tool as opposed to having a more robust conversation about philanthropy with their clients. What is someone's philanthropic goal? There needs to be a more robust conversation.[197]

To foster deeper engagement, advisors can move beyond transactional discussions about tools and vehicles. Instead, they guide clients through structured, exploratory conversations about their charitable vision, impact aspirations, and long-term philanthropic strategies.

Tailoring Strategies for Client Segments

Fidelity Charitable reports that women often take a more holistic approach to philanthropy, integrating charitable giving with volunteering, impact investing, and community engagement. Additionally, younger investors are twice as likely to seek philanthropic guidance from their advisors. By understanding

---

[196] Cafferata, R. Interview with Ted Hart, September 11, 2024.
[197] Hennessy, A. Interview with Ted Hart, August 19, 2024.

these trends, advisors can tailor strategies to align with clients' long-term goals, integrating socially responsible investing (SRI) and impact-driven charitable planning.[198]

Proactively aligning philanthropic discussions with these preferences allows advisors to strengthen client relationships and position themselves as key partners in single-generation or multigenerational wealth and legacy planning.

Guided Conversations for Strategic Giving

Once trust is established and philanthropic values are explored, advisors can guide clients toward structured decision-making. Thoughtful questions help refine donor intent, clarify giving priorities, and create a strategic framework for v These conversations are not just about understanding clients' goals; they are about transforming aspirations into action.

Helpful Questions to Guide Philanthropic Conversations

- What causes or issues are you most passionate about?
- How do you envision your philanthropic legacy?
- Are there specific communities or populations you want to support?
- How involved do you want to be in the grantmaking process?
- Do you want to involve your family or future generations in your giving?
- Do you prefer structured, ongoing philanthropy or larger, one-time contributions?
- Would you like your giving to be public, or is anonymity important?

These questions help advisors uncover the heart of a client's philanthropic vision, building a giving strategy that is both meaningful and aligned with their values.

Transitioning to Structuring a Giving Strategy Using DAFs

Engaging conversations are only the first step in a well-designed philanthropic plan. Once donor intent, values, and strategic goals are clearly defined, advisors can help clients transition from discussion to implementation.

DAFs are powerful tools for structuring giving strategies, offering clients the flexibility to give over time while maximizing tax benefits and philanthropic impact. Advisors can help clients:

---

[198] Fidelity Charitable. 2021 Women and Giving and Study Finds Next-Generation Investors Are Seeking Financial Advisor Guidance on Charitable Planning. Accessed June 2025. https://www.fidelitycharitable.org

- **Optimize contributions** by using appreciated assets or bundling donations in high-income years.
- **Align grants with nonprofit sustainability,** helping build toward long-term impact.
- **Involve family members** to foster multigenerational giving and legacy planning.

In the next section, we explore how to structure a giving strategy using DAFs, which helps every contribution to become optimized for impact, financial efficiency, and long-term legacy planning.

The Wright family's experience illustrates how early, proactive philanthropic conversations, guided by trust and clarity, can produce elegant, tax-efficient solutions that honor each generation's values.

CASE STUDY: STRATEGIC PHILANTHROPY

By Jane Peebles. Based on actual client transactions.[199]

Chuck Wright grew up in a philanthropic neighborhood devoted to religious denomination #1 ("RD#1"),[200] where his parents instilled in him the importance of generosity and service. Alongside his wife, Mona, and their three children, David (marketing), Ruth (accounting), and Robert (operations), Chuck built a highly successful consumer goods business based on one of his own inventions.

As they prepared to sell the business, valued at $500 million, Chuck and Mona worked closely with their advisor to chart a thoughtful philanthropic path. Before the sale, they made discounted gifts totaling $8 million in trust for their children, utilizing nearly all of their joint lifetime gift tax exclusion and preserving just $1 million.

To address capital gains and achieve their charitable goals, they designed a multi-layered plan that included:

- Establishing a private nonoperating foundation, funded with $40 million from the business sale proceeds
- Maintaining an existing commercial DAF held by Chuck, valued at $4 million

---

[199] Case Study provided by Jane Peebles, Partner Emerita, Karlin & Peebles, LLP. Used with permission under license to Theodore R. Hart and TEDHART.COM LLC.
[200] RD#1" refers to an anonymized religious denomination, as used in the original case study by Jane Peebles to protect client confidentiality.

- Creating three new DAFs, one for each child, using non-taxable internal transfers from Chuck and Mona's DAF

With limited exclusion remaining, they could not afford to make direct gifts to their children without triggering gift tax. However, transferring $1 million from their DAF to each child's new DAF was not considered a taxable gift, an elegant solution confirmed through careful tax counsel.

Important structural insights guided their strategy:

- A DAF cannot make a grant to a private nonoperating foundation.
- A private foundation may make a grant to a DAF, as DAFs qualify as public charities.
- A DAF may make a grant to another DAF, and a donor-advisor may recommend such transfers, pending the policies of both DAF sponsors, for strategic, administrative, or legacy planning purposes.

Chuck and Mona retained $1 million in their own DAF for future anonymous giving. Meanwhile, David later chose to grant out the majority of his DAF's assets to a private operating foundation he co-founded with a close friend. This foundation serves as a religious community center for members of RD#1, offering programming that promotes shared faith, mutual support, and cultural cohesion. Though the DAF-to-foundation grant did not result in an additional income tax deduction, it powerfully aligned with David's personal mission.

Notably, despite their differing roles in the family business, none of the children sought greater shares or recognition. David never claimed more for leading marketing; Ruth did not ask for more due to her accounting work. Their mutual respect and shared values made it possible to implement this plan with transparency and trust.

The family's humility and unity throughout the process serve as a powerful reminder: strategic philanthropy achieves its highest impact when rooted in long-term vision, thoughtful planning, and genuine family collaboration.

ADVISOR CHECKLIST #3: STRUCTURING A GIVING STRATEGY

Advisors have a unique opportunity to integrate donor-advised funds (DAFs) into holistic financial planning, helping clients achieve their philanthropic goals alongside tax and financial benefits. As Kirk Hoopingarner, Partner at Quarles & Brady, LLP, and Chair of the Evanston, IL Community Foundation, emphasizes:

> The popularity of donor-advised funds stems from their simplicity and efficiency, especially for end-of-year contributions involving complex assets, which offer donors substantial tax benefits.[201]

This quote highlights why DAFs have become a cornerstone of modern philanthropy, offering donors a flexible, efficient, and tax-advantaged vehicle to simplify the giving process while amplifying their impact.

The 3 categories of DAF Sponsors

- ## National DAFs
- ## Community Foundations
- ## Faith/Mission Based

Understanding DAF Mechanics

Advisors who develop a working understanding of DAFs, including the differences between national, community, and faith/mission-based sponsors, are better equipped to guide clients through their charitable giving options. This knowledge enables advisors to provide tailored recommendations on contributions, investment growth, and grantmaking, helping donors achieve both their philanthropic goals and financial objectives.

Choosing the Right DAF Sponsor

Selecting the right DAF sponsor can significantly impact donor satisfaction and philanthropic effectiveness. While finding the right alignment is essential, it's important to note that this decision isn't final; donors can maintain multiple DAFs across different sponsors to address both short-term and long-term giving needs.

Donors may recommend grants from one DAF to another, though such transfers are subject to the policies of both sponsors and may not always be permitted. DAF sponsors are unlikely to refuse transfers, although extenuating circumstances, such as conflicts of interest or policy restrictions, could arise.

---

[201] Hoopingarner, K. Interview with Ted Hart, December 4, 2024.

Comparing National, Community, and Faith/Mission-Based DAF Sponsors

DAF sponsors generally fall into three categories, each offering distinct advantages tailored to different donor priorities:

1. National DAFs

- Broad investment options and streamlined administration
- Many national DAFs also offer advisor-managed options, allowing donors to retain their financial advisors to manage the DAF's investments, subject to the sponsor's oversight and policies.
- Ideal for donors seeking scale and convenience

2. Community Foundations

- Specialize in place-based philanthropy, offering personalized service and deep local knowledge
- Strong connections to nonprofits within specific geographic areas
- Best for donors focused on local impact

3. Faith/Mission-Based DAF Sponsors (single-issue charities)

- Align giving with religious values, ethical principles, or cause-specific missions (e.g., social justice, environmental impact, education, or a specific university).
- Provide a values-driven approach to philanthropy, prioritizing community-driven impact.
- Ideal for donors seeking to integrate their faith or mission into their giving strategy

Regardless of sponsor type, the advisor's role is to help clients select organizations that adhere to best practices in transparency, stewardship, and impact, principles explored in *Chapter 4: Making a Difference: Best Practices for DAFs*, applicable across all DAF sponsors.

Evaluating Key Factors

The evaluation should begin with an understanding of the sponsor's core capabilities, such as charitable planning support, acceptance of complex or illiquid assets, educational tools, and donor engagement programs, and how these align with the donor's philanthropic goals.

When choosing a DAF sponsor, donors and advisors should evaluate these critical factors:

- **Anonymity Preferences:** Most sponsors allow donors to remain anonymous, if desired.
- **Investment Options:** Sponsors vary in the flexibility and diversity of investment choices they provide.
- **Fee Structures:** Administrative and investment fees differ based on account size and management complexity.
- **Grantmaking Flexibility:** How quickly can grants be processed? Are there restrictions on the types of nonprofits supported?
- **Donor Services:** Does the sponsor offer personalized support, such as philanthropic advising, impact reporting, or international grantmaking?
- **Technology and Tools:** Does the sponsor provide user-friendly platforms for managing the DAF, tracking grants, and measuring impact?
- **Successor Planning:** Does the sponsor allow for the designation of successor advisors, and what are the policies for transferring responsibilities?

By carefully considering these factors, advisors can help donors select a DAF sponsor that aligns with their philanthropic vision, financial goals, and values, ensuring a seamless and impactful giving experience.

The Importance of Charitable Planning Guidance

Philanthropic planning is about more than maximizing tax deductions; it's about creating a donor roadmap for meaningful, lasting impact. Advisors play a pivotal role in helping donors define their charitable vision and bring it to life through structured giving strategies, compliance with tax laws, and alignment with broader financial goals.

Behavioral research cited in a recent annual report published by DAFFY reveals that individuals who set charitable giving goals donate, on average, 32% more annually. This could potentially result in an additional $1.6 trillion in charitable giving over the next decade. By helping clients establish structured giving goals through their DAFs, advisors can reinforce philanthropy as a core component of holistic financial planning. [202]

---

[202] DAFFY. Daffy Year in Review 2024. DAFFY Charitable Fund. January 30, 2025. https://www.daffy.org/annual-report-2024

A well-structured DAF strategy integrates philanthropy with a donor's values, financial objectives, and long-term vision. Rather than serving as passive charitable accounts, DAFs can be powerful tools for intentional and sustained giving, enabling donors to make a lasting impact on the causes they care about.

Four Key Areas for Structuring an Effective DAF Strategy

Advisors who wish to help clients make the most of their donor-advised funds can focus on four interconnected areas that together form the backbone of an effective giving strategy. The first is aligning giving with the donor's values and goals. This begins with in-depth conversations to uncover a client's core beliefs, passions, and long-term philanthropic vision. Advisors can then work with donors to define clear priorities and document these through tools such as values-alignment exercises or philanthropic mission statements. When this alignment is achieved, contributions and grant recommendations reflect personal priorities and intent, making the giving experience both meaningful and fulfilling.

A second key area is staying current on regulatory and tax considerations. Advisors must remain informed about IRS regulations, including rules around eligible grant recipients, self-dealing, and international giving compliance. Partnering with tax and legal professionals allows charitable strategies to be integrated seamlessly with estate, retirement, and business succession planning. By ensuring ongoing compliance with evolving laws, advisors help donors maximize tax advantages while avoiding costly penalties.

The third area involves encouraging active grantmaking. Advisors can guide clients in setting structured giving goals, such as annual grant targets or multi-year commitments, and prompt them to review their DAF balances regularly to ensure assets are being actively deployed. Introducing donors to grant dashboards and impact reports provided by their sponsors can reinforce engagement and demonstrate the tangible results of their generosity.

Finally, fostering transparency and communication is essential to sustaining a successful DAF strategy. Advisors should maintain open, ongoing dialogue to adapt giving plans as a donor's financial and charitable priorities evolve. Providing regular updates on the impact of grants and encouraging donors to share their philanthropic journey with family members can inspire a culture of giving that extends across generations. This combination of openness, adaptability, and shared purpose strengthens the advisor-client relationship and ensures that the donor's philanthropic legacy continues to grow over time.

Comparative Analysis of Charitable Giving Vehicles

The philanthropic landscape offers several vehicles for donors to channel their generosity, including DAFs, private foundations, and charitable trusts. Each has distinct features, advantages, and limitations, making it crucial for donors and advisors to evaluate which aligns best with their philanthropic goals and operational preferences.

Criteria	DAFs	Private Foundations (PFs)	Charitable Trusts (CRT/CLT)
Setup Complexity	Simple, requires minimal paperwork with a DAF sponsor	Complex, requires legal setup and IRS registration	Complex, requires legal setup, and a trust agreement
Tax Deductibility	Up to 60% of AGI (cash)	Up to 30% of AGI	Up to 50% of AGI for CRTs; varies for CLTs
Tax Deductibility Limits (Appreciated Assets)	Up to 30% of AGI	Up to 20% of AGI	Up to 30% of AGI
Control Over Funds	Donors advise but the sponsor has final authority	Full control by donor or board	Donor sets terms but trustee manages
Privacy	High: grants can be made anonymously	Low: public disclosureof activities	Moderate: trust documents are private but some disclosures are required
Administrative Burden	Low: managed by DAF sponsor	High: requires tax filings, grant due diligence, potential for multigenerational involvement	Moderate to high: depends on trust type and trustee involvement

Criteria	DAFs	Private Foundations (PFs)	Charitable Trusts (CRT/CLT)
Annual Distribution Requirement	None	5% of assets annually	None for CRTs (there is a required annuity payment to a non-charitable beneficiary); varies for CLTs
Setup and Operating Costs	Low: typically 0.1% to 1% of assets annually	High: startup and ongoing costs significant	Moderate to high: includes trustee fees and setup costs

The above table provides a side-by-side comparison to help inform these decisions:[203]

KEY INSIGHTS FROM THE COMPARISON

This comparison highlights the distinct roles these vehicles play in philanthropy:

- **DAFs** offer simplicity, flexibility, and broad accessibility, making them an ideal choice for donors seeking a streamlined, low-cost way to engage in philanthropy. They are particularly well-suited for donors prioritizing privacy and those who prefer to focus on impact rather than administrative tasks.
- **Private Foundations** provide unparalleled control and flexibility, allowing donors to set their own grantmaking priorities and directly manage philanthropic activities. However, their higher costs, regulatory requirements, and public disclosures make them best suited for donors with significant resources and a desire for complete end-to-end control.
- **Charitable Trusts,** such as Charitable Remainder Trusts (CRTs) or Charitable Lead Trusts (CLTs), excel in estate planning. They offer tax benefits while allowing donors to balance personal income needs with philanthropic goals. However, their relative complexity and limited flexibility in grantmaking may appeal more to donors with specific financial or estate-planning objectives.

---

[203] Rockefeller Philanthropy Advisors. Operating for Impact: Choosing a Giving Vehicle. 2025. https://www.rockpa.org

Making an Informed Decision

Choosing the right giving vehicle is a pivotal step in any donor's philanthropic journey. Advisors and donors should begin by clarifying their goals, financial capacity, and desired level of involvement.

For those seeking a streamlined, cost-effective, and flexible approach DAFs stand out as a powerful option. They combine professional management with low barriers to entry, allowing donors to focus on impact without being weighed down by administrative burdens. Private foundations offer greater control and visibility, while charitable trusts serve as valuable tools for estate planning and intergenerational wealth strategies.

With expert guidance and a clear understanding of the strengths and limitations of each vehicle, donors can craft a philanthropic strategy that reflects their values, advances their legacy, and delivers lasting impact on the causes they care about most.

Mission-Aligned Investing: SRI and Recoverable Grants

DAFs are increasingly used not only for strategic grantmaking but also for mission-aligned investing. Two of the most common approaches that DAF sponsors offer are Socially Responsible Investing (SRI) and recoverable grants.

Socially Responsible Investing (SRI) involves allocating assets to investment portfolios that reflect ethical, environmental, social or other defined values. These portfolios may screen out industries such as fossil fuels or tobacco, while actively supporting areas like renewable energy or fair labor practices. For example, a DAF might invest in a fund that excludes oil companies and prioritizes wind energy startups, ensuring that charitable assets reinforce, rather than contradict, the donor's philanthropic mission.

Recoverable grants are used by some DAF sponsors as a mission-aligned strategy to extend charitable capital with the possibility of repayment. These grants are made with the expectation, though not the legal obligation, of repayment, allowing the funds, if returned, to support future charitable activity While recoverable grants may resemble low- or no-interest loans in structure and intent, there is no IRS guidance that defines or governs recoverable grants within DAFs. Their accounting treatment is not standardized and may vary by sponsor based on internal policy and audit interpretation.

This model is conceptually aligned with Program-Related Investments (PRIs), as defined under Internal Revenue Code §4944(c), which are used by private foundations to further charitable objectives where financial return is secondary to mission alignment. Though PRIs and recoverable grants differ in legal structure and accounting treatment, both reflect a shared commitment to amplifying charitable capital through mission-first reuse.[204]

For instance, a DAF might issue a recoverable grant to help a nonprofit develop affordable housing. The loan enables the project to move forward while preserving the capital for future mission-aligned use. When structured with oversight and charitable intent, recoverable grants enhance both immediate impact and long-term sustainability, showcasing how DAFs can be leveraged as dynamic tools for systemic change.[205]

Balancing Impact and Charity

The IRS has raised concerns that if too much DAF capital is tied up in long-term investments, it could delay funds from reaching active charities, undermining the core purpose of donor-advised giving. To address this, leading DAF sponsors encourage donors to:

1. Pair impact investments with regular grantmaking, ensuring nonprofits still receive timely support.
2. Set clear timelines for recoverable grants, so repaid funds are reinvested in charity within a reasonable period.
3. Avoid treating DAFs as indefinite holding accounts. Impact investing should accelerate giving, not replace it.

What's Possible Depends on Your DAF Sponsor

Some sponsors offer advanced tools, such as socially responsible investment (SRI) options or recoverable grants, but others may not permit them. These strategies are legal when used to further a charitable purpose, but their application is subject to sponsor policies and professional judgment. Donors and advisors should consult both the DAF sponsor and legal counsel before pursuing mission-aligned investments or recoverable grantmaking.

---

[204] Internal Revenue Service. "Program-Related Investments." IRS.gov. Accessed January 16, 2025. https://www.irs.gov/charities-non-profits/private-foundations/program-related-investments
[205] Bernstein. "Recoverable Grants: The Gifts That Keep on Giving." Published March 2024. Accessed March 5, 2025. https://www.bernstein.com/our-insights/insights/2024/articles/recoverable-grants-the-gifts-that-keep-on-giving.html

The Bottom Line

Impact investing in DAFs, whether through SRI screens, recoverable grants, or other strategies, can amplify your philanthropy by ensuring every dollar does good while it grows. The key is balance: these investments should complement, not replace, the essential work of timely nonprofit funding. Best practices, not mandates, have driven DAFs to outperform private foundations in payout behavior.[206]

Transparent policies on grant distribution schedules and investment purpose verification help maintain compliance and reinforce the philanthropic integrity of donor-advised funds. To encourage timely charitable activity, most DAF sponsors have adopted inactivity policies that require donors to recommend at least one grant within a set period, typically between one and three years. If no grant is made during that timeframe, the sponsor often contacts the donor and may ultimately make grants aligned with the donor's previously stated intent or the organization's charitable mission. These practices help ensure that philanthropic capital is put to work while preserving donor flexibility.[207]

Proactive donor engagement strategies, such as regular outreach, tailored grant suggestions, and educational programming, can further motivate ongoing granting. Many sponsors also encourage unrestricted giving, allowing nonprofits to meet critical needs and maintain operational stability. To support donor decision-making, some sponsors provide curated lists of high-impact organizations or offer thematic funds aligned with specific causes.

Legal Guardrails for Impact Investing

Under IRS guidelines, DAF investments must serve charitable purposes and avoid impermissible private benefit pursuant to IRC §4958. To reinforce mission alignment, many sponsors voluntarily apply private foundation standards, such as the jeopardizing investment rules of IRC §4944 and PRI documentation practices, to demonstrate that charitable purpose drives investment choices. DAFs are not subject to the excess business holding limits of IRC §4943, yet many sponsors adopt similar safeguards. They evaluate contributed business

---

[206] National Philanthropic Trust. (2024). 2024 Donor-Advised Fund Report. Jenkintown, PA: National Philanthropic Trust. https://www.nptrust.org/reports/daf-report
[207] Philanthropy Roundtable. Donor-Advised Funds: Payout Trends, Inactivity Policies, and Accessibility. March 13, 2025.
https://www.philanthropyroundtable.org/resource/donor-advised-funds-payout-trends-inactivity-policies-and-accessibility

interests to prevent donor control or self-dealing, ensuring that assets are managed appropriately and charitable integrity is preserved.[208]

In addition to these investment-focused guardrails, DAF sponsors must navigate excise-tax provisions designed to deter improper distributions and self-dealing. Under IRC §4966, if a DAF sponsor distributes funds to non-qualified organizations or fails to conduct proper expenditure responsibility, it may be subject to a 20% excise tax on the grant. Any fund manager who knowingly authorizes such a distribution may be personally liable for a 5% excise tax. Sponsors must ensure all distributions comply with IRS rules and are properly validated to avoid these penalties.Under IRC §4967, prohibited self-dealing transactions trigger a 125% excise tax on the value of the benefit conferred, plus a 10% (up to $20,000) excise tax on any manager who knowingly or recklessly approves the transaction. Sponsors mitigate these risks through clear anti-abuse policies, rigorous due diligence, regular account reviews, staff training on IRC §§4966 and 4967 compliance, and thorough documentation of all investment and grant-making decisions.

Transitioning to Multigenerational Philanthropy

As donors clarify their philanthropic goals, many begin looking beyond individual giving to build a legacy through family engagement. The next checklist explores how advisors can support multigenerational philanthropic planning using DAFs.

Beyond the financial blueprint, many donors seek to pass on values, not just assets. Advisors can guide families in crafting a shared philanthropic identity.

ADVISOR CHECKLIST #4: MULTIGENERATIONAL

Engaging Successors in DAF Planning

Without thoughtful preparation, a donor's philanthropic vision can fade over time. Advisors play a pivotal role in ensuring that generosity endures by helping clients designate and prepare successor advisors, whether family members, trusted friends, or professional partners, who are equipped to carry out the donor's intent.

Succession planning is more than a handoff; it's an intentional process of instilling values, cultivating stewardship skills, and maintaining alignment with

---

[208] Vanguard Charitable Granting Policies and Guidelines. Accessed March 2025., https://www.vanguardchar-itable.org/granting

long-term charitable goals. By guiding clients through this process, advisors create a durable framework for sustained, mission-driven giving that extends well beyond the donor's lifetime.

As Holly Welch Stubbing, Chief Executive Officer of National Philanthropic Trust, observes,

> DAFs enable donors to plan thoughtfully, partner effectively, and amplify their impact over time, especially when sponsors provide tools and guidance that help donors turn good intentions into meaningful results.[209]

> # Millennials gravitate toward DAFs due to their lower administrative burden and seamless integration with their digital lives.
> - Stanford Center on Philanthropy and Civil Society (PACS)

Advisors who help families build a shared philanthropic vision not only deepen impact but also strengthen intergenerational relationships. Notably, advisors who engage heirs in charitable planning are significantly more likely to retain the family as clients across generations. By positioning philanthropy as a shared family value, advisors foster continuity, trust, and long-term engagement that extends beyond financial management into legacy-building.

Engaging the Next Generation

Philanthropy isn't just about today's impact; donors can have the option to cultivate a legacy that endures. Advisors play a key role in helping families pass down charitable values by meaningfully involving the next generation in giving decisions.

A major challenge in multigenerational philanthropy is helping younger family members feel authentically connected to the family's mission. Millennials and

---

[209] Stubbing, H.W. Interview with Ted Hart, May 6, 2025.

Gen Z often bring fresh priorities to the table, favoring social impact, innovation, and hands-on involvement. Advisors can bridge these generational differences by:

- Facilitating open conversations about family values and philanthropic goals
- Designing engagement opportunities aligned with younger generations' interests
- Using technology to meet their desire for transparency, collaboration, and measurable results

A 2020 study from the Stanford Center on Philanthropy and Civil Society (PACS) highlights that high-capacity Bay Area millennials are not only proactive in their giving but strongly value convenience, flexibility, and the ability to measure impact. They gravitate toward DAFs over family foundations due to DAFs' lower administrative burden and seamless integration with their digital lives. Advisors who understand these motivations can better help younger donors align their philanthropic plans with personal values, engage family members, and design multi-year giving strategies that reflect both local and global concerns.[210] This data equips advisors to better tailor conversations and tools that meet next-generation donors where they are, strengthening both family relationships and long-term philanthropic engagement. For advisors, this means offering not just tools, but a mindset shift, one that integrates next-generation preferences into every aspect of multigenerational philanthropic planning. Jane Wales, Co-Chair, National Generosity Commission and Vice President, The Aspen Institute underscores:

> The future of philanthropy will be about inclusivity and creating pathways for people from all walks of life to make a difference.[211]

DAFs also offer a practical way to teach broader financial skills, such as budgeting, investing, and long-term planning, within a charitable context.

As explored in *Chapter 2: DAFs: Redefining Modern Philanthropy*, next-generation donors are reshaping philanthropy through tools like direct giving platforms, impact investing, and AI-powered dashboards. Advisors can support their evolving preferences by introducing real-time grant tracking, personalized recommendations, and collaborative donor portals. These tools keep younger

[210] Park, J., & Shankar, K. Bay Area Millennial Giving: Current Trends, Challenges, and Opportunities. Effective Philanthropy Learning Initiative, Stanford PACS, 2020.
[211] Wales, J. Interview with Ted Hart, September 11, 2024.

donors actively engaged and deepen their sense of connection to causes they care about.

By integrating these strategies, advisors help families build a resilient philanthropic culture that evolves with each generation, ensuring that giving remains dynamic, relevant, and purpose-driven.

Successor Advisors and Beneficiaries

Most DAF sponsors allow donors to designate successor advisors to continue recommending grants after the donor's lifetime. However, policies vary, so it's essential that donors understand the specific terms and choose a sponsor aligned with their legacy goals.

A clear succession plan helps philanthropic assets remain active and true to the donor's intent. Without one, DAFs risk becoming dormant. Many sponsors have inactive account policies that dictate how funds will be distributed if no grants are made within a set timeframe. Knowing these rules is critical to protecting the donor's long-term charitable vision.

Engaging Successor Advisors Early

Involving successor advisors early builds commitment and creates a smoother transition of grantmaking responsibilities. Advisors can assist by:

- Educating successors on philanthropic planning, nonprofit engagement, and strategic giving
- Encouraging shared decision-making through family giving councils or rotating grantmaking roles
- Facilitating hands-on learning, such as nonprofit site visits or grant evaluations, to deepen understanding of charitable impact

These steps not only prepare successors to carry out the donor's mission, but also strengthen family bonds through shared values and purpose. As Adam Nash, CEO and Co-Founder of Daffy, puts it,

> Generational giving is more than a financial goal; it's about teaching children and grandchildren to give, creating a legacy of values and impact.[212]

Advisors who foster a culture of giving help philanthropy continue across generations, if that is desired, not just through financial planning, but by cultivating lasting, intentional engagement.

---

[212] Nash, A. Interview with Ted Hart, October 4, 2024.

Engaging younger generations in philanthropy begins with open, ongoing conversations. Advisors can help by encouraging families to share their philanthropic philosophy, values, and motivations. When these discussions are woven into daily life rather than framed as formal obligations, young people are more likely to feel personally connected to giving.

Providing Leadership and Hands-On Experience

Empowering younger family members to take active roles in philanthropy builds long-term commitment. Advisors can support this by facilitating or advising on:

- **The assignment of leadership roles** within family discussions and grant recommendations
- **The allocation of a portion of the DAF** for next-generation members to advise, enabling them to support causes they care about
- **The planning of hands-on experiences**, such as volunteer work, nonprofit site visits, or travel-based philanthropy that provide direct exposure to impact

Leveraging Digital Tools and Social Engagement

Today's rising donors often turn to digital platforms to amplify their giving. Advisors can help families integrate:

- Online fundraising and crowdfunding campaigns
- Impact-tracking tools to measure results
- Participation in DAF-sponsored networks that support collaborative giving and nonprofit validation

These strategies are offered as adaptable approaches, not one-size-fits-all requirements, so sponsors and advisors can adopt what best fits their governance model and donor relationships.

CASE STUDY: COLLABORATIVE GIVING

In 2024, a multi-generational family office partnered with CapShift to transform two donor-advised funds into platforms for collaborative, mission-aligned impact investing. Working closely with their advisor and DAF sponsor, the family deployed $100 million toward climate innovation and $40 million toward emerging market solutions, including pooled investments in over 36 high-impact companies and funds.

CapShift served as the coordinating hub, liaising among the family, advisor, and fund managers, while providing due diligence and thematic portfolio design. This structure enabled the family to advise on strategic direction, benefit from pooled expertise, and drive systemic change aligned with their values. The case illustrates how digital tools, curated partnerships, and collaborative structures can elevate a DAF from a grantmaking account into an engine for long-term, values-aligned change.[213]

Creating a Long-Term Vision for Philanthropy

DAFs are a powerful tool for extending charitable impact beyond a single generation. However, not all are designed for perpetuity. Many function as spend-down vehicles, offering immediate tax benefits and flexible grantmaking, which often deplete during the donor's lifetime.

In contrast, endowed DAFs are structured to preserve principal while making annual grant distributions, similar to a private foundation or university endowment. This approach enables donors to sustain their philanthropic vision indefinitely.

Key Differences Between Traditional DAFs and Endowed DAFs

Structuring a DAF for Perpetual Giving

Advisors can help families establish an endowed DAF by:

- Engaging heirs in grantmaking and leadership roles
- Guiding the creation of a written philanthropic mission statement that outlines values, goals, and priorities
- Structuring a DAF to function like an endowment, working closely with the DAF sponsor that will own the endowment, ensuring ongoing impact beyond the donor's lifetime

Funding an Endowed DAF

Endowed DAFs offer a sustainable way to preserve charitable capital while distributing grants over time. Advisors can guide donors in funding these vehicles through several tax-efficient mechanisms, listed below.

- Lifetime Contributions: Cash, appreciated securities, real estate, or business interests

---

213 CapShift. "Case Study: Turn Your Donor-Advised Fund Into an Impact Powerhouse." 2025. https://capshift.com/wp-content/uploads/2025/06/Case-Study-Family.pdf

- Bequests via Will or Trust: Enables a seamless transfer of philanthropic intent
- Life Insurance: Name the DAF sponsor as beneficiary to direct policy proceeds
- Retirement Accounts (IRA, 401(k), 403(b)): DAFs receive assets tax-free when named as beneficiary
- Charitable Trusts:
  - Charitable Remainder Trusts (CRTs): Provide payments to the donor (or others) for a set period; remainder to the DAF
  - **Charitable Lead Trusts (CLTs):** Income goes to the DAF for a set term; remaining assets pass to one or more non-charitable beneficiaries.

Feature	Traditional DAF	Endowed DAF
Grantmaking Approach	Flexible, can be spent down over time	Grants are distributed as a percentage of fund value annually
Longevity	May be fully distributed within donor's lifetime	Designed for perpetual giving
Successor Planning	Donors can name successors or charities to receive funds after their lifetime	Successors oversee fund growth and annual grantmaking
Investment Strategy	Based on donor's giving timeline	Focused on long-term sustainability

How the Endowment DAF Works

Unlike a traditional DAF, where donors may grant funds at their discretion, an endowed DAF follows a structured payout model:

- **Fund Management:** Assets are invested by the sponsor to support long-term growth, guided by best practices and standards like the Uniform Prudent Management of Institutional Funds Act (UPMIFA). As detailed in Chapter 3, UPMIFA balances prudent spending and donor intent.[214]
- **Grantmaking Structure:** Grants are typically distributed annually as a set percentage of the endowment's value, similar to foundation payout models.
- **Successor Designation:** Donors may appoint trusted individuals, including family members, to oversee the fund's growth and continue recommending grants.
- **Defined Charitable Purpose:** Donors can specify causes or issue areas, ensuring their giving stays aligned with their values over time.

Benefits of an Endowed DAF

- **Perpetual Giving:** Supports causes indefinitely through annual grant distributions
- **Tax Efficiency:** Offers immediate deductions; assets grow tax-free within the DAF
- **Ease of Administration:** No separate tax filings or regulatory burdens
- **Strategic Flexibility:** Enables evolving grant priorities while preserving donor intent

A well-structured endowed DAF allows donors to extend their philanthropic vision far beyond their lifetime. By integrating successor advisors, thoughtful governance, and long-term planning, donors can sustain their values while responding to the changing needs of the communities they care about.

What Happens if No Successor or Beneficiary Is Named?

If a donor fails to name a successor advisor or designate a charitable beneficiary for their DAF, most sponsors will follow their default inactive account policy. These vary but typically involve the sponsor's board allocating the remaining

---

[214] UPMIFA, adopted in 2006 by the Uniform Law Commission, modernized nonprofit fund management by emphasizing prudent investment, sustainable spending, and donor intent. It replaced the Uniform Management of Institutional Funds Act (UMIFA) of 1972.

funds to qualified charities that align with the sponsor's mission or to a general grantmaking fund.

Advisors should consider proactively guiding clients to:

- Name one or more successor advisors
- Establish a backup charitable beneficiary
- Understand the sponsor's inactive account or default distribution policy

Planning ahead prevents charitable intent from being lost and ensures the donor's legacy is preserved, even in unforeseen circumstances.

While family engagement is essential, every giving plan must rest on a solid compliance foundation. Advisors should be equipped to guide donors through key regulatory considerations.

ADVISOR CHECKLIST #5: COMPLIANCE

A working understanding of compliance and due diligence is helpful for advisors guiding clients through legally sound and strategically effective philanthropy. While DAF sponsors are responsible for regulatory compliance, advisors who are well-versed in the legal and procedural landscape can provide more informed guidance, set realistic expectations, and navigate complex giving scenarios with confidence.

Under IRC §4966, DAFs are prohibited from making grants directly to individuals. Grants must go to an IRS-qualified public charity, unless proper expenditure responsibility procedures are followed. While DAFs cannot fund scholarships or aid directly, they may support such programs when administered exclusively by a qualified charity that retains full control over selection and distribution. Sponsors typically maintain robust validation systems, and advisors can help their clients understand and navigate these legal boundaries.[215]

By understanding compliance frameworks and regulatory obligations, advisors can help donors align their charitable giving with both their values and regulatory requirements. This knowledge allows advisors to proactively address donor concerns, reinforce best practices, and provide strategic guidance that maximizes both charitable impact and compliance.

---

[215] IRC §4966; IRS Publication 3833.

Key Areas of Compliance and Due Diligence for Advisors

To effectively guide donors, advisors will focus on the following critical areas of compliance and due diligence:

A. Eligible Grant Recipients

The IRS requires that DAF grants be directed to charitable projects and eligible nonprofit organizations, which include:

- IRS-recognized public charities (501(c)(3) organizations) under IRC §170(c)(2)
- Government entities such as schools and municipalities, under IRC §170(c)(1)
- Religious institutions under IRC §170(c)(2)(B)
- Foreign organizations that have been properly validated to ensure charitable use of funds, typically through procedures such as equivalency determination, expenditure responsibility, or similar protocol established by the DAF sponsor

DAF sponsors verify nonprofit eligibility to ensure compliance with these requirements and avoid penalties under IRC §4966 (governing taxable distributions) and IRC §4967 (prohibiting impermissible benefits).

Advisor Action Steps

Advisors can also direct clients to publicly available tools such as the IRS Exempt Organizations Select Check and Candid's GuideStar Database to confirm a nonprofit's tax-exempt status and review governance, financials, and impact reports.

B. Self-Dealing and Prohibited Benefits

IRS rules strictly prohibit donors and related parties from receiving "impermissible benefits" from a DAF grant (IRC §4967). This includes any direct or indirect benefit (e.g., event tickets, scholarships for family members, or quid pro quo arrangements). Unlike private foundations, which are governed by IRC §4941, DAFs are subject to IRC §4967, which prohibits more than incidental benefits to donors, advisors, or related parties. In addition to IRC §4967, which governs impermissible benefits specific to DAFs, advisors should also be aware of IRC §4958(c)(2), which defines excess benefit transactions and may apply in cases where disqualified persons receive more than reasonable compensation or other undue benefits.

Advisor Action Steps

- Clarify that DAFs are not subject to private foundation self-dealing rules (§4941). Instead, emphasize compliance with IRC §4967, which bans impermissible benefits.
- Ensure donors understand that DAF grants must be made solely for charitable purposes, with no personal or private benefit.
- Help donors understand that grants must be made exclusively for charitable purposes, with no quid pro quo arrangements.

While DAF sponsors enforce these regulations, advisors play a critical role in helping donors structure their grants to avoid unintentional results.

C. Fulfilling Pledges

While IRS rules have historically prohibited using DAF grants to satisfy a legally binding pledge, IRS Notice 2017–73 clarified that such grants may be permissible under specific conditions, opening the door for a more practical and donor-friendly approach.

According to Notice 2017–73, a DAF sponsor may approve a grant that is applied to a prior pledge if:

- The grant letter makes no reference to the pledge.
- The donor receives no impermissible benefit (e.g., event tickets, naming rights, or other quid pro quo benefits).
- The charity receiving the grant does not issue a written acknowledgment that the pledge has been satisfied by the grant.

This guidance allows for a more flexible and compliant path for donors to fulfill their commitments without undermining IRS regulations or exposing themselves or the DAF sponsor to penalties.

Advisor Action Steps

- **Educate clients** on the practical application of IRS Notice 2017–73 and how to structure gifts accordingly.
- **Avoid any language** in correspondence, grant recommendations, or acknowledgments that explicitly ties a DAF grant to the fulfillment of a pledge. While DAFs may be used in this context under certain conditions, linking the grant too directly to the pledge could raise compliance concerns.

- **Coordinate with the recipient charity to ensure it does not issue a written acknowledgment** to the donor for income tax purposes. While Notice 2017–73 does not require the DAF sponsor to block such acknowledgments, the burden falls on the donor to avoid claiming a deduction if one is received.
- **Reinforce compliance by clarifying roles:** Advising both the donor and the charity on best practices can prevent missteps.

D. International Grantmaking

Grants to international NGOs require additional legal and regulatory diligence. Advisors should be aware that while DAFs are not legally required to follow private foundation rules; most sponsors voluntarily adopt IRS-recognized frameworks such as ED and ER. As Allison Fine reminds us,

Taking the friction out of international giving is a good thing for humanity.[216]

A full analysis of international grantmaking compliance, including country-specific risks and emerging best practices, is provided in *Chapter 7: International Grantmaking: A Worldwide Blueprint.*

E. Grants to Private Non-Operating Foundations

Grants from DAFs to private non-operating foundations are subject to strict IRS limitations and are generally treated as taxable distributions under IRC §4966 unless structured to meet expenditure responsibility requirements. This means the grant must be restricted to specific charitable programs, projects, or activities, with proper monitoring and reporting to ensure compliance. Such grants must not provide any undue benefit to the donor or related parties. Because these grants are complex and may require additional documentation and oversight, donors typically work closely with legal counsel and the DAF sponsor when such strategies are proposed. In most cases, supporting public charities directly through a DAF remains a simpler and more flexible alternative.

F. Scholarship Programs

Supporting scholarships is a meaningful way to expand access to education, but when funded through DAFs, strict IRS compliance is required. DAFs cannot make grants directly to individuals, and donors or related parties may not select

---

[216] Fine, A. Interview with Ted Hart, August 23, 2024.

recipients or control scholarship decisions. These restrictions are governed by IRC §4966 (prohibiting taxable distributions) and IRC §4967 (prohibiting more than incidental benefit to donors).

To remain compliant:

- All scholarship grants must be made to a qualified public charity (such as a university or community foundation) that has exclusive authority over the scholarship's selection process, award terms, and governance. The administering organization must independently manage the program without donor influence, including through side agreements or informal expectations.

Funding a scholarship via a DAF requires strict IRS compliance.

- Donors, their family members, advisors, or any related parties must have no role in the recipient selection process, even in an advisory or non-voting capacity, to avoid violating IRC §4967's prohibition on 'more than incidental benefit.'
- Selection criteria must be objective, nondiscriminatory, and serve a broad charitable class.

Violating these rules may result in excise taxes of up to 200% of the benefit under IRC §4967, levied on both the donor and the DAF sponsor. In egregious cases, the DAF's tax-exempt status could be jeopardized.

Donors may support existing scholarship programs or establish new funds with public charities. In either case, advisors should ensure donors avoid conflicts of interest and uphold the integrity of the charitable purpose.[217]

G. Fee Structures and Payout Rates

DAF sponsors charge administrative and investment fees, which vary based on account size and management complexity. Advisors can help donors evaluate these costs to make certain they align with the donor's philanthropic goals.

---

[217] "A Guide to Using Donor-Advised Funds for Scholarships," Bold.org, January 8, 2025. https://bold.org/blog/donor-advised-funds-for-scholarships/

Advisor Action Steps

- Compare fee structures across different DAF sponsors, including national charities, community foundations, and faith/mission-based organizations.
- Highlight the impact of fees on the donor's ability to maximize charitable impact.

Understanding payout rates and administrative costs helps donors make informed decisions about where to establish their DAF.

H. Nonprofit-Specific Compliance

Advisors should be aware that nonprofits face their own compliance responsibilities in receipting DAF gifts, avoiding bifurcated *acknowledgments, and reporting contribut*ions accurately; a more detailed discussion of these nonprofit-specific requirements is provided in *Chapter 6: The Nonprofit Guide to DAFs.*

ADVISOR CHECKLIST #6: STRATEGIC GRANTMAKING

Advisors as Strategic Partners in Grantmaking

Advisors play a crucial role in helping donors connect with the right philanthropic partners. By cultivating strong relationships with both DAF sponsors and nonprofits, advisors can enhance donor impact, ensure compliance, and promote sustainable philanthropy.

Compliance is an essential aspect of effective grantmaking. While DAF sponsors are responsible for verifying nonprofit eligibility and ensuring regulatory compliance, advisors can help donors make informed decisions by understanding these requirements. Once donors are aware of these safeguards, advisors can focus on aligning donor intent with nonprofit needs.

A key advantage of DAFs is their ability to streamline grant administration without the burden of managing a private foundation's complex infrastructure. Unlike private foundations, which require legal structuring and annual filings, DAF sponsors handle compliance, due diligence, and reporting, reducing costs and administrative hurdles for donors.

Collaborating with Nonprofits for Greater Impact

DAF sponsors handle compliance, allowing donors to focus on strategic grantmaking. Here's how advisors can facilitate stronger nonprofit engagement:

- **Bridge the knowledge gap:** Many nonprofits are unfamiliar with how to engage DAF donors. Advisors can help educate nonprofit leaders on effective strategies for connecting with DAF donors.
- **Facilitate strategic giving:** Help donors structure grants that align with nonprofit funding needs, such as multi-year commitments or unrestricted gifts.
- **Strengthen nonprofit relationships:** Encourage site visits, impact reporting, and direct communication between donors and nonprofits to build lasting, trust-based partnerships.

By fostering active engagement between donors and nonprofits, advisors help philanthropy remain both meaningful and sustainable, creating impact for both donors and beneficiaries.

Balancing Donor Intent with Nonprofit Needs

A well-executed DAF strategy aligns donor intent with the operational realities of nonprofits. DAFs offer donors the flexibility to give strategically, ensuring funds are deployed thoughtfully rather than reactively.

To support both donors and nonprofits, advisors can:

- Encourage active grantmaking: Help donors create a structured grantmaking plan that reflects their philanthropic priorities while ensuring nonprofits receive support when it is most needed.
- Promote communication: Facilitate open dialogue between donors and nonprofits to strengthen trust and support the effective use of charitable funds.

By integrating intentional giving strategies into financial planning, advisors help clients transform DAFs from passive charitable accounts into proactive vehicles for philanthropy, ensuring funds are actively deployed.

Balancing Immediate Needs with Long-Term Goals

Effective philanthropy requires balancing short-term needs with long-term sustainability. While immediate giving addresses urgent social issues, long-term commitments provide nonprofits with financial stability and the ability to plan for the future. By integrating both approaches, advisors help donors maximize their philanthropic impact while aligning disbursements with their broader vision for change. This structured strategy not only enhances donor engagement but also helps nonprofits receive the consistent, mission-driven support they need to thrive.

Donor Privacy and Anonymity in Philanthropy

Donor privacy is a core principle of modern philanthropy, balancing the benefits of public recognition with the desire for discretion. At its core, donor privacy serves as an extension of free expression, ensuring that individuals can support social movements, advocacy efforts, and charitable causes without fear of coercion, retaliation, or undue public scrutiny. Just as free speech allows for open or anonymous discourse, donor privacy ensures that philanthropy remains a protected form of civic engagement.

Unlike private foundations, which must disclose all grantees on IRS Form 990-PF, DAFs report grants in aggregate on IRS Form 990, preserving donor anonymity. This structure allows donors to support causes without mandatory public disclosure of individual grants, reducing unsolicited funding requests and safeguarding personal privacy.

While donor anonymity is essential for many, it has also led to debates about transparency. Critics argue that without disclosure requirements, it can be challenging to track charitable dollars from DAFs to nonprofits. However, many DAF sponsors voluntarily publish aggregated grant data, and donors themselves can choose to share their giving through impact reports or donor recognition programs.

For many donors, confidentiality is not about secrecy but about focusing on impact rather than visibility. According to the National Philanthropic Trust, some donors choose to give anonymously to avoid public recognition, protect their privacy, or ensure that the focus remains on the cause rather than the donor.[218]

Strategic Stewardship for Long-Term Philanthropy

With foundational planning, family engagement, and sponsor selection in place, the advisor's role shifts from architect to steward. The focus turns to guiding donors toward sustainable, impactful giving over time. As philanthropic landscapes shift and donor priorities evolve, successful DAF strategy requires ongoing adaptation, creative structuring, and a commitment to donor intent.

By helping donors integrate DAFs into comprehensive financial plans, including

---

[218] National Philanthropic Trust (NPT), 2024 Donor-Advised Fund Report. November 12, 2024.

private foundations, complex assets, and impact-aligned investments, advisors can transform charitable giving into enduring legacies. Flexible and donor-driven, DAFs remain one of the most versatile tools available to support both immediate needs and long-term mission sustainability.

Sustained engagement is key. Donors who remain actively involved in their giving are more likely to evolve their strategies, deepen their impact, and stay connected to their values. Advisors play a vital role in fostering this connection, strengthening nonprofit relationships, and reinforcing meaningful, ongoing commitment.

With an active grantmaking strategy in place, advisors can deepen value by aligning giving with larger financial and tax objectives.

ADVISOR CHECKLIST #7: FINANCIAL AND TAX PLANNING

Strategic Alignment: Maximizing Philanthropic and Financial Impact

A well-structured philanthropic plan not only advances charitable goals but also aligns with a donor's broader financial and tax strategies. By working together, advisors and DAF sponsors can help donors seamlessly integrate philanthropy into wealth management, estate planning, and tax optimization, ensuring their giving is both impactful and financially strategic. Ken Nopar, Vice President and Senior Philanthropic Advisor at American Endowment Foundation, highlights the increasing value advisors place on DAFs as a planning tool:

> DAFs have gained popularity as more advisors recognize the benefits they offer both to their clients and to themselves.[219]

This dual benefit, enhancing client satisfaction while simplifying the advisor's role, has made DAFs a valuable tool in philanthropic planning.

The appeal of DAFs goes well beyond tax advantages. Their flexibility makes them ideal for donors seeking to optimize giving over time, manage charitable commitments, and efficiently transfer wealth. As outlined in Checklist #4, this flexibility also makes DAFs a powerful tool for engaging multiple generations in long-term charitable planning. Turney P. Berry, Partner at Wyatt, Tarrant & Combs, LLP, underscores this point:

---

[219] Nopar, K. Interview with Ted Hart, November 15, 2025.

What makes donor-advised funds so attractive is their simplicity. They allow donors to give, accumulate, and manage funds without the complexities of establishing a private foundation. You can merge them, change them, or give it all away, all without significant legal and administrative burdens.[220]

This adaptability enables advisors to craft philanthropic strategies that evolve alongside their clients' financial goals.

Tax-Efficient Giving Strategies

Donors who contribute long-term appreciated assets, including stocks, cryptocurrency, real estate, or many other types of assets may receive a double tax benefit:

> **"With DAFs, you can merge them, change them, or give it all away, all without significant legal and administrative burdens."**
> - Turney P. Berry

- Avoid capital gains tax: Donating appreciated assets directly to a DAF avoids capital gains taxes on the appreciation, allowing the full fair market value to support charitable causes.

- Receive an immediate charitable deduction: Donors may deduct the fair market value of the asset at the time of contribution, subject to IRS limits. These limits are generally 30% of AGI for non-cash gifts and 60% for cash. Excess deductions may be carried forward for up to five years.

In exchange for relinquishing control of the donated asset, donors gain greater tax advantages than private foundations offer, with far fewer administrative burdens.

Strategic Timing and Liquidity Events

DAFs provide powerful planning flexibility during periods of market volatility, year-end tax strategy, or major liquidity events, such as business exits or stock sales. Advisors often recommend:

---

[220] Berry, T.P. Interview with Ted Hart, November 15, 2024.

- Bundling donations in high-income years
- Timing gifts around liquidity events
- Donating appreciated assets instead of cash
- Planning around deduction ceilings and carryforward rules

Contributions to DAFs are irrevocable, but grantmaking does not need to be immediate. This separation between the tax event and philanthropic deployment allows for more thoughtful, long-term giving strategies.

CASE STUDY: PIERRE & PAM OMIDYAR

In 2004, Pierre and Pam Omidyar, founders of the Omidyar Network and eBay philanthropists, contributed $100 million in appreciated eBay stock to a DAF at the Silicon Valley Community Foundation (SVCF). Their decision illustrates how high-net-worth donors can leverage DAFs to achieve financial efficiency and philanthropic flexibility.[221]

Their strategic use of a DAF allowed them to:

- Avoid capital gains taxes: The appreciated stock was donated directly, maximizing its charitable value.
- Minimize administrative burden: SVCF managed compliance, investments, and grant processing.
- Maintain strategic flexibility: They were able to recommend grants over time, supporting causes, including education, microfinance, and human rights.

This example demonstrates how DAFs empower donors to focus on mission rather than management, while still retaining meaningful advisory privileges over their giving.

ADVISOR CHECKLIST #8: COMPLEMENT PRIVATE FOUNDATION

Philanthropy is not a one-size-fits-all endeavor. For many donors, the choice between a DAF and a private foundation is not an either/or decision, it's a strategic combination. By leveraging the unique strengths of both vehicles, donors can achieve greater flexibility, tax efficiency, and long-term impact Private foundations offer greater control, governance oversight, and a structured approach to legacy philanthropy, making them ideal for donors who wish to involve family members, support complex initiatives, or shape long-term grantmaking strategies. In contrast, DAFs provide efficiency and simplicity, with lower administrative burdens, immediate tax benefits, and the ability to respond quickly to emerging needs.

Advisors note that private foundations have a 5% annual payout mandate, but the average DAF grant rate is higher. According to the National Philanthropic Trust, DAFs annually distribute more than 20% (four times higher than private foundations). This distinction is critical when weighing philanthropic impact versus administrative burden.[222] For many clients, DAFs offer both the flexibility and generosity of purpose that private foundations can struggle to match.

This dual-vehicle approach is especially valuable in global philanthropy, where private foundations often encounter regulatory hurdles when funding foreign charities directly. DAFs, provide a streamlined mechanism for international giving, enabling donors to channel grants through U.S.-based DAF sponsors while adhering to IRS regulations and foreign funding laws.

DAFs and Private Foundations: Key Differences and Strategic Synergies

While DAFs and private foundations differ in structure, governance, and tax treatment, they are not mutually exclusive. In fact, Sunil Garga, Executive Advisor at Fairshare Ads and former CEO and President at Foundation Source, reminds us that:

> Combining private foundations and donor-advised funds can help families achieve specific philanthropic goals, offering anonymity through DAFs while fulfilling regulatory needs with foundations.[223]

Below are the key differences between DAFs and private foundations, followed by ways they can be used together strategically.

Important Compliance Considerations

Feature	Donor-Advised Fund (DAF)	Private Foundation
Governance	Managed by a public charity; donor provides recommendations.	Independent board with full control.

---

[222] National Philanthropic Trust. 2024 Donor-Advised Fund Report. November, 12, 2024. https://www.nptrust.org/reports/daf-report

[223] Garga, S. Interview with Ted Hart, September 16, 2024.

Feature	Donor-Advised Fund (DAF)	Private Foundation
Administrative Burden	Minimal; managed by the sponsoring organization.	High; requires tax filings, meetings, and recordkeeping.
Tax Deduction Limits	Up to 60% of AGI for cash gifts, 30% for appreciated assets.	Up to 30% of AGI for cash gifts, 20% for appreciated assets.
Payout Requirements	No mandatory payout.	Must distribute 5% annually.
Anonymity	Grants can be made anonymously.	Public disclosure of grants and financials.
Investment Control	Managed by the sponsoring organization.	Full investment control.
International Giving	Requires detailed expenditure responsibility or equivalency determination.	Requires detailed expenditure responsibility or equivalency determination.

While earlier sections addressed some of these considerations, it's helpful to reiterate the critical points here so donors and advisors fully understand the distinctions and responsibilities when utilizing both DAFs and private foundations.

Investment Oversight

Private foundations retain direct oversight of their investments, while DAF assets are managed by the DAF sponsor. Advisors can help donors understand the implications of relinquishing direct control over DAF investments, including the potential trade-offs in flexibility and investment options.

DAF Grants and Minimum Distribution Requirements

While current IRS regulations do not prohibit grants from private foundations to donor-advised funds (DAFs), there is no binding IRS guidance that clearly establishes when such grants count toward the 5% distribution requirement. In 2023, *the U.S. Treasury proposed new regulations that would require grants to DAFs to:*

- Be used for charitable purposes by the end of the following taxable year
- Not involve retained advisory privileges by the foundation or its disqualified persons
- Be accompanied by documentation of timely charitable use

These proposals have not been finalized, and many experts consider them controversial. Until final rules are issued, foundations making grants to DAFs should proceed with caution and consult legal counsel to assess whether such grants are likely to be considered qualifying distributions under current IRS interpretations.[224]

Strategic Applications of DAFs with Private Foundations

DAFs and private foundations can work together to offer donors a mix of flexibility, oversight, and streamlined giving. Each vehicle brings unique advantages that, when combined, can help donors achieve a balanced, impactful philanthropic strategy.

- **Anonymous giving.** Donors who wish to give anonymously, whether due to religious convictions or privacy concerns, can use a DAF to make grants without being subject to the more detailed public disclosure requirements of a private foundation. This approach is ideal for individuals who value discretion in their philanthropy.
- **Responsive philanthropy.** When speed is critical, DAFs allow donors to react quickly to emerging opportunities or urgent needs. By leveraging the efficiency of a DAF, donors can complement the deliberate, long-term approach of a private foundation with fast, effective grantmaking.
- **Simplified administration.** DAFs reduce administrative complexity, freeing donors from the annual tax filings and board meeting requirements of a private foundation. This lighter administrative load enables donors to focus on their charitable goals rather than operational tasks.
- **Facilitating international giving.** While private foundations face stringent compliance and reporting obligations when making international grants, DAF sponsors often handle these processes on behalf of foun-

---

[224] U.S. Department of the Treasury, Proposed Regulations under Sections 4966 and 4942, REG-142338-07, 88 Fed. Reg. 83790 (Nov. 21, 2023); see also IRS Notice 2017-73, 2017-51 I.R.B. 562.

dations. This capability allows foundations to reach global causes more easily and efficiently.

- **Enabling multi-generational involvement.** Both private foundations and DAFs can play a role in fostering family engagement in philanthropy. Private foundations provide a governance framework for long-term family involvement, while DAFs offer an accessible entry point for younger family members to participate in charitable giving. Combining these vehicles helps philanthropy become a shared, multi-generational legacy.

By strategically using DAFs alongside private foundations, donors can enhance their philanthropic flexibility, reduce administrative burdens, and engage their families more deeply. This dual-vehicle approach offers a way to achieve immediate impact, maintain oversight, and helps giving remain aligned with evolving goals.

CASE STUDY: CATALYST FOR TRANSITION

Over the years, many private foundation founders have realized that the administrative demands of maintaining a foundation can overshadow the joy of philanthropy. David Scott Sloan, head of the National Private Wealth Services group at Holland & Knight, observes this growing trend:

> During the past several years, we've had more and more clients inquire about terminating private foundations. For some founders, the administrative burden and cost of running a foundation ultimately outweigh the initial thrill of giving like a Carnegie. It's easy to get bogged down with day-to-day details, like overseeing investments, monitoring income and expenditures, and making the required distribution of at least 5% of the entity's assets each year.

One entrepreneur, who had funded his private foundation with $10 million in post-IPO stock, initially found satisfaction in direct grantmaking. However, as the years passed, he found it increasingly difficult to keep up with the operational requirements, including tax filings, compliance with IRS regulations, and the mandated minimum payout. After consultation with advisors, he transitioned his remaining endowment into a DAF, eliminating much of the administrative work while maintaining the flexibility to advise grants.

This case highlights a broader shift in high-net-worth philanthropy: while private foundations provide autonomy, they require substantial management. DAFs offer an alternative that preserves donor intent while reducing regulatory complexity and administrative overhead. As more philanthropists recognize this, transitions from private foundations to DAFs are becoming a mainstream strategy in charitable planning.[225] Courtney Murphy, Senior Director, Head of Strategy and Grants, Global Impact Citizenship, BNY, underscores this point,

> DAFs can be a good substitute for a private foundation, especially for family foundations converting to DAFs because they don't necessarily need the governance structure.[226]

Her observation reflects a growing movement toward simplifying operations while maintaining flexibility and strategic intent, a shift that continues to reshape how families structure their long-term giving.

DAFs and private foundations offer distinct but complementary advantages. By thoughtfully combining both vehicles, donors can balance short-term flexibility with long-term governance and legacy. Advisors play a crucial role in helping clients align these tools with evolving goals, enabling a unified and resilient philanthropic strategy.

ADVISOR CHECKLIST #9: FLEXIBILITY AND EFFICIENCY
Maximizing Client Impact through DAFs

Through strategic contributions, donors can enhance their giving capacity, reduce tax liabilities, and align charitable goals with broader financial and estate planning strategies. This section explores donating appreciated securities and understanding the roles of successors, beneficiaries, and philanthropy funds.

CASE STUDY: USING DAFS FOR IMPACT INVESTING

The Bronx Defenders, a nonprofit legal services organization, faced a severe cash-flow crisis when its commercial bank declined to renew a credit line. Essential services were at risk of shutting down. FJC, a foundation of philanthropic funds, stepped in and issued a $4 million emergency bridge loan from DAF assets earmarked for impact investing.

This timely intervention kept the organization operating and allowed it to secure a long-term banking relationship. Justine Olderman, Executive Director of The Bronx Defenders, noted:

---

[225] David Scott Sloan, quoted in Deborah L. Jacobs, "Making the Transition Out of a Private Foundation," Fidelity Charitable Services, June 16, 2008. Reprinted with permission from Holland & Knight. Accessed February 11, 2025.
[226] Murphy, C. Interview with Ted Hart, August 13, 2024.

The loan could not have come at a better time. We had run out of options and were facing the possibility of having to close our doors and turn away New Yorkers in dire need of our services.[227]

This example illustrates how DAFs can extend beyond traditional grantmaking by providing catalytic financing that sustains nonprofits during liquidity challenges and strengthens long-term resilience.

Practical Guidance: Impact Investing Through DAFs

DAFs offer unique opportunities for mission-aligned and impact-oriented investing. The IRS maintains strict guardrails to ensure that charitable assets are used to further public benefit and are not diverted to private interests. Advisors help clients navigate three key dimensions:

- **IRS restrictions:** Charitable assets must serve public, not private, interests. Avoid excess benefit transactions under IRC §4958, private inurement, or undue donor control.
- **Sponsor policies:** Not all DAF sponsors permit custom investment strategies or alternative assets. Compare policies and review approval processes before selecting a sponsor.
- **Strategic alternatives:** In some cases, other vehicles may be more effective, such as private foundations, charitable remainder trusts, or charitable lead trusts.

Navigating IRS Restrictions

DAF investments must primarily serve public, not private, interests. Under IRC §4958, any excess benefit provided to a disqualified person, such as a donor, donor advisor, or related party may trigger excise taxes. DAF sponsors must also ensure that investment strategies do not result in private inurement, violate charitable purpose requirements under IRC §4966, or confer undue control to donors.

While program-related investments (PRIs) are defined and permitted under IRC §4944(c) for private foundations, there is currently no IRS provision that applies PRIs to DAFs. However, some DAF sponsors voluntarily adopt PRI-like policies to guide mission-aligned investing. These typically include:

---

[227] FJC. "Bridge Loan Maintains Vital Programs at The Bronx Defenders." FJC, May 31, 2022. https://fjc.org/news/bridge-loan-maintains-vital-programs-at-the-bronx-defenders/

- A primary purpose test to ensure alignment with specific charitable goals
- A secondary profit motive, where financial return is not the primary driver
- Clear documentation of charitable intent, purpose, and outcomes

These practices are not mandated by law but may reduce regulatory risk when properly implemented.

Key Compliance Considerations

Risk Area	Legal Context	Advisor Action
Unrelated Business Income Tax (UBIT)	21% tax on unrelated business income	Evaluate pass-through or leveraged investments for UBIT exposure
Private Benefit and Excess Benefit Transactions	IRC §4958 and general §501(c)(3) restrictions	Avoid investments that benefit disqualified persons
Donor Control	DAF assets must be controlled by the sponsor	Recommend use of intermediaries or blind investment pools when needed

Implementing Strategies

To effectively implement an impact investing strategy through a DAF, donors and their advisors must take several key steps. First, selecting the right sponsor is critical. Not all DAF sponsors offer the same flexibility or support for mission-aligned investments. It is important to compare sponsor policies to determine which ones allow for custom investment options or support nontraditional assets. Understanding the sponsor's review and approval processes, especially for assets outside of standard investment pools, can help ensure the strategy is both viable and aligned with the donor's goals.

Equally important is establishing a strong documentation framework. Donors should maintain a clearly articulated charitable purpose statement and revisit it annually to ensure relevance and alignment with their philanthropic priorities. Outcome measurement tools can be developed to assess the impact of grants and investments, providing data that reinforces the fund's mission. In some cases, donors may also wish to request expenditure responsibility reports or grant impact summaries from recipient organizations to enhance transparency and evaluation.

However, it is important to recognize that DAFs may not be the most effective vehicle for every philanthropic scenario. In certain cases, alternative giving structures may better serve the donor's objectives. For example, those who desire full control over both investment decisions and grantmaking might consider establishing a private foundation. Donors seeking immediate charitable impact, particularly those aged 70½ or older, might benefit from direct giving strategies, such as qualified charitable distributions from an IRA. For more complex planning needs, such as those involving income streams or estate planning, charitable remainder trusts or charitable lead trusts may offer more appropriate solutions.

Strategic Timing of Contributions and Grants

One of the key advantages of DAFs is the ability to contribute assets at tax-advantageous moments while distributing grants on a personalized schedule. These moments of windfall wealth, such as a business sale or unexpected inheritance, represent one of the most powerful applications of DAFs. When clients experience sudden financial gains, whether from business sales, inheritances, or stock windfalls, they may be highly motivated to give but unsure where or how to direct their philanthropy. A DAF enables them to secure an immediate tax deduction in the year of the windfall, while giving them time to reflect on long-term philanthropic goals.

Advisor Insight: Encourage donors to contribute assets during peak earning years or in conjunction with liquidity events to maximize tax benefits.

ADVISOR CHECKLIST #10. LONG-TERM ENGAGEMENT

Advisors as Catalysts for Client Success

Philanthropic advisors play a crucial role in modern giving, guiding donors to maximize impact, maintain compliance, and align charitable giving with financial strategies. Their influence extends beyond facilitating transactions; they shape legacies of generosity by fostering multigenerational giving and strategic grantmaking. As explored in Checklist #4, engaging successor advisors and involving family members can deepen donor satisfaction and preserve charitable intent across generations.

A key advantage of DAFs is their ability to simplify charitable giving by reducing many of the legal, reporting, and overhead costs that private foundations incur. The shared services structure of DAFs helps direct a greater proportion of charitable contributions toward mission-driven impact rather than operational expenses. By leveraging DAFs, advisors can assist clients in reducing administrative burdens, enhancing cost efficiency, and increasing the effectiveness of their philanthropy.

Advisors who embrace their role as philanthropic strategists can drive meaningful social change. By actively engaging clients in values-driven giving and leveraging DAFs effectively, they help shape the future of philanthropy. Now is the time for advisors to lead with expertise, integrity, and vision, empowering donors to give boldly, intentionally, and with purpose.

Measuring What Matters

Today's philanthropists increasingly seek transparency about how their contributions create change. Savvy donors leverage resources like Charity Navigator and Candid/GuideStar to evaluate nonprofits' financial health and operational effectiveness. Beyond third-party ratings, forward-looking donors request outcome reports from grantees and track key performance indicators tied to their missions. This data-driven approach transforms charitable giving from a transactional exercise into a strategic endeavor, ensuring every dollar delivers measurable impact.

The Human Dimension: Building Relationships with Beneficiaries

The most impactful philanthropy often emerges from authentic connections between donors and the communities they support. Regular communication with grant recipients provides invaluable insights into evolving needs and demonstrates how funding creates tangible change. These relationships foster mutual understanding: Nonprofits gain a partner attuned to their challenges, while donors develop deeper satisfaction from seeing their values in action.

Creating Lasting Legacy

By combining structured engagement, rigorous impact measurement, and meaningful beneficiary relationships, donors move beyond check-writing to curate a philanthropic legacy. This holistic approach ensures charitable dollars reflect the donor's vision while adapting to changing circumstances. For professional advisors, implementing this framework transforms the DAF from a giving vehicle into a dynamic tool for values realization, where strategic planning, empirical analysis, and human connection converge to multiply impact.

KEY TAKEAWAYS

Philanthropic advisors play a pivotal role in helping clients integrate charitable giving with financial, estate, and legacy planning. DAFs serve as versatile platforms for achieving tax efficiency, regulatory compliance, and long-term philanthropic goals.

This chapter outlined practical strategies that enable advisors to move beyond transactional giving and design comprehensive philanthropic plans. These include selecting the right DAF sponsor, incorporating family succession planning, leveraging impact-aligned investments, and promoting timely and values-based grantmaking.

The Philanthropic Advisor's DAF Success Checklist and related compliance frameworks equip advisors to guide clients with clarity, confidence, and purpose. When approached strategically, DAFs preserve donor intent, foster multigenerational engagement, and ensure that generosity delivers meaningful community impact.

CHAPTER

06

The Nonprofit Guide to DAFs

Executive Summary

Donor-Advised Fund (DAF)-powered donors are shaping the future of philanthropy, offering nonprofits a powerful opportunity to secure sustained, flexible funding. Yet many organizations still struggle to engage DAF donors effectively or build lasting relationships with sponsoring organizations and financial advisors. This chapter presents **10 Proven Strategies to Maximize Support,** a practical framework designed to help nonprofit leaders, fundraisers, and board members turn DAFs into reliable engines of philanthropic support. From strengthening donor stewardship and addressing DAF anonymity to aligning with sponsor priorities and encouraging multi-year commitments, each strategy is grounded in real-world practice and supported by expert insight. Whether you are building your first DAF strategy or refining an existing approach, this chapter offers the tools and structure to move beyond passive receipt of DAF grants and toward intentional engagement that advances your mission.

The Nonprofit Advantage

DAFs are opening new pathways for nonprofit engagement and long-term financial sustainability, yet many nonprofits perceive DAFs as both an opportunity and a challenge. Estimates of the total number of DAF accounts in the United States range from 1.4 million to nearly 2 million.[228] While exact figures vary due to differences in data collection and reporting methods, the overall trend is unmistakable. DAF adoption is accelerating, and these vehicles are playing an increasingly central role in charitable funding.

With charitable assets in DAFs now totaling hundreds of billions of dollars and annual grant distributions in the tens of billions, these accounts represent a significant and renewable source of philanthropic capital for nonprofits that know how to engage effectively.[229] A key point for nonprofits to understand is that once a donor contributes assets to a DAF, they legally relinquish ownership and control over those funds. The DAF sponsor retains final authority over grant distributions, meaning proactively engaging donors and DAF sponsors can help develop a steady flow of contributions.

---

[228] Estimates derived from the National Philanthropic Trust. 2024 Donor-Advised Fund Report. Jenkintown, PA: NPT, November 12, 2024, reporting 1,782,281 DAF accounts in 2023; and IRS Form 990 filings (2019–2023), which document over 1.4 million discrete accounts, with potential undercounting due to sponsor-level aggregation practices.
[229] Donor Advised Fund Research Collaborative. Independent Report on Donor-Advised Funds. April 3, 2025. https://www.dafresearchcollaborative.org/national-study-dafs

Fundraising expert Kay Sprinkel Grace, Founder and Principal of Transforming Philanthropy, LLC, underscores the importance of working closely with DAF sponsors to increase visibility within donor networks:

> Work with DAF managers and foundation CEOs. Fund managers and advisors are the people who will recommend your organization if asked. Let them know what you are doing. Share your dreams and big ideas.[230]

By proactively building relationships, demonstrating impact, and stewarding donors effectively, nonprofits can strengthen long-term donor engagement and secure sustained DAF support.

One of the most compelling advantages of DAFs is their ability to simplify administrative and compliance processes for both donors and nonprofits. Unlike direct donations, which may require the nonprofit to manage complex asset transfers, valuation, and tax documentation, DAF sponsors handle these tasks on behalf of the donor.

> # Fund managers and advisors are the people who will recommend your organization if asked.
>
> - Kay Sprinkel Grace

This creates a kind of centralized infrastructure where financial, legal, and transactional responsibilities are managed by the DAF sponsor. For nonprofits, it reduces administrative burdens, ensuring proper receipting, and lowers risk, especially when dealing with appreciated assets or non-cash gifts. This approach functions as a shared services model, where DAF sponsors provide back-office efficiency and financial expertise that benefits all parties involved.

For nonprofits, this data reinforces the importance of strategically engaging with DAF donors and sponsors to develop philanthropic support. Understanding these trends allows organizations to align their fundraising strategies with donor behaviors, maximizing opportunities to secure recurring grants and long-term partnerships. The following chart presents a six-year overview of key DAF

---

[230] Grace, K.S. Interview with Ted Hart, August 20. 2024.

metrics from that report, including charitable assets, grants distributed, and contributions received.

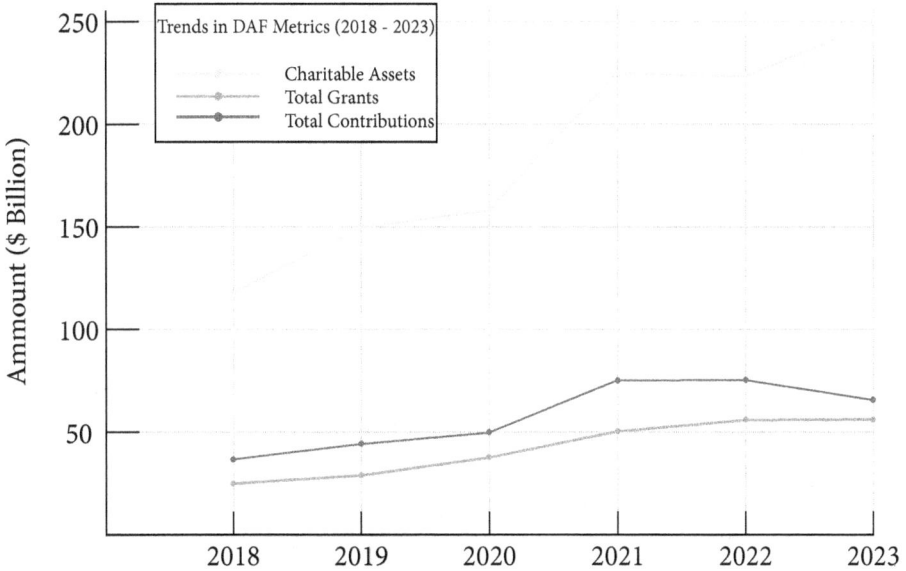

Trends in DAF Metrics (2018 - 2023)

These figures illustrate the steady growth and financial resilience of DAFs despite fluctuations in contributions and grantmaking. The continued increase in charitable assets and the number of DAF accounts signal a strong commitment from donors.

Nonprofits should also be aware of the broad services many DAF sponsors offer in liquidating complex or illiquid assets, such as closely held stock, real estate, or limited partnership interests. These assets are converted into cash within the DAF, which can then be granted to the nonprofit. Donors who take advantage of this benefit often avoid capital gains taxes of up to 20%, while still receiving a charitable gift receipt for the asset's full fair market value at the time of contribution.[231]

Beyond simplifying administrative tasks, nonprofits that take a proactive approach, educating DAF donors, demonstrating impact, and fostering long-term relationships, can encourage more consistent giving. By strategically engaging

---

[231] Trend data drawn from National Philanthropic Trust, 2019 Donor-Advised Fund Report (Jenkintown, PA: National Philanthropic Trust, 2019), and National Philanthropic Trust, 2024 Donor-Advised Fund Report (Jenkintown, PA: National Philanthropic Trust, 2024),

DAF donors, nonprofits can transition from occasional contributions to ongoing philanthropic support. Encouraging donors to consider multi-year commitments or recurring grants can help organizations build stronger, mission-aligned funding strategies. DAF donors can often be encouraged to make unrestricted grants, which can provide nonprofits with critical financial stability and flexibility to allocate funds where they are needed most.

Maximizing the potential of DAFs requires a strategic approach. While DAFs create avenues for substantial, recurring support, they require nonprofits to engage intentionally in order to cultivate long-term donor relationships. Nonprofits that build strong relationships with DAF sponsors, demonstrate impact through transparent reporting, and invest in donor stewardship can unlock sustained financial support.

This chapter explores how organizations can move beyond uncertainty and leverage DAFs as a cornerstone of sustainable fundraising. Through proven strategies, best practices, and case studies, nonprofits will gain essential tools to access, sustain, and maximize these valuable philanthropic funds.

CASE STUDY: REAL-WORLD TRANSFORMATION: HOW ONE FOUNDATION ACTIVATED ITS DAF POTENTIAL

By Tracy Hart, CEO, Osteogenesis Imperfecta Foundation (OIF)
Background

Th OIF relies on individual donors, industry partners, and government grants to support individuals with a rare bone disease. While OIF occasionally received DAF gifts from Fidelity Charitable, these were sporadic and difficult to track, due to donor anonymity.

The Discovery: Engaging the Donor
A conversation with a recurring DAF donor revealed three key insights:

- He preferred managing his philanthropy through a DAF for tracking, tax benefits, and long-term giving stability.
- Many donors in OIF's community likely held DAFs but had never considered using them for OIF simply because they were never asked.
- DAFs provided an opportunity for recurring gifts, which OIF had not yet promoted.

The Solution: Educating and Engaging DAF Donors
In Fall 2023, OIF launched a DAF education initiative that included:

- A quarterly newsletter article explaining how DAFs could be used to support OIF
- Step-by-step instructions on making a DAF contribution
- A dedicated DAF donation section on OIF's website
- Encouragement for recurring DAF gifts to turn one-time donors into sustained supporters

Results: Transforming DAF Contributions into a Reliable Funding Stream

By the end of 2024, OIF achieved:

- Fifteen DAF gifts from various providers (Fidelity, Vanguard, etc.), compared to only two gifts the previous year.
- A 500% increase in total DAF contributions, growing from $15,000 in 2023 to over $100,000 in 2024.
- The ability to expand outreach and services, enhancing educational programs and direct support for families affected by osteogenesis imperfecta.

Ongoing Strategy and Future Plans
Given this success, OIF remains committed to DAF education and now regularly reminds donors about this giving option in newsletters, emails, and on its website. Tracy Hart, CEO, Osteogenesis Imperfecta Foundation, noted:

> Many donors have the capacity to give but need clear guidance on how to do so. By educating donors on DAFs, nonprofits can unlock new sources of funding, increase engagement, and sustain long-term philanthropic partnerships.[232]

Recent survey data supports the urgency of strategic engagement. According to a recent FreeWill DAF Report, only 16% of nonprofits have a formal DAF stewardship plan, despite the rapid growth of DAFs. More than 70% of fundraisers believe DAFs will become more important in the next five years, yet just 32% segment DAF donors in their CRM systems. Even more concerning, only 18% of fundraisers proactively talk to donors about giving through a DAF. These gaps underscore a critical disconnect between fundraisers' awareness and their operational readiness, leaving billions of potential philanthropic dollars

---

[232] Hart, T. Interview with Ted Hart, December 18, 2024.

underleveraged. Closing this gap through education, technology, and intentional outreach is not only an opportunity but a necessity for sustained success.[233]

With the growing scale and influence of donor-advised funds, nonprofit leaders can adopt a deliberate, informed strategy to fully engage this evolving source of philanthropic capital. The following section outlines 10 proven strategies that can help nonprofits move beyond passive grant receipt and toward intentional, long-term cultivation of DAF donors and sponsors. Each strategy is designed to be practical, flexible, and adaptable across organization sizes and missions.

10 Proven Strategies to Maximize Support

DAFs offer nonprofits a powerful opportunity, but success requires more than passively receiving grants. These ten strategies are not theoretical; they are drawn from real-world experience across a broad spectrum of successful organizations. To harness their full potential, nonprofits must engage with strategic intent and operational readiness. Whether you are building your first DAF-focused campaign or refining an advanced stewardship program, these proven practices will help you increase support, strengthen relationships, and avoid common pitfalls. The pages that follow offer a roadmap for turning DAF potential into lasting impact.

Proven Strategy #1. Candid GuideStar Seal

What DAF donors know about your nonprofit may very well be determined by the information available in the Candid GuideStar database. The good news is that your organization can dramatically strengthen its profile and visibility using the free tools provided to every 501(c)(3) nonprofit listed on this powerful platform.

Among the quickest credibility boosters for attracting DAF grants is to earn a GuideStar Seal of Transparency, offered by Candid. These Seals: Bronze, Silver, Gold, and Platinum, signal a nonprofit's commitment to transparency and accountability. Among them, the Platinum Seal of Transparency represents the highest standard and is rapidly becoming an expectation of DAF donors.

More than 1,100 DAF programs are powered by or integrated with Candid's GuideStar database. This includes platforms used by Fidelity Charitable, Schwab

[233] FreeWill. "2025 DAF Report: Fundraising Trends, Data & Insights." FreeWill, Inc., May 2025, https://www.nonprofits.freewill.com/resources/reports/2025-daf-report

Charitable's DAFgiving360, Vanguard Charitable, and the National Philanthropic Trust (NPT). These sponsors use GuideStar profiles to help donors search for, evaluate, and engage with nonprofits. Appearing in their systems with a Platinum Seal increases your organization's chances of being discovered, trusted, and potentially recommended for grants.[234]

What the Platinum Seal Signifies: Why it Matters

- **Comprehensive information:** Organizations must provide detailed insights into their mission, programs, strategies, and leadership.
- **Impact measurement:** Platinum Seal holders share meaningful metrics that demonstrate progress over time, often using data from multiple years.
- **Commitment to transparency:** Platinum status signals a high level of accountability, which builds trust with donors, advisors, and institutional funders.
- **Top-tier visibility:** It places a nonprofit in the top tier of GuideStar-recognized organizations and makes it more attractive to DAF donors and their advisors.

How to Earn the Platinum Seal

1. **Claim and update your GuideStar profile**
   Ensure your organization's basic information and contact details are current.
2. **Share strategic information**
   Upload a strategic plan or complete questions about your goals, strategies, and capabilities.
3. **Provide metrics**
   Include one to twenty metrics from annual reports, grant applications, or evaluations that track progress toward your mission.
4. **Demonstrate recent impact**
   At least one metric must be from the past year to show current effectiveness.
5. **Disclose financial and governance data**
   Share your most recent financials, 990s, and board demographics to round out your transparency profile.

Research from Villanova University and the University of Wisconsin–Milwaukee claims transparency pays off. Nonprofits that earned a GuideStar Seal received 53% more in contributions the following year than those without a seal.

---

[234] Candid. "GuideStar Seals of Transparency." Accessed June 2025. https://www.guidestar.org/profile/seals

Additionally, Candid reports that Gold and Platinum profiles receive twice the visibility as others. In an era where donor trust is paramount, showcasing your accomplishments and financial transparency is not just good practice; it's a powerful fundraising strategy.[235]

The Platinum Seal demonstrates that a nonprofit is not only disclosing basic organizational details. It also actively proves its impact through measurable outcomes and clear strategic planning. This seal helps DAF sponsors and advisors confirm your nonprofit's credibility and makes your organization easier to recommend in donor portals. For nonprofits looking to expand their DAF support, this is a vital first step. It can set you apart in a growing, competitive philanthropic landscape.

PROVEN STRATEGY #2. RELATIONSHIPS WITH DAF

DAF sponsors facilitate grants and connect nonprofits with donors. Research shows that nonprofits that actively cultivate partnerships with DAF sponsors benefit from increased visibility, enhanced credibility, and more frequent repeat grant recommendations. Establishing these relationships is key to long-term sustainability and philanthropic success.

Understanding and Engaging DAF Sponsors
For nonprofits seeking long-term, sustainable funding through DAFs, building strong relationships with DAF sponsors is essential. These organizations do more than process grants; they serve as philanthropic intermediaries, often advising donors, recommending grantees, and helping align giving with donor intent.

DAF sponsors vary widely in structure, priorities, and engagement models, but most fall into three broad categories: national sponsors, community foundations, and faith or mission-based sponsors.

National DAF Sponsors
Many national DAF sponsors are affiliated with investment firms, manage billions in assets, and serve donors across the country. Their platforms are digital, streamlined, and efficient, appealing to donors who value low fees and flexibility. Nonprofits that work proactively with wealth advisors and make DAF giving easy through their websites can increase visibility and grant potential.

---

[235] Candid. "Update Your Nonprofit Profile to Earn a Seal of Transparency." Accessed June 2025. https://www.guidestar.org/UpdateNonprofitProfile/transparency

How Nonprofits Can Engage

- Many donors using national DAFs have financial advisors who influence their philanthropic decisions. Developing relationships with wealth advisors can help position your nonprofit as a recommended recipient.
- DAF giving options should be clear and easy to find on your website, including direct links to DAF sponsors' grant recommendation portals.

DAF sponsors vary widely in structure, priorities, and engagement models

Community Foundations

Community foundations focus on regional impact and donor engagement. These sponsors often provide philanthropic advising services and take an active role in connecting donors to local needs. Attending events, sharing local success stories, and involving foundation staff in your programs can position your organization as a trusted community partner. As Courtney Murphy, Senior Director, Head of Strategy and Grants, Global Impact Citizenship, BNY, observed,

> DAFs can be really impactful for local giving, especially through community foundations that provide guidance to DAF holders.[236]

Her insight underscores the importance of local relationship-building, as community foundations serve not only as grant administrators but also as philanthropic advisors who help donors align giving with regional needs. These DAF sponsors prioritize community impact and typically encourage grantees to engage with donors through reports, site visits, and collaborative philanthropy initiatives. Karen Heald, Vice President at Fidelity Charitable, shares:

> National DAFs resonate with many families, especially if their relatives are spread across different regions. At the same time, these families maintain strong ties with their local community foundations, valuing their expertise.[237]

---

[236] Murphy, C. Interview with Ted Hart, August 13, 2024.
[237] Heald, K. Interview with Ted Hart, August 27, 2024.

How Nonprofits Can Engage
- Attend community foundation events to build visibility with both donors and fund managers.
- Proactively share impact updates and local success stories with foundation staff to increase your chances of being recommended for grants.

Faith/Mission-Based DAFs
Faith/mission-based DAFs guide giving in alignment with deeply held beliefs and long-term social priorities. Faith-based DAFs often emphasize community care and alignment with moral teachings. Secular mission-based sponsors may focus on social justice, environmental action, or other system-level change. In both cases, nonprofits are most effective when they mirror the sponsor's values, provide clear impact narratives, and demonstrate alignment with donor priorities.

- Faith/mission-based DAFs prioritize charitable giving that aligns with religious teachings and community support initiatives. These funds often facilitate lasting partnerships with nonprofits aligned to the donor's faith or mission-oriented goals
- Mission-driven DAFs support donors who prioritize social justice, environmental sustainability, or other systemic change. These funds are non-religious and focus on high-impact philanthropy that advances cause-related efforts and initiatives.

How Nonprofits Can Engage
- Faith/mission-based DAFs: Tailor messaging to align with religious values and community engagement priorities.
- Mission-driven DAFs: Highlight measurable impact, systemic change efforts, alignment with cause-related advocacy efforts, and grassroots initiatives supported by the DAF.
- Encourage donors to communicate their giving priorities directly to the DAF sponsor, potentially streamlining grant approval.

Building relationships with DAF sponsors is not about accessing a grant portal; it's about cultivating trust. Through tailored messaging, transparent reporting, and meaningful invitations to engage, nonprofits can unlock consistent support, deepen donor relationships, and become valued partners in philanthropy.

How Nonprofits Can Engage

Building strong relationships with DAF sponsors requires intentional engagement, clear communication, and shared value creation. Nonprofits can take the following steps to enhance these partnerships:

1. **Participate in Sponsor-Led Events and Initiatives**
   Attend networking events, donor engagement opportunities, and giving campaigns hosted by DAF sponsors. These gatherings offer direct access to fund managers and donor networks, increasing visibility and the likelihood of future grant recommendations.

2. **Maintain Open Communication and Provide Regular Reporting**
   DAF sponsors prioritize transparency and measurable outcomes. Sharing timely impact reports, updates on grant utilization, and tailored recognition materials helps build trust and encourages repeat giving. Consistent communication reinforces the nonprofit's credibility as a responsible and effective partner.

3. **Develop Relationships with Fund Managers and Advisors**
   Forming personal connections with DAF sponsor associated fund managers and financial advisors can lead to more frequent recommendations. These professionals often influence their clients' philanthropic decisions and are more inclined to recommend organizations they know and trust.

4. **Collaborate on Donor Education and Stewardship**
   Partner with DAF sponsors to co-host webinars, offer virtual site visits, or participate in recognition events. These efforts not only educate donors but also strengthen ties with sponsors by showcasing your organization's mission, funding priorities, and impact, making it easier for sponsors to recommend your nonprofit to their donor base.

Nonprofits that proactively educate DAF sponsors about their mission and impact tend to receive higher-value and more frequent grants. By investing in these relationships, nonprofits can secure long-term sustainability, increased donor engagement, and expanded philanthropic reach.[238]

---

[238] Donor-Advised Fund Research Collaborative. National Study on Donor-Advised Funds. February 15, 2024. https://www.dafresearchcollaborative.org/national-study-dafs

Building Strong Relationships with Donor Advisors
Bleu Blakslee, IPA, International Advisors in Philanthropy (AiP) Board underscores an often-overlooked opportunity:

> Anonymous doesn't mean unreachable. When nonprofits strategically feed impact data to community foundations and institutional sponsors, those intermediaries become the bridge to anonymous donors. Donors may remain private, but they still expect to see results. Consistent reporting equips intermediaries to keep donors engaged and inspired to give again.[239]

This wisdom highlights the critical role donor advisors and intermediaries play in shaping philanthropic decisions. Advisors not only connect donors to causes but also carry the responsibility of stewarding relationships and demonstrating impact on their clients' behalf. Nonprofits that cultivate strong, trust-based partnerships with these professionals can significantly expand their DAF funding potential. Effective engagement strategies include:

- Developing educational resources specifically for donor advisors, outlining the nonprofit's mission, financial health, and strategic goals
- Hosting informational webinars or in-person events where advisors can learn about the organization's impact and funding opportunities
- Providing data-driven reports and case studies to help advisors understand how their clients' contributions create meaningful change
- Establishing these relationships sets the stage for another critical best practice, properly tracking and acknowledging the grants they generate.

PROVEN STRATEGY #3. TRACK AND ACKNOWLEDGE DAF CONTRIBUTIONS

Tracking and acknowledging DAF contributions is essential for maintaining compliance, building donor trust, and fostering long-term engagement. Since DAF grants are issued by the DAF sponsor, not directly by the donor, nonprofits should not provide a tax receipt. However, it remains important to recognize and thank donors personally, ensuring they feel appreciated for their generosity.[240]

---

[239] Blakslee, B. Interview with Ted Hart, April 25, 2025
[240] Internal Revenue Service. Publication 526: Charitable Contributions. Washington, D.C.: Department of the Treasury, 2023. https://www.irs.gov/pub/irs-pdf/p526.pdf.

Anonymous Grants and Donor Stewardship
While a small percentage of donors choose to recommend grants anonymously, nonprofits should not assume a grant is anonymous unless it is explicitly stated. In many cases, the donor has authorized the DAF sponsor to release contact details.

To ensure proper stewardship, fundraising and finance teams should work closely to interpret any acknowledgment instructions and determine whether donor information is available. If unclear, reaching out directly to the DAF sponsor is both appropriate and advisable. This allows the organization to thank the donor appropriately, respect their privacy preferences, and strengthen the relationship.

A thoughtful, privacy-conscious approach builds trust and may pave the way for deeper engagement and long-term support.

Tax Considerations for Nonprofits
For nonprofits, understanding DAF-related tax and compliance requirements is crucial for effective donor engagement and financial stewardship. The following practices help ensure compliance and avoid common pitfalls when acknowledging and managing DAF grants.

1. Proper Acknowledgment of DAF Grants
Nonprofits must not issue charitable tax receipts or tax substantiation letters to individuals who recommend grants from DAFs. The donor receives a tax deduction when contributing to the DAF sponsor, not when the grant is made to the nonprofit. Issuing a receipt that implies a tax benefit may lead to donor confusion or an improper duplicate deduction. IRS Notice 2006–109 confirms that, while thank-you letters and general acknowledgments are permitted, they must not include language suggesting the gift is tax-deductible.[241]

Specific Guidance for Nonprofits
Acknowledge the Grant Appropriately
Send a formal acknowledgment to the DAF sponsor, and, if the donor's identity is disclosed, consider sending a thank-you letter to the donor. This acknowledgment can express appreciation and describe the grant's intended use.

---

[241] See IRS Notice 2006-109, 2006-51 I.R.B. 1121, https://www.irs.gov/pub/irs-drop/n-06-109.pdf (advising that recipient charities should not issue tax substantiation for DAF grants); see also 26 U.S.C. §6714 (imposing penalties for knowing violations of donor-advised fund rules).

Use Clear, IRS-Compliant Language. Include a statement such as:

> This acknowledgment is not a tax receipt. The tax deduction was provided by [DAF Sponsor Name] at the time of your contribution to the donor-advised fund.

Educate Donors and Staff

Help donors understand that no additional tax deduction is available when a DAF grant is made. Train staff, particularly in development and finance roles, to avoid issuing improper receipts and to follow IRS guidance on DAF compliance.

Why This Matters

Providing a second tax receipt for a DAF grant, even inadvertently, could allow a donor to claim a duplicate charitable deduction. Under Section 6714 of the Internal Revenue Code, nonprofits that knowingly participate in improper DAF activities, including issuing tax receipts that support double deductions, may be subject to penalties of up to $10,000 per incident.[242]

Although enforcement is rare and typically focuses on willful violations, organizations should implement clear internal policies and staff training to ensure compliance. While the legal responsibility for an improper deduction rests with the donor, the nonprofit may still face reputational harm or IRS scrutiny for facilitating noncompliant behavior. By following these best practices, nonprofits reduce risk, stay in full regulatory compliance, and build stronger relationships with both DAF sponsors and donors.

DAFs simplify the process of donating complex assets.

Compliance and Reporting Requirements

Nonprofits are generally not responsible for tax reporting on grants received from DAFs, since the DAF sponsor handles all required IRS documentation. While most DAF sponsors do not request reports on grant usage, they may do so in specific circumstances, such as when concerns arise about potential fraud, conflicts of interest, or regulatory compliance. To maintain transparency and demonstrate accountability, nonprofits should keep accurate financial records and be prepared to provide clear, timely

---

[242] 26 U.S.C. §6714 (establishing penalties for knowing violations of DAF rules).

reports if requested. Even when reporting is not routinely required, a willingness to share impact information can strengthen trust with both DAF sponsors and donors. In addition, strong internal grant tracking helps build long-term funder relationships and provides the data needed to showcase meaningful results.

Additional Opportunities

Handling Complex and Illiquid Asset Contributions
DAFs simplify the process of donating complex assets such as real estate, private business interests, and appreciated securities. Donors should be reminded to comply with IRS requirements, including obtaining a qualified appraisal when required under Publication 561 and completing Form 8283 for non-cash charitable contributions exceeding $500. As Joe Fisher, President and CEO at REN, notes,

> The story that often goes untold is the value DAFs bring to nonprofits by handling complex asset gifts that charities can't manage directly, like having a herd of cattle donated.[243]

By managing these challenging gifts, DAFs provide nonprofits with ready-to-use funds, enabling organizations to focus more directly on their mission-driven activities rather than navigating the complexities of asset liquidation and compliance. Nonprofits can strengthen donor engagement by actively educating donors, particularly high-net-worth individuals, about the significant advantages of using DAFs to contribute complex assets.

Proven Strategy #4. Encouraging Repeat Giving

DAF donors seek tangible impact and long-term engagement. Clear, measurable outcomes strengthen donor trust and encourage repeat giving. By effectively demonstrating impact through transparent communication and meaningful stewardship, nonprofits can strengthen donor relationships and encourage repeat giving.

---

[243] Fisher, J. Interview with Ted Hart, February 13, 2025.

CASE STUDY: FRED HUTCHINSON CANCER RESEARCH CENTER

The Fred Hutchinson Cancer Research Center implemented a comprehensive stewardship strategy to engage DAF donors, building long-term relationships and sustained giving.

As part of their approach, the Fred Hutchinson Cancer Research Center developed personalized stewardship plans tailored specifically for DAF donors. These customized engagement strategies provided donors with individualized communication detailing how their contributions were being used. By providing donors with a clear connection between their gifts and tangible outcomes, the organization strengthened trust and donor retention.

A key component of their strategy was transparent impact reporting. The center provided detailed reports that outlined how DAF contributions advanced cancer research, enhanced patient care, and supported medical breakthroughs. By demonstrating the real-world impact of donor funding, the organization reinforced donor confidence and encouraged ongoing philanthropic investment.

To further cultivate relationships, the Fred Hutchinson Cancer Research Center created dedicated donor liaison roles, making it easier for DAF donors to engage directly with the organization. These dedicated contacts provided a personalized point of connection, allowing donors to ask questions, receive updates, and feel more actively involved in the mission. This level of engagement deepened relationships and led to higher donor retention and repeat giving.

Additionally, DAF giving was seamlessly integrated into the research center's overall fundraising communications. The organization actively promoted DAF contributions through direct mail, digital outreach, and donor communications, helping donors clearly understand how to use their DAFs to support the organization's mission. This multi-channel strategy increased awareness, accessibility, and donor participation, leading to a significant rise in DAF-recommended grants.

Through personalized stewardship, transparent impact reporting, dedicated donor engagement, and strategic DAF communication, the Fred Hutchinson Cancer Research Center successfully cultivated long-term relationships with DAF donors, increasing the likelihood these contributions would remain a reliable and growing source of support for their mission.

How Nonprofits Can Implement Similar Strategies

To effectively engage DAF donors and encourage repeat giving, nonprofits can prioritize clear, compelling impact communication that builds donor confidence and strengthens long-term relationships.

A crucial first step involves showcasing the tangible impact of DAF contributions. Sharing real-world stories, key data, and detailed reports that demonstrate how DAF gifts support the organization's mission helps reinforce the value of donor support. Concrete examples of progress and measurable success inspire continued and increased giving.

Beyond impact reporting, offering exclusive donor engagement opportunities helps create a deeper connection between donors and the cause. Behind-the-scenes access to funded projects, virtual site visits, and special appreciation events foster a sense of community and meaningful involvement.

Personalized stewardship also plays a vital role in sustaining engagement. Tailoring updates and outreach to DAF donors helps them feel valued and appreciated. This can include regular updates on funded initiatives, personalized thank-you messages, and public recognition opportunities (with the donor's consent).

Additionally, transparent reporting on DAF grants is critical for reinforcing trust. Nonprofits will provide clear, detailed breakdowns outlining how DAF funds were allocated, the outcomes achieved, and the long-term benefits of donor contributions. By maintaining accountability and transparency, nonprofits can cultivate stronger relationships with DAF donors, demonstrate their philanthropic impact, and encourage sustained and increased giving over time.

Through a combination of impact storytelling, exclusive engagement opportunities, personalized stewardship, and transparent reporting, nonprofits can help DAF donors remain actively engaged and committed to their cause.

By implementing these strategies, nonprofits can foster trust, deepen donor engagement, and establish long-term giving partnerships with DAF donors.[244]

---

[244] Kurdzos, R. A Case Study in Focused Donor Advised Fund Fundraising. Fred Hutchinson Cancer Research Center, PG Calc Webinar, May 27, 2021.

PROVEN STRATEGY #5. PROMOTE COMPLEX ASSET DONATIONS

Nonprofits have the opportunity to significantly expand their fundraising potential by encouraging donors to contribute illiquid and complex assets through DAFs. Complex assets are non-cash gifts such as real estate, privately held business interests, cryptocurrency, or high-value collectibles. Many high-net-worth donors hold these types of assets, including real estate, stock, or art, and may not realize they can donate them through a DAF.

DAFs offer a structured and tax-advantaged approach to handling complex charitable gifts, helping donors navigate liquidation, valuation, and compliance requirements. By educating donors about this strategic giving option, nonprofits can unlock larger and more sustainable contributions. Non-cash contributions to DAFs must comply with substantiation and appraisal rules under IRS §170(f)(11) and may require Form 8283 and a qualified appraisal. See IRS Pub. 561 (Determining the Value of Donated Property) and Form 8283 Instructions.

However, not all DAF sponsors accept every asset type. Contributions of illiquid or complex property must undergo due diligence to determine suitability, ensure valuation compliance, and meet IRS substantiation rules for non-cash gifts.[245]

How Nonprofits Can Encourage Complex Asset Donations
To unlock transformational giving, nonprofits must proactively educate and engage donors around the option to contribute complex assets, such as real estate, business interests, or high-value collectibles, through DAFs. Many donors are unaware these gifts are possible, making donor education a vital first step.

Educate Donors About Non-Cash Giving
Develop donor-facing materials that explain how non-cash contributions work and the mutual benefits they provide. These may include:

- FAQs on donating complex assets via DAFs
- Donor stories featuring gifts of stock, real estate, or other assets.
- Step-by-step guides outlining how DAFs facilitate asset liquidation and grantmaking

Engage High-Net-Worth Donors and Their Advisors
Financial advisors, estate planners, and wealth managers are essential allies. By building strong relationships, nonprofits position themselves as preferred partners for DAF-funded giving. Strategies include:

---

[245] IRS Instructions for Form 8283; IRS Pub. 561.

- Supplying advisors with client-ready tools on tax benefits and DAF structures
- Offering storytelling assets (e.g., donor profiles) to illustrate impact
- Hosting private briefings or appreciation events for advisor partners
- Co-sponsoring webinars or seminars focused on complex giving strategies

Leverage Multi-Channel Marketing
Promote complex giving opportunities across platforms:

- Feature dedicated web content on DAF-funded non-cash gifts.
- Share success stories via newsletters and social media.
- Include educational content at donor events and wealth-planning seminars.

Partner with DAF Sponsors and Gatekeepers
Many DAF sponsors already accept complex assets, easing the path for donors. Collaborate with sponsors and advisors to amplify awareness and streamline the giving process. When effectively communicated and supported, this strategy can deliver measurable benefits for nonprofit growth and long-term sustainability.

The Impact of Promoting Complex Gifts

Promoting complex gifts opens a powerful pathway to sustainability and growth. These non-cash contributions, from closely held business interests to real estate and cryptocurrency, are often overlooked yet can be transformational. By moving beyond traditional cash giving, nonprofits can diversify revenue, reduce reliance on short-term fundraising, and build stronger partnerships with wealth advisors, estate planners, and high-net-worth donors seeking tax-efficient, values-driven ways to create lasting impact.

PROVEN STRATEGY #6. INTEGRATE DAFS INTO FUNDRAISING

To maximize DAF giving, successful nonprofits integrate it into their core fundraising efforts. Instead of treating DAF contributions as a passive funding source, they actively promote them across all donor engagement channels to increase visibility, accessibility, and ease of use. Featuring DAFs as a giving option in annual appeals, capital campaigns, and special events positions them as a primary method of support. Promoting DAF contributions during peak fundraising periods aligns with donor intent, boosts participation, and encourages larger, repeat gifts.

CASE STUDY: BRIGHAM AND WOMEN'S HOSPITAL

A standout example of effective DAF integration comes from Brigham and Women's Hospital (BWH). In 2019, BWH partnered with RKD Group to develop a data-driven campaign that educated donors about the benefits of DAF contributions, stock gifts, and IRA giving.

As part of this strategy, the hospital sent targeted postcards to donors who were most likely to contribute through DAFs, providing clear instructions on how to recommend grants and maximize the impact of their gifts.

The results were remarkable:

- Total DAF donations increased from 556 in 2017 to 912 in 2021
- DAF gifts between $10,000–$100,000 grew from 92 to 172.
- DAF gifts of $1,000,000+ increased from 0 to 4.

This case study demonstrates how targeted donor education and strategic outreach can drive DAF engagement, major gifts, and repeat contributions.

How Nonprofits Can Implement Similar Strategies

To integrate DAF giving effectively, nonprofits should make it visible, accessible, and strategically promoted across multiple donor engagement channels.

A key step is to feature DAFs prominently in all fundraising campaigns, including direct mail appeals and digital fundraising, so donors consistently see them as a giving option.

Regular reminders also help increase engagement. Incorporate consistent messaging across all communications, explaining how donors can give through their DAFs and providing clear, step-by-step instructions for recommending grants. Many donors have DAF accounts but are not in the habit of using them, so regular reinforcement can lead to greater participation.

Educating donors on the benefits of DAFs encourages use. Highlight advantages such as tax efficiency, flexibility in grant recommendations, and the potential for larger gifts. Clear communication of these benefits can motivate more supporters to give through their DAFs.

Because DAFs are often used by affluent donors, targeting high-net-worth individuals and financial advisors is also important. Estate planners, wealth managers, and financial consultants frequently guide donor giving decisions.

Partnering with these professionals can position DAF contributions
as a tax-advantaged, high-impact
giving strategy aligned with long-
term goals.

Leveraging key fundraising moments can further boost DAF giving. High-engagement periods,
such as #DAFDay (October), Giving Tuesday, year-end giving, and
capital campaigns, are ideal times
to remind donors to make a DAF
grant before year-end. This creates
urgency and can increase participation.

Successful nonprofits make DAFs a prominent giving option in all fundraising campaigns.

Finally, tracking and analyzing DAF giving trends is essential for long-term success. Monitoring contributions enables nonprofits to refine outreach, measure messaging effectiveness, and identify opportunities to grow their DAF donor base.

Encouraging Recurring and Multi-Year Commitments

Nonprofits can strengthen financial stability by encouraging donors to make recurring grants or multi-year commitments through their DAFs. Rather than treating these contributions as one-time windfalls, successful organizations take a proactive approach to building sustained relationships.

Encouraging donors to recommend grants on a regular schedule helps convert occasional generosity into a reliable, mission-aligned funding stream. As Marco Corona, Director of Individual Giving at the Southern Environmental Law Center, explains:

> When we discover that a donor has a DAF, we immediately perk up. That tells us they're already thinking strategically; they've taken a deliberate step by choosing a specific giving vehicle. For us, that's almost an automatic qualifier. We know this is someone worth building a relationship with. They've already committed to giving; now the opportunity is to inspire them to give to us.[246]

---

[246] Corona, M. Interview with Ted Hart, May 14, 2025.

Recognizing that many donors value ease and clarity, ensure your giving process is DAF-friendly. Clearly state that you accept DAF grants and provide all necessary information for making a contribution.

CASE STUDY: THE UNIVERSITY OF MARYLAND

A best-in-class example of DAF donor education comes from the University of Maryland, which offers both a dedicated webpage and a downloadable guide to help donors understand how DAFs work. Their Your Giving with Donor Advised Funds guide provides step-by-step instructions on:

- Setting up a DAF account with a DAF sponsor
- Making tax-deductible contributions to the fund
- Recommending grants to the university and other nonprofits
- Naming favorite charities as beneficiaries of the DAF
- Understanding the tax advantages and administrative fees associated with DAFs

This comprehensive approach helps donors not only understand how to contribute but also feel confident in using their DAFs to support the causes they care about. Effective educational materials will also explain the tax benefits of DAFs in simple terms, such as how contributions are tax-deductible and grow tax-free, and could include a comparison chart of different DAF sponsors, highlighting their fees, investment options, and grantmaking processes.[247]

PROVEN STRATEGY #7. LEVERAGE TECHNOLOGY

Technology simplifies and enhances the DAF giving experience. To maximize DAF contributions, nonprofits can optimize their digital infrastructure to support seamless and efficient transactions.

A key step is to improve donation forms and online giving pages with a dedicated DAF donation button. Providing clear, step-by-step instructions on how to recommend a grant helps donors navigate the process, removing confusion and minimizing barriers to giving. Digital platforms such as DAFpay, DAFDirect, and DAFwidget allow donors to recommend grants with just a few clicks, reducing friction and making it easier to give through their DAF accounts.

---

[247] University of Maryland. Centralize Your Giving with Donor Advised Funds. Accessed March 18, 2025. https:// giftplanning.umd.edu/

As technology advances, it is reshaping how donors interact with DAFs. Shannon Scott, SVP and CFO at NCTA, The Internet & Television Association, notes:

> The future of DAFs lies in their ability to integrate technology seamlessly, not just to streamline administration but to enhance the donor experience.[248]

The rise of digital giving platforms has made DAFs more accessible, allowing nonprofits to:

- **Expand donor outreach** with digital engagement tools.
- **Automate donor interactions** with CRM integrations and grant tracking.
- **Optimize donor retention** by leveraging data-driven impact reporting.

As DAFs continue to evolve, their influence on philanthropy will only grow, spanning multiple generations of donors. The next section explores the trends driving their continued success. The tools that streamline donor interactions are also reshaping donor expectations toward real-time impact, personalized giving, and responsiveness to urgent needs.

CASE STUDY: THE AMERICAN CANCER SOCIETY

A strong example of leveraging technology for DAF giving is the American Cancer Society (ACS), which partnered with DAFpay to integrate secure and efficient DAF donations into its website.

With this new system, donors can now initiate a grant in just three clicks from over 1,000 DAF providers, including Fidelity Charitable, Schwab's DAFGiving360, and Vanguard Charitable. This streamlined process eliminates common donor concerns, such as:

- Real-time grant requests with an intuitive, user-friendly interface
- End-to-end encryption, ensuring secure transactions
- Avoiding lost checks, mailing delays, and processing errors

By adopting DAFpay, ACS removed barriers to giving, making it easier for supporters to contribute toward advocacy, research, and patient care.[249]

How Nonprofits Can Implement Similar Strategies
To fully leverage technology and maximize DAF contributions, nonprofits benefit from creating a seamless, efficient, and donor-friendly digital giving experience.

---

[248] Scott, S. Interview with Ted Hart, October 7, 2024.
[249] American Cancer Society. Donor-Advised Fund Giving. Accessed February 19, 2025. cancer.org.

A strategic approach to digital optimization helps organizations increase participation rates, reduce administrative burdens, and enhance donor engagement.

One essential step in optimizing DAF giving is to make certain online donation pages prominently display DAF options and simplify the giving process. A well-designed DAF donation page includes a dedicated DAF button that allows donors to easily access grant recommendation tools. Providing step-by-step instructions helps guide donors through the process of initiating a DAF grant, making the experience smooth and user-friendly. A clear explanation of how DAF contributions support the organization's mission reinforces the impact of each gift.

Some DAF sponsors are also integrating artificial intelligence (AI) to personalize donor engagement. For example, Daffy's "Quick Donate" tool uses AI to enable natural language giving while tailoring outreach based on giving history and fund balances. Staying informed about these developments and exploring partnerships with AI-enabled DAF sponsors can further enhance donor relationships and support more timely, values-aligned giving.

By harnessing these emerging technologies, nonprofits can increase DAF contributions, improve the donor experience, and streamline fundraising operations, ultimately directing more funding toward their mission efficiently and effectively.

As nonprofits adopt more advanced tools to manage donor relationships and automate giving, it becomes even more essential to ensure that these strategies operate within legal and ethical boundaries. The next strategy highlights key compliance principles that all organizations must follow when engaging with DAF donors.

PROVEN STRATEGY #8. EXPLORE IMPACT INVESTMENT OPTIONS

DAFs are now key vehicles for impact investing, allowing donors to align giving with financial and social goals. More donors are aligning their philanthropic assets with investments that generate both financial returns and measurable social or environmental benefits. Many DAF sponsors now offer impact-first investing options, allowing funds to not only grow tax-free but also contribute to meaningful change.

For nonprofits, this shift presents a unique opportunity to access capital beyond conventional grants, offering financial stability and scalability for initiatives that align with donor values. By tapping into DAF-supported impact investments, nonprofits can attract donors who seek both financial sustainability and measurable social impact.

Important: Nonprofits using donor-advised fund (DAF) grants for impact investments must ensure compliance with IRC §4966 to avoid taxable distributions. Investments must avoid impermissible private benefit (to donors, advisors, or other disqualified persons); and must ensure investments further their charitable mission exclusively. Financial returns cannot benefit private interests. Misuse of DAF funds for non-charitable purposes may trigger excise taxes, penalties, or loss of tax-exempt status. Consult IRS guidance or legal counsel to review specific transactions.[250]

CASE STUDIES: IMPACT INVESTMENTS HELP NONPROFITS

1. Tenement Museum: Restructuring Debt to Preserve a Cultural Institution
Challenge: The Tenement Museum, a historic site reliant on ticket sales, **faced** financial hardship during the COVID-19 pandemic, struggling with a $585,000 annual mortgage payment as revenue sharply declined.

Solution: A DAF donor purchased the museum's tax-exempt bond, restructuring the mortgage to interest-only payments at 1% per year.

Impact: The new financing structure saved the museum $2.5 million over five years, securing its ability to continue operations and adapt its financial strategy. This case illustrates how DAF-supported impact investments can sustain nonprofit infrastructure during financial uncertainty.

2. Fortune Society: Funding Affordable Housing for Justice-Involved Individuals
Challenge: The Fortune Society, which provides housing and services for formerly incarcerated individuals, needed predevelopment capital to initiate affordable housing projects but faced barriers in securing traditional loans.

Solution: A low-interest revolving fund was established by a coalition of DAF donors at FJC (A Foundation of Philanthropic Funds), providing the necessary capital for zoning approvals and planning phases.

---

[250] Internal Revenue Code §4966 and §4944 (26 U.S.C. §4966, §4944). Restrictions on Donor-Advised Funds and Jeopardizing Investments. U.S. Government Publishing Office, 2023. https://www.govinfo.gov/content/pkg/USCODE-2023-title26/pdf/USCODE-2023-title26.pdf.

Impact: This flexible funding structure accelerated housing development, demonstrating how DAFs can drive mission-aligned investments that create long-term impact.[251]

Why Nonprofits Should Leverage Impact Investment Options
By integrating impact investing strategies into their funding models, nonprofits can attract DAF donors who prioritize long-term sustainability over one-time charitable gifts. These donors are not just looking to make a philanthropic contribution; they seek opportunities where their DAF funds can both support a nonprofit's mission and generate meaningful financial and social returns.

For nonprofits, adopting an impact investment approach provides several key benefits. First, it offers access to mission-aligned capital, enabling organizations to expand programs and scale initiatives with a sustainable financial backing that extends beyond traditional grants. Second, it enhances financial stability by diversifying revenue streams through structured investments, reducing reliance on unpredictable grant cycles. Finally, it positions nonprofits to appeal to socially conscious donors, particularly DAF holders who actively seek to invest in impact-driven solutions that align with their values.

By positioning themselves as investment-ready organizations, nonprofits can unlock new pathways for sustainable, long-term funding. This approach allows them to align with forward-thinking DAF donors who wish to achieve both financial sustainability and measurable philanthropic impact, building a stronger, more resilient future for their mission-driven work. As digital tools make giving easier than ever, it's equally important to ensure that all engagement with DAF donors aligns with current regulations and ethical standards.

PROVEN STRATEGY #9. FOSTER LEGACY GIVING

DAFs are a powerful tool for legacy giving, enabling donors to extend their philanthropic impact beyond their lifetimes, often at no cost during their lifetime. Naming a nonprofit as a beneficiary of a DAF is a simple, low-barrier option for planned giving, allowing any remaining fund balance to be directed to charitable purposes after the donor's passing. By incorporating DAFs into estate planning, donors can create a lasting charitable legacy that supports their chosen causes for generations.

---

[251] Marks, S. (2024). Donor-advised funds and impact investing: A practitioner's view — With 2024 prologue. The Foundation Review, 16(1). (Original work published 2022.) https://doi.org/10.9707/1944-5660.1695

To encourage legacy giving through DAFs, nonprofits will actively educate donors about the option to name their organization as a beneficiary of their DAF account in their estate plans. This approach directs any remaining funds in the DAF toward charitable purposes after the donor's lifetime. Additionally, organizations can partner with financial advisors, estate planners, and community foundations to facilitate discussions on planned giving and assist donors in developing a philanthropic strategy that aligns with their values.

By proactively engaging donors in legacy planning conversations, nonprofits can help individuals create a sustained impact that continues well beyond their lifetimes.

CASE STUDY: JEWISH COMMUNAL FUND (JCF)

A compelling example of legacy giving through DAFs comes from the Jewish Communal Fund (JCF), which encourages donors to establish philanthropic legacies by naming either charitable organizations or successors, trusted individuals who will direct giving after the donor's passing, as beneficiaries of their DAF accounts. Donors should confirm specific successor and beneficiary policies with their DAF sponsor to ensure their intentions are carried out.

One notable case is the Anita K. Hersh Philanthropic Fund. Anita Hersh, a dedicated philanthropist, established a DAF with JCF and took a distinctive approach to legacy giving. Instead of solely leaving her charitable contributions to be distributed after her passing, she appointed two close friends as successors to her fund. These successors were empowered to continue her charitable work, make philanthropic decisions in her name, and ensure her donations were allocated in alignment with her values.

> **DAFs are a powerful tool for legacy giving.**

By structuring her DAF as a legacy tool, Anita Hersh not only honored her life-long commitment to philanthropy but also ensured her mission would continue for years to come. This model demonstrates the flexibility and enduring impact that DAFs can provide as part of a planned giving strategy.[252]

Why Nonprofits Should Leverage Legacy Giving Through DAFs
As more donors look for ways to make a lasting impact aligned with their values, DAF legacy gifts are emerging as a vital part of planned giving programs.

By encouraging donors to name the nonprofit as a beneficiary of their DAF, organizations can unlock future funding that extends far beyond the donor's lifetime. This approach positions the nonprofit as a steward of the donor's values, building trust and reinforcing a long-term philanthropic partnership. To fully leverage this opportunity, nonprofits should adopt a proactive strategy that combines education, outreach, and personalized stewardship.

- **Educate donors** about the ability to name the nonprofit as a DAF beneficiary through clear website content, donor guides, and one-on-one conversations. Many supporters are unaware this is an option.
- **Partner with estate planners, financial advisors, and community foundations** to guide donors in incorporating DAFs into their estate plans. These professionals play a key role in helping donors structure legacy gifts that reflect their personal and family values.
- **Host workshops and webinars** on legacy giving, featuring estate planning experts or donor testimonials. These sessions offer a welcoming space for donors to explore their options and visualize the long-term impact they can have.
- **Develop dedicated legacy giving materials,** such as brochures and educational videos, that clearly explain how DAFs can serve as vehicles for lasting impact.
- **Encourage multi-generational philanthropy** by inviting donors to name successors to their DAFs. This enables charitable missions to continue across generations and strengthens family engagement in giving.

By actively promoting DAF legacy giving, nonprofits can create a sustainable future while offering donors a meaningful way to extend their philanthropic values beyond their lifetimes.

---

[252] Jewish Communal Fund. Legacy Planning Beyond Family: The Power of a Donor-Advised Fund.

PROVEN STRATEGY #10. MONITOR CHANGING POLICIES

DAF regulations continue to evolve, with ongoing discussions around mandatory payout requirements, donor disclosure rules, and increased transparency measures. As changes are possible over time, nonprofits benefit from staying informed and adjusting their strategies to remain compliant.

To navigate this shifting landscape effectively, nonprofits can monitor legislative updates and work toward alignment with IRS regulations when accepting DAF grants. Failing to do so may lead to operational disruptions or missed funding opportunities.

Proactively communicating relevant regulatory changes to donors and stakeholders also helps maintain trust. Many donors may be unaware of how policy developments could affect their giving strategies, so offering timely guidance and clarity can build confidence and reinforce the organization's role as a trusted philanthropic partner.

This kind of preparedness calls for more than just passive observation. It requires a proactive framework that blends policy awareness, expert guidance, donor education, and sector advocacy into an ongoing cycle of institutional readiness.

Monitoring developments from trusted sources is a vital starting point. Resources such as the IRS, the Council on Foundations, and Independent Sector regularly publish updates on legislative trends and policy guidance. While federal policy often receives the most attention, state-level regulations are also emerging in areas such as transparency, reporting, and charitable oversight. Nonprofits that keep pace with these changes are better positioned to adapt quickly and confidently.

In addition to monitoring, direct engagement with legal and financial experts is critical. By consulting with advisors and hosting internal training, organizations can equip staff across departments to interpret regulatory shifts and apply best practices. This ensures that development, finance, and executive leadership teams remain aligned and informed.

Clear communication with donors is equally important. Many supporters may be unaware of how regulatory changes affect their DAF giving. Offering accessible materials, facilitating conversations, and hosting informational sessions can help donors navigate these changes while reinforcing the organization's role as a trusted philanthropic partner.

Finally, nonprofits have a role to play in shaping the future of DAF policy. By joining advocacy coalitions, participating in sector-wide initiatives, and sharing their perspectives with lawmakers, organizations contribute to a more thoughtful and balanced regulatory environment, one that recognizes the needs of both donors and the missions they support.

Remaining informed is not just a matter of compliance. It is an investment in the long-term sustainability of the nonprofit's DAF strategy, and in its ability to serve donors and communities with clarity, integrity, and purpose.

Addressing Common Questions about DAFs

DAFs offer significant benefits to nonprofits, yet persistent misconceptions about how they function can create hesitation or confusion. Two of the most common myths involve donor anonymity and the notion that DAFs serve as "charitable warehouses" where funds sit unused. In reality, DAFs are highly active grant-making vehicles that support long-term donor engagement and meaningful philanthropic outcomes.

Myth #1: DAFs Are Primarily Anonymous Giving Vehicles
A common concern among nonprofits is that many DAF grants are anonymous, making it difficult to steward donors. However, research tells a different story. According to the DAF Research Collaborative's National Study on Donor-Advised Funds, 96% of DAF donors want nonprofits to receive their contact information, and fewer than 4% of grants are made truly anonymously.[253]

Fidelity Charitable, for example, reported that 95% of its 2024 grants included donor attribution. Furthermore, 80% of those grants were directed to charities the donor had previously supported, underscoring that most DAF donors seek ongoing, relationship-based giving.[254]

Myth #2: DAFs Keep Money Away From Nonprofits
Some critics argue that donor-advised funds tie up charitable dollars, keeping them from reaching nonprofits in a timely manner. In reality, both the funds themselves and the donors who use them are among the most active sources of philanthropic support.

[253] DAF Research Collaborative. National Study on Donor-Advised Funds. February 16, 2024. https://www.dafresearchcollaborative.org/national-study-dafs
[254] Fidelity Charitable. 2025 Giving Report. Accessed April 22, 2025. https://www.fidelitycharitable.org/content/dam/fc-public/docs/insights/2025-giving-report.pdf

Far from sitting idle, donor-advised funds consistently send more than 20% of their assets to nonprofits each year, according to the National Philanthropic Trust, more than four times the minimum distribution rate required of private foundations. This high level of activity is reflected not just in aggregate payout rates but also in individual donor behavior. Rebecca Moffett, President of Vanguard Charitable, notes that,

> donor-advised fund donors granted two and a half times more on average than non-DAF donors — about $1,500 versus $815 — and were significantly more likely to say they plan to increase their giving in the next six months: 68 percent compared to just 35 percent.[255]

Phil Purcell, Director of Planned Giving at The Salvation Army, provides helpful context:

> My experience with donors accumulating funds in their donor-advised funds, sometimes called stockpiling, has shown that donors often haven't yet determined where they want to grant. In many cases, they are preparing for a significant gift or campaign that requires careful planning.[256]

A COMPREHENSIVE GUIDE FOR NONPROFITS

DAFs have transformed modern philanthropy, making charitable giving easier, faster, and more flexible for donors. As Matt Nash, Executive Director, The Blackbaud Giving Fund, puts it,

> DAFs have taken a lot of the sand out of the gears of giving... They've made it very simple for donors to give.[257]

This ease of use has fueled widespread adoption, positioning DAFs as one of the most powerful tools for philanthropy today.

---

[255] Moffett, R. Interview with Ted Hart, August 4, 2025. Survey Method: This survey was conducted online within the United States by The Harris Poll on behalf of Vanguard Charitable from June 17-19, 2025, among 2,100 adults ages 18 and older, among whom 1,443 have donated money to charity in the past 6 months (i.e., donors), of which 141 have a DAF. The sampling precision of Harris online polls is measured by using a Bayesian credible interval. For this study, the sample data is accurate to within +/-2.5 percentage points using a 95% confidence level. This credible interval will be wider among subsets of the surveyed population of interest. https://www.vanguardcharitable.org/news/new-survey-americans-believe-charitable-giving-civic-duty-especiallyduring-times-uncertainty
[256] Purcell, P. Interview with Ted Hart, November 19, 2024.
[257] Nash, M. Interview with Ted Hart, August 8, 2024.

To fully leverage the benefits of DAFs, nonprofits should understand how they work and why they appeal to a broad range of donors. DAFs provide:

- **Efficiency:** Contributions can take the form of cash, securities, or complex assets while being professionally managed.
- **Tax advantages:** Donors receive an immediate tax deduction upon contribution, even if grants are recommended later.
- **Flexibility:** Unlike direct donations, DAFs allow donors to distribute funds over time, keeping pace with their changing philanthropic goals.

Beyond Tax Considerations: DAFs as a Philanthropic Tool
While tax benefits drive much of the growth of DAFs, their flexibility and responsiveness make them a powerful tool for addressing urgent social challenges. Dan Heist, Assistant Professor at Brigham Young University, notes:

> The flexibility of DAFs allows donors to pivot their giving strategies as needs arise, making them a critical tool in addressing urgent social challenges.[258]

Unlike traditional giving models, DAFs enable donors to:

- **Respond quickly to crises** (e.g., disaster relief, healthcare emergencies)
- **Adapt their grantmaking strategy** based on evolving priorities
- **Fund long-term initiatives** while maintaining flexibility in timing and impact

For nonprofits, engaging with DAF donors effectively means emphasizing timely needs, impact-driven programs, and strategic partnerships with DAF sponsors.

Handling Bifurcated Gifts and Pledge Payments
Nonprofits need to exercise caution when accepting DAF grants for events and pledges, as IRS regulations prohibit any transaction that provides more than incidental benefit to the donor. DAF grants cannot be used for gifts that include both charitable and non-charitable components. For example, if a donor sponsors a fundraising gala and plans to attend, they must make two separate payments: one from their DAF for the deductible sponsorship, and a personal payment for the ticket or any associated benefits.

---

[258] Heist, D. Interview with Ted Hart, September 17, 2024.

Even if a donor waives the benefit, using a DAF grant for events like galas, golf outings, or dinners may still trigger excise tax penalties under IRC §4967. These types of transactions are categorically ineligible for DAF funding. Clear communication is essential to set expectations and prevent inadvertent violations.

Events providing more than incidental donor benefits are categorically ineligible for DAF funding.

Similarly, IRS Notice 2017–73 prohibits using DAF grants to fulfill legally binding pledges. Although a narrow safe harbor exists, the general rule is that nonprofits cannot reference a donor's pledge in acknowledgment letters or imply that a DAF gift satisfies such a commitment. Donors may still recommend a grant for the same charitable purpose, as long as there is no explicit or implied link to the pledge.[259] As Dave Shevlin, Partner at Simpson Thacher & Bartlett LLP, explains:

> The IRS rules create a nuanced distinction; while DAFs can support the same charitable purpose as a pledge, there must be no explicit connection between the two.[260]

To maintain compliance, nonprofits need to avoid referencing pledges in any DAF-related correspondence and exclude language in fundraising materials that suggest DAF funds can meet personal giving commitments. Educating both donors and development staff is key to upholding IRS guidelines and avoiding penalties.

Establishing a Compliance Foundation for DAF Readiness
To build long-term DAF readiness, nonprofits, especially smaller or all-volunteer organizations, will adopt core compliance practices that demonstrate professionalism and prepare them for sustainable growth. These foundational

---

[259] Internal Revenue Service. Notice 2017–73: Donor-Advised Funds: Proposed Guidelines on Pledge Fulfillment and Bifurcated Gifts. Washington, D.C.: Department of the Treasury, 2017. https://www.irs.gov/pub/irs-drop/n-17-73.pdf.
[260] Shevlin, D. Interview with Ted Hart, November 22, 2024.

steps apply, whether or not an organization is currently receiving DAF grants, and are essential for donor confidence and institutional credibility.

- **Register to Fundraise**
  Thirty-six U.S. states plus the District of Columbia require charitable solicitation registration before an organization may legally request donations, even online.[261] Organizations must be properly registered in their home state and any other jurisdictions where they plan to solicit contributions. Many states accept the Unified Registration Statement (URS), which simplifies multi-state compliance.[262]
- **Follow IRS-Compliant Gift Acknowledgment Practices**
  Organizations must issue appropriate tax receipts for direct donations.[263] However, for DAF grants, nonprofits must never issue tax receipts, as the donor has already received their deduction from the DAF sponsor.[264]
- **Implement Basic Internal Controls and Gift Acceptance Procedures**
  Even modest organizations benefit from having written policies that clarify how they handle donations, distinguish restricted from unrestricted gifts, and document board oversight. These practices promote financial integrity and risk reduction, and they support future audit readiness.[265]

These foundational steps represent best practices and demonstrate a nonprofit's commitment to transparency and good governance. They also create the infrastructure necessary to engage responsibly with DAF donors, DAF sponsors, and the broader philanthropic ecosystem.

Educating Staff on DAF Compliance and Stewardship
Maintaining compliance and transparency requires ongoing staff education. Development, finance, and donor relations teams should receive training on:

- Best practices for handling DAF contributions, including IRS compliance and reporting requirements

---

[261] COGENCY GLOBAL, "Charitable Solicitation Registration Chart by State," updated February 2025. https://www.cogencyglobal.com/wp-content/uploads/2025/02/Charitable-Registration-Map.pdf
[262] Multistate Registration Information from the Unified Registration Statement. Accessed September 18, 2024. https://www.multistatefiling.org
[263] IRS Publication 1771, Charitable Contributions: Substantiation and Disclosure Requirements, Department of the Treasury, rev. 2016. https://www.irs.gov/pub/irs-pdf/p1771.pdf
[264] IRS Notice 2006-109, Internal Revenue Bulletin: 2006-51, December 18, 2006. https://www.irs.gov/irb/2006-51_IRB
[265] National Council of Nonprofits. "Financial Management Policies." Accessed June 2025. https://www.councilofnonprofits.org/tools-resources/financial-management

- Proper donor acknowledgment protocols; make certain that DAF gifts are recognized appropriately without issuing tax receipts
- Strategies for cultivating strong relationships with both donors and DAF sponsors

By equipping staff with the necessary knowledge, nonprofits can avoid regulatory pitfalls while fostering a culture of donor stewardship that strengthens DAF engagement.

LONG-TERM IMPACT OF COMPLIANCE AND STEWARDSHIP

A well-structured approach to compliance, donor engagement, and stewardship helps nonprofits:

- **Maintain transparency and trust** with donors, DAF sponsors, and regulatory agencies.
- **Encourage sustained DAF contributions,** turning one-time grants into regular funding streams.
- **Position themselves as preferred recipients** for future DAF grants by demonstrating financial accountability and impact.

> # Sustained compliance depends on a well-trained staff.

By integrating compliance with donor stewardship, nonprofits can maximize DAF funding while reinforcing lasting relationships with donors, advisors, and DAF sponsors. The result is a sustainable approach to DAF fundraising that enhances long-term philanthropic impact.

Stewardship and Recognition: Creating a Meaningful Experience for DAF Donors
Long-term stewardship plays a vital role in retaining and growing DAF support. While some donors prefer anonymity, many welcome thoughtful engagement that reflects their values and impact. Personalized updates, mission-focused recognition, and meaningful touchpoints help foster lasting relationships.

To cultivate stronger connections with DAF donors,
nonprofits can prioritize
transparency, sincere ac-
knowledgment, and personalized engagement. Since DAF
gifts do not permit transactional benefits like event
tickets or memberships, mission-driven experiences become essential in reinforcing
donor impact.

For nonprofits, understanding how to engage with DAF donors is essential.

- Elliot B. Karp

Fostering Long-Term Commitment and Advocacy

Encouraging DAF donor participation in organizational events, mission-driven
discussions, and volunteer opportunities strengthen long-term engagement
and donor loyalty. Nonprofits that provide ongoing updates, exclusive impact
reports, and personalized experiences create an environment where DAF donors feel like partners in philanthropy, rather than just financial contributors.
Elliot B. Karp, Director of Philanthropy at Temple Emanu-El of Westfield, NJ,
emphasizes this point:

> For nonprofits, understanding how to engage with DAF donors is essential;
> it's a two-way street of value creation.[266]

KEY TAKEAWAYS

DAFs are no longer a peripheral giving vehicle; they are a primary driver of
modern philanthropy. Successful nonprofits recognize this reality and approach
DAF engagement with strategy, structure, and cross-departmental readiness.
This chapter outlined 10 proven strategies to help nonprofits maximize support
from DAF donors. These include building strong relationships with sponsors
and advisors, training staff to interpret grant documentation correctly, tracking
contributions accurately, and acknowledging grants in full compliance with IRS
rules. Avoiding prohibited benefits and issuing appropriate acknowledgments
are legal necessities that also build donor trust.

---

[266] Karp, E.B. Interview with Ted Hart, September 13, 2024.

Organizations that excel in this space are those that embrace transparency, welcome complex or mission-aligned gifts, and make it easy for DAF donors to give. Internal alignment across development, finance, and leadership teams is essential to positioning your nonprofit as a preferred philanthropic partner. By integrating these strategies into your fundraising and operational approach, your organization can enhance its DAF readiness and deepen relationships with today's most generous and engaged donors.

International Grantmaking: A Worldwide Blueprint

EXECUTIVE SUMMARY

The desire to give internationally has never been stronger, and the barriers to success have never been higher. Donor-advised funds (DAFs) are transforming the landscape of global philanthropy, enabling individuals, families, corporations, and foundations to support causes around the world with both generosity and strategic intent. Yet making grants outside the United States introduces a complex set of legal, tax, and operational considerations for all involved.

This chapter provides a **Readiness Assessment** for a diverse group of stakeholders involved in international philanthropy. It is designed to support donors who wish to make charitable gifts outside the United States using a DAF, as well as advisors who are helping clients navigate the complexities of cross-border giving. It also speaks directly to foreign charities that are seeking to access U.S.-based philanthropic support and need to understand the expectations and processes involved. Finally, it offers guidance for DAF sponsors aiming to strengthen or expand their global grantmaking programs. This may include conducting internal compliance reviews, increasing operational efficiency, or developing cooperative relationships with other DAF providers.

Whether you are initiating your first international grant or managing a sophisticated cross-border portfolio, you will find here a clear and actionable roadmap. Topics covered include proven due diligence protocols such as Equivalency Determination (ED) and Expenditure Responsibility (ER), global data privacy and anti-money laundering (AML) requirements, DAF-to-DAF transfers, and country-specific legal barriers.

This chapter also features compliance assessment and best practices to demystify the inner workings of U.S. regulatory standards. It offers behind-the-scenes insights for DAF sponsors alongside accessible guidance for external stakeholders, highlighting how each contributes to safe, effective, and compliant worldwide grantmaking.

Global grantmaking is not just a technical exercise. It is a shared opportunity. When DAF sponsor systems provide robust compliance, donors give with confidence, advisors guide with clarity, and foreign charities partner with trust, the result is a worldwide philanthropic ecosystem rooted in accountability and shared purpose.

Borderless DAF Grantmaking

In an increasingly interconnected world, the challenges that define our time transcend national borders. As awareness of global issues grows, so too does the philanthropic response. American donors are supporting efforts worldwide that improve lives, strengthen communities, and respond to complex global challenges with compassion and purpose.

Corporations want to engage employees and communities around the world. Foundations want to respond to needs wherever they may arise. And individual donors are passionate about causes that transcend borders.

> # The moment a donor wants to grant outside the U.S., the complexity skyrockets.

But the moment a donor wants to grant outside the U.S., the complexity skyrockets. Each jurisdiction comes with its own legal framework for charitable giving. What qualifies as charity in one country might not in another. And to add to that: banking restrictions, currency conversion, anti-terrorism regulations, reputation risks, and it becomes very clear why so many donors get stuck.

But beyond the legal and logistical hurdles, there is a human side to granting. Donors, whether individuals, corporations, or institutions, are often left feeling frustrated. They have the resources. They have the will to make a difference. But they face delays, uncertainty, and difficulty building trust across cultures and time zones. Sampriti Ganguli of Ganguli Associates, LLC, and former CEO of Arabella Advisors, puts this in perspective by sharing:

> When it comes to cross-border giving, compliance isn't just about checking boxes. It's about understanding the cultural and regulatory nuances of each region.[267]

---

[267] Ganguli, S. Interview with Ted Hart, September 11, 2024

The rise in cross-border philanthropy reflects a meaningful shift in donor priorities. While international giving typically represents less than 6% of total annual U.S. charitable contributions, it has often outpaced domestic giving growth.[268] Donors are increasingly motivated by personal ties, global crises, and intergenerational values that span both local and global causes. Younger donors, in particular, are embracing global causes while seeking to align their charitable giving with their values.

DAFs are uniquely positioned to meet this moment. As flexible, tax-advantaged charitable giving vehicles, DAFs allow individuals, families, foundations, and corporations to support international efforts with the same efficiency and strategic intent as domestic giving. DAF sponsors play a crucial role in translating donor intent into effective and compliant global impact. Daryl Upsall, President, Upsall International, www.darylupsall.com, shares:

> I think DAFs could be the tool to engage higher-level philanthropists, especially in countries where they don't have established philanthropic infrastructure.[269]

Many corporations, foundations, families, and individuals rely on DAF sponsors to handle the complexity of cross-border giving. This includes navigating legal requirements, validating foreign grantees, ensuring compliance with IRS regulations, and mitigating risks, such as terrorism financing, corruption, and shifting foreign laws. When executed well, international DAF grantmaking amplifies a philanthropic organization's reach while preserving both regulatory integrity and alignment with its mission. As Hillel Korin, President of Korin Development Associates, explains:

> DAFs are increasingly critical in cross-border giving, where compliance and alignment with local regulations matter just as much as donor intent.[270]

DAFs are not limited to domestic giving; they are becoming an important force in global philanthropy. As international crises and opportunities reshape the donor landscape, DAF sponsors who step into this role with purpose and compliance will help define the future of charitable giving worldwide. Christopher Carnie, Director, Factary (UK) and Fundacio Terra (Spain) notes,

---

[268] Giving USA Foundation. Giving USA 2023: The Annual Report on Philanthropy for the Year 2022. Chicago: Giving USA Foundation, 2023.
[269] Upsall, D. Interview with Ted Hart, August 13, 2024.
[270] Korin, H. Interview with Ted Hart, September 11, 2024.

Donor advised funds are still a relatively new concept in Europe, especially outside the UK. While the community of people familiar with DAFs remains small, there is tremendous potential for growth, provided there is more education to bridge the gap. Across the continent, private banks are beginning to encourage clients to use tools like DAFs to structure philanthropic giving, an early sign that the model may become a cornerstone of European philanthropy.[271]

CASE STUDY: COLLABORATIVE FUNDING AT SCALE: THE AUDACIOUS MODEL

Launched at TED in 2018, The Audacious Project was designed to match bold social change ideas with catalytic levels of funding. It convenes more than three dozen major funders, including MacKenzie Scott, the Gates Foundation, and the Skoll Foundation, into a pooled model that identifies high-impact initiatives and funds them in multi-year cohorts. In 2021 alone, Audacious moved $920 million into the global social sector, supporting causes from climate change to immigration justice.

While The Audacious Project is not itself a donor-advised fund sponsor, many of its participating funders channel their charitable dollars through DAFs. This linkage underscores how donor-advised funds can serve as the financial backbone for collaborative, large-scale philanthropy that transcends borders and unites donors around shared priorities. In 2021 alone, The Audacious Project moved more than $920 million into the global social sector, illustrating the scale that can be achieved when visionary initiatives are supported by compliant, flexible, and trusted giving infrastructure. Together, The Audacious Project and its DAF funders demonstrate how modern philanthropic tools can transform generosity into coordinated, borderless impact.

DAF sponsors and donors can draw lessons from this model. When aligned around shared priorities and backed by secure, compliant giving infrastructure, generosity becomes not just borderless but transformational.[272]

---

[271] Carnie, C. Interview with Ted Hart, November 14, 2024.
[272] Tamela Spicer and Malik Robinson, "Collaborative Funding Is Uniting Efforts in the Nonprofit Sector," Dorothy A. Johnson Center for Philanthropy, January 18, 2023, https://johnsoncenter.org/blog/11-trends-in-philanthropy-for-2023/

WHY READINESS MATTERS IN GLOBAL GRANTMAKING

Even well-structured international grantmaking programs can fall into avoidable compliance traps. One common risk involves making grants without a written memorandum of understanding (MOU), which can create ambiguity when regranting through international NGOs or other charitable entities. Without sufficient oversight, the original grant framework may break down, increasing the risk of misused or untraceable funds.

Another concern arises when donors have a direct relationship with the foreign grantees they recommend. This is entirely permissible but must be managed with integrity and transparency to avoid any risk of violating IRS rules prohibiting private benefit and self-dealing. DAF sponsors must retain full discretion and ensure that decision-making authority remains with the granting organization.

Transmitting or storing personal data across borders without explicit consent may violate local data sovereignty laws, including the GDPR, China's PIPL, and similar regulations elsewhere. Separately, anonymous cryptocurrency disbursements can raise AML and sanctions compliance concerns, especially when donor or recipient identities are unclear.

Avoiding these regulatory traps requires more than technical compliance. It demands operational discipline, transparency, and a strong commitment to donor trust and principled stewardship.

To operationalize the principles of risk management and compliance discussed above, DAF sponsors can apply the following Readiness Assessment Framework. This tool outlines the foundational elements necessary to build a legally sound and mission-aligned global giving program.

READINESS ASSESSMENT

Supporting charitable work around the world is one of the most powerful services DAFs can offer. But with this opportunity comes the responsibility to uphold legal, ethical, and operational standards that vary widely across borders. From tax compliance and due diligence to data privacy and local registration, the overall process is not difficult, but it is precise, and the consequences of getting it wrong can be serious.

To meet this challenge, DAF sponsors are advised to move beyond case-by-case decision-making and adopt a proactive, system-wide approach to global grant-making. This begins with a full assessment of internal capacity and readiness.

This readiness assessment provides a structured way to evaluate whether a DAF program is equipped for responsible international grantmaking. It highlights the essential building blocks, from IRS-recognized compliance protocols to cybersecurity and partner validation, that form the foundation of any globally effective grantmaking program.

The tool can also help donors and advisors evaluate the readiness of a DAF sponsor they may wish to work with to support international grantmaking ambitions. Likewise, it offers insight to foreign charities on what to expect from a U.S.-based DAF provider operating within regulatory compliance boundaries. And for DAF sponsors, it can be used to identify areas of strength and uncover gaps that require attention when launching or refreshing a cross-border grant-making program.

As you move through each section of the chapter, you will find in-depth guidance, expert insights, and actionable strategies to help you assess whether international grantmaking practices are aligned with current regulatory frameworks, operational best practices, and principled stewardship.

READINESS ASSESSMENT: A LEARNING TOOL

Use this 10-point framework as a guide to strengthen international grantmaking readiness. Whether you are a sponsor, donor, advisor, or nonprofit partner, review each area, identify gaps, and build a path toward more effective cross-border giving.

Rate the organization on each of the following dimensions ($\checkmark$ = Operational, X = Needs Work):

Scoring:
8–10 $\checkmark$ = Future-Ready Global DAF Program
5–7 $\checkmark$ = Good Foundation, Prioritize Strategic Gaps
0–4 $\checkmark$ = Urgent Need for International Compliance Overhaul

✓ / X	Assessment Item	Assessment Question
	Regulatory Compliance	Have they established a documented internal protocol for international grantmaking that either meets or exceeds IRS expectations? Do they default to using ED and ER as their standard compliance frameworks?
	Documentation	Are their international grant files organized, complete, and audit-ready, with annual reviews to ensure up-to-date compliance across all grants?
	Privacy and Data	Have they implemented policies and safeguards to comply with foreign data sovereignty and privacy laws such as GDPR, LGPD, and others relevant to grantee jurisdictions?
	Subgranting	Do their grant agreements address downstream use of funds, including explicit terms for regranting, fiscal sponsorship, and required disclosures?
	Donor Education	Does their global grant portfolio incorporate feedback from local communities and reflect the voice and leadership of their in-country partners?
	Localization	Have they implemented policies and safeguards to comply with foreign data sovereignty and privacy laws such as GDPR, LGPD, and others relevant to grantee jurisdictions?
	Risk Monitoring	Do they have a structured process to regularly screen international grantees for sanctions lists, reputational concerns, and other legal and operational red flags?

✓ / X	Assessment Item	Assessment Question
	Digital Infrastructure	Are their grant management systems capable of tracking compliance steps, securely storing regulatory compliance documentation, and supporting international workflows?
	Policy Watch/ Registration/ Schedule F	Do they actively monitor legal, tax, and regulatory developments in the United States and in countries where they support grantees?
	Cultural Intelligence	Are their staff trained and systems equipped to engage with local norms, avoid cultural imposition, and promote equitable, respectful partnerships?

HOW TO USE THIS ASSESSMENT

This readiness assessment is a practical tool for evaluating the capacity and preparedness of a DAF sponsor to engage in responsible international grantmaking. While originally designed as a self-audit for DAF sponsors, it is equally useful to donors, advisors, and foreign charities seeking to understand the inner workings of global DAF operations.

- **DAF sponsors** can use this assessment to identify operational strengths, compliance gaps, and areas for improvement in their cross-border grantmaking processes.
- **Donors and advisors** may use it to evaluate whether a DAF sponsor is equipped to support international giving goals with appropriate legal and operational safeguards.
- **Foreign charities** can gain insight into the systems and expectations of U.S.-based DAF sponsors, helping them better prepare for successful partnerships and meet due diligence requirements.

For each category, assess whether the necessary protocols, systems, and controls are in place. Use the ✓ and X indicators to identify strengths and areas that may require additional oversight or development. This assessment does not replace legal counsel, but it will help surface key questions, clarify expectations, and guide practical next steps.

Each section of the chapter provides deeper context, expert commentary, and actionable strategies aligned with the assessment items to help ensure your approach to international grantmaking is both effective and compliant.

Assessment #1: Regulatory Compliance

DAFs and International Grant Compliance

Though originally developed as legal requirements for private foundations, ED and ER have become a de facto standard among DAF sponsors engaged in international grantmaking. This section explores what the law does and does not require for DAFs, and what donors, advisors, and foreign grantees need to understand about how U.S.-based DAF sponsors maintain compliance in international grantmaking.

What the Law Says (and Doesn't Say)

DAFs are not subject to the same statutory restrictions as private foundations under IRC §4945. The IRS has not issued regulations mandating that DAF sponsors use ED or ER when making grants to foreign organizations. However, this absence of explicit legal obligation does not mean DAFs operate in a compliance vacuum.

DAFs are required to ensure that:

- All grants serve a legitimate charitable purpose.[273] No grant provides impermissible private benefit or constitutes self-dealing.[274]
- Funds are not used to support terrorism or violate U.S. sanctions.[275]
- The DAF sponsor maintains adequate records and oversight to justify its exempt status.[276]

This regulatory landscape may evolve. In November 2023, the IRS issued proposed regulations (REG-142338-07) that, if finalized, could reshape DAF-to-DAF transfers and international grantmaking practices. The proposal would treat most DAF-to-DAF grants as "taxable distributions" unless the recipient DAF sponsor exercises sufficient discretion and control over the funds and ensures that subsequent grants meet IRS charitable purpose standards. For international

---

[273] 26 U.S.C. §170(c)(2)(B); Treas. Reg. §1.501(c)(3)–1(d)(2).
[274] 26 U.S.C. §501(c)(3); Treas. Reg. §1.501(c)(3)–1(c)(1).
[275] 31 C.F.R. pt. 594 (OFAC regulations); IRS Form 990, Part V, line 2.
[276] 26 U.S.C. §6001; Treas. Reg. §1.6001–1(a).

giving, the proposed rules would limit the use of ER in certain contexts, for example, prohibiting ER-funded grants from being used to support distributions to individuals or direct payments to service providers abroad. These proposals underscore the IRS's growing scrutiny of DAF practices and may require sponsors to rely more heavily on ED for grants to foreign organizations, particularly those supporting humanitarian aid or scholarships. While not final, the proposed regulations signal a clear intent to tighten compliance expectations and increase accountability in cross-border DAF operations.[277]

In this context, ED and ER serve as tested frameworks that demonstrate good-faith compliance with IRS expectations. They offer structure, consistency, and documentary protection against the risks of misused grants, reputational damage, or audit exposure. By proactively adopting ED or ER protocols, sponsors can anticipate potential future requirements and align with the standards already applied to private foundations.

Ignoring these frameworks altogether invites serious risk. Grants made to foreign entities without appropriate due diligence may trigger conduit concerns, where the DAF is seen as simply passing through donor instructions, and could jeopardize the sponsor's 501(c)(3) status[278], trigger excise taxes, or result in the disallowance of the donor's charitable deduction.

Alternative Protocols for DAF Sponsors

While ED and ER provide robust frameworks for international grantmaking, some DAF sponsors, particularly those with specialized legal or global expertise, have adapted these models to better suit their operational needs. These alternative protocols aim to reduce administrative burdens without compromising compliance.

For instance, sponsors working with low-risk, recurring grantees might adopt an "ER-lite" approach. Instead of full ER documentation, they conduct a streamlined due diligence review, require a basic grant agreement, and perform periodic financial checks. This balances efficiency with accountability, especially for trusted partners.

Other sponsors leverage in-house resources to replicate ED processes internally. By employing legal counsel or standardized templates, they generate ED-like

---

[277] IRS Proposed Regulations, REG-142338–07, 88 Fed. Reg. 77472. Nov. 13, 2023.
[278] IRS EO CPE Text 2019–03 at 52–54 (discussing exemption revocation for inadequate oversight).

opinions without outsourcing the work, a cost-effective solution for organizations with the capacity to manage it.

Still others implement risk-tiered systems, classifying grantees into categories (e.g., high-, medium-, or low-risk) and adjusting due diligence accordingly. A newly established NGO in a politically volatile region, for example, might trigger heightened scrutiny, while a decades-old, government-validated charity could qualify for simplified steps.

At their core, these adaptations reflect the same principles as ED and ER: defining charitable intent, validating recipients, monitoring funds, and documenting compliance. But when faced with uncertainty, such as grants to unregistered entities or unfamiliar jurisdictions, sponsors are wise to default to formal ED or ER. In global philanthropy, rigor is not optional. It is the foundation for achieving both meaningful impact and ethical integrity. Whether using ED, ER, or an adapted protocol, DAF sponsors must uphold standards that protect their mission and comply with evolving regulations.

Why Do DAFs Default to ED and ER?

In the absence of an equally robust and IRS-acceptable protocol, ED and ER remain the only formally recognized compliance frameworks for cross-border grantmaking. Most DAF sponsors choose to follow them because they:

- Provide legal protection by documenting compliance with IRS requirements.
- Preserve tax-exempt status by mitigating risks of private benefit or non-charitable use.
- Reduce audit exposure through structured due diligence and reporting.
- Align with industry best practices and donor expectations for transparency.

Some DAF sponsors are exploring alternative approaches, such as risk-tiered reviews or in-house legal assessments. Yet ED and ER continue to provide a proven, defensible framework in today's regulatory environment.

What This Means for Charities Outside the United States

Be prepared to provide legal and financial documentation if a DAF sponsor initiates an ED process, or to submit progress and financial reports if ER is used. Understanding these pathways improves your readiness and strengthens trust.

Legal Foundations of ED and ER

ED and ER are not just procedural tools; they are the product of a legal framework developed to protect the integrity of cross-border philanthropy.[279]

As first outlined in *Chapter 3: The History of the DAF Revolution*, the Tax Reform Act of 1969 was originally codified to address concerns about oversight and misuse of funds by private foundations. Most sponsors have embraced ED and ER as essential guardrails, shaping how they assess risk, validate foreign grantees, and demonstrate regulatory compliance.[280] This section traces the historical roots of ED and ER, highlights key milestones in their development, and explains why these legal structures continue to offer clarity and credibility in a complex global grantmaking landscape.

Laying the Groundwork for ED and ER

The framework for modern ER was established by the Tax Reform Act of 1969, a landmark overhaul of nonprofit tax law.[281] Driven by congressional concerns over self-dealing, lax oversight, and misuse of charitable assets, particularly in international grants, Sections 4941 through 4945 of the Internal Revenue Code imposed strict new rules on private foundations. While the 1969 Act formally established ER as the primary compliance mechanism, the foundations for ED emerged later. In 1992, Revenue Procedure 92-94 marked the IRS's first official recognition of ED, permitting foundations to rely on qualified opinions of counsel or other documentation to verify a foreign organization's equivalence to §501(c)(3) status. This administrative guidance laid the groundwork for ED to develop as a standardized alternative to ER, though it wouldn't be fully codified until Revenue Procedure 2017-53.[282] Jacqui Valouch, Head of Wealth Planning and Philanthropy at Deutsche Bank Wealth Management, notes:

> DAFs make international giving much easier, but they do require careful navigation to ensure compliance with regulations like equivalency determination and expenditure responsibility.[283]

---

[279] IRS Revenue Ruling 92–94 and Rev. Proc. 2017–53.

[280] See IRS Notice 2017–73 (indicating IRS interest in potential future regulation of DAF distributions, but confirming that no such rules currently exist).281 Tax Reform Act of 1969, Pub. L. No. 91-172, 83

[281] Tax Reform Act of 1969, Pub. L. No. 91-172, 83 Stat. 487, 1969.

[282] Internal Revenue Service, *Revenue Procedure 92-94*, 1992-2 C.B. 507 (1992), first formally permitting equivalency determination (ED) for foreign grantees; see also Internal Revenue Service, *Revenue Procedure 2017-53*, 2017-43 I.R.B. 377 (2017), codifying ED standards.

[283] Valouch, J. Interview with Ted Hart, August 8, 2024.

Under IRC §4945(d)(4) and §4945(h), private foundations were barred from making grants to foreign organizations unless they:

- Obtain a determination that the recipient is the equivalent of a U.S. §501(c)(3) organization (typically assessed as public charity equivalence through ED), or[284]
- Exercise expenditure responsibility (ER), which requires pre-grant due diligence, written agreements, and ongoing monitoring to ensure charitable use.[285]

These two mechanisms, now formalized as ED and ER, remain widely used tools for cross-border grantmaking compliance. While rooted in private foundation law, they are not legally required for donor-advised funds. However, many DAF sponsors adopt them as effective ways to meet their obligation to ensure that grants are used exclusively for charitable purposes.[286]

Evolution and IRS Codification (2015 Regulations)

In 2015, the IRS issued final regulations[287] that modernized both ED and ER practices. Key updates included:

Expanded authority for ED opinions: Sponsors may now rely on ED opinions from qualified tax practitioners (CPAs, enrolled agents) with expertise in nonprofit tax law, in addition to attorneys. These professionals, whether employed by DAF sponsors or retained externally, are expected to adhere to IRS Circular 230 standards[288], ensuring rigorous tax compliance and due diligence.

Recognition of both methods: The IRS reiterated that ED and ER remain equally valid for compliance[289], with the choice depending on grantee type and risk tolerance.

By expanding the pool of qualified ED opinion providers, the rules reduced compliance costs[290], while maintaining rigor. As the IRS noted the rules were

---

[284] Rev. Proc. 92–94, 1992–2 C.B. 507 (guidance on foreign equivalency determinations).

[285] IRS Pub. 578 (Rev. 2021), Expenditure Responsibility Guidelines.

[286] See Rev. Proc. 2017–53 (regarding ED) and IRC §4945(h) (regarding ER for private foundations). For DAFs, neither ED nor ER is required by law or regulation. See also IRS Notice 2006–109, which confirms that DAF sponsors must ensure charitable use of grant funds, but allows flexibility in how this is achieved. Proposed regulations under IRC §4966 further reinforce that ED and ER are not mandatory for DAFs, though widely accepted as best practices.

[287] U.S. Department of the Treasury. "Final Regulations on Equivalency Determination and Expenditure Responsibility." Treasury Decision 9740. 80 FR 57709, September 25, 2015.

[288] 31 C.F.R. pt. 10 (2023) (Circular 230 standards for tax practitioners).

[289] Rev. Proc. 2017–53, 2017–42 I.R.B. 1 (affirming continued validity of both approaches).

[290] Council on Foundations, International Grantmaking Update 12 (survey showing 27% cost reduction for DAF sponsors post-2015), 2016.

designed to offer flexibility while maintaining accountability.[281] Today, ED and ER function as complementary strategies: DAF sponsors offering international grantmaking typically offer both options, selecting the approach that aligns with the donor's intent, the grantee's legal status, and the transaction's risk profile.[292]

How to Conduct Equivalency Determination

ED is one of two IRS-recognized methods that U.S. grantmakers can use to determine whether a foreign nonprofit qualifies as the equivalent of a U.S. public charity. Although not required by law or regulation for DAFs, it provides a reliable and efficient way to ensure compliance, particularly when working with recurring international grantees that have a stable legal and financial presence.

How to Conduct Equivalency Determination.

When to Use ED

ED is the preferred method in these scenarios:

- The foreign organization is a known, recurring grantee or part of a strategic long-term partnership.
- The organization operates transparently and maintains up-to-date legal, financial, and governance documentation.
- The DAF sponsor prefers to complete compliance upfront with a legal opinion rather than monitor ongoing grant use.

Because ED offers a defensible, IRS-recognized path for demonstrating public charity equivalency, it is especially useful for sustained or expanding donor relationships.[293]

[281] 80 Fed. Reg. at 71,381.
[292] IRS EO CPE Text 2019–03 at 45 (noting 78% of large sponsors now offer both ED/ER options).
[293] See IRS Rev. Proc. 92–94 and T.D. 9740 (Preamble to Final Regulations issued in 2015), which confirm that U.S. grantmakers, including DAF sponsors, may use ED or ER to ensure foreign grantee compliance. ED is not required by law but provides a reliable path to demonstrating public charity equivalency.

What's Required for a Valid Equivalency Determination

To issue an ED, the grantmaker or a qualified third-party provider must obtain and review the following:

- Organizing documents: These include the foreign nonprofit's articles of incorporation, governing statutes, or other legal formation documents that confirm a charitable purpose and a public benefit mission.
- Financial statements: Typically, two to three years of audited or reliable financial records are reviewed to assess transparency, fiscal responsibility, and whether a significant portion of income supports charitable activities.
- Operational information: This includes details about board composition, key staff, funding sources, and descriptions of recent and planned programs to evaluate alignment with U.S. charitable standards.

If this documentation supports the conclusion that the foreign organization would qualify as a U.S. public charity under IRS rules, then a written legal opinion, known as an ED, is issued.

Originally set forth in IRS Revenue Procedure 92-94, this framework was expanded in Revenue Procedure 2017-53, which permits such opinions to be issued by a qualified U.S.-based attorney, CPA, or enrolled agent with appropriate nonprofit tax expertise.[294]

Validity Period and Renewal Best Practices

Although ED opinions do not have a fixed statutory expiration date, they are valid until material details have changed, however most DAF sponsors and private foundations treat them as valid for two years. This convention reflects the evolving legal and operational landscape of foreign nonprofits.

Recommended best practices for maintaining compliance with ED include scheduling renewals every two years for all ED-certified grantees to ensure that documentation remains current and accurate. If there is any material change in the grantee's leadership, organizational purpose, or legal status, the ED should be promptly updated to reflect those developments. Sponsors should also maintain complete and organized documentation for audit purposes. This includes

---

[294] IRS Rev. Proc. 92-94, 1992-2 C.B. 507 (initial framework), and Rev. Proc. 2017-53, 2017-40 I.R.B. 263, which confirm that a legal opinion for ED may be issued by a U.S. attorney, CPA, or enrolled agent with appropriate nonprofit tax expertise.

retaining the original legal opinion, all supporting materials, and written confirmation that the grantee continues to meet the standards required by the IRS.

How to Conduct Expenditure Responsibility

How to Conduct Expenditure Responsibility.

ER is the IRS-sanctioned alternative to ED for making grants to foreign organizations or other entities that do not qualify as the equivalent of a U.S. public charity. Although originally designed for private foundations under IRC §4945(h) and Treasury Regulations §53.4945–5, many DAF sponsors voluntarily adopt ER protocols, especially when working with new or emerging organizations, pooled funds, social enterprises, or intermediaries lacking sufficient documentation for ED.

ER is more administratively intensive than ED, but it offers a clear, defensible path for compliant international giving when ED is not viable.

When to Use ER

DAF sponsors typically rely on ER in the following scenarios:

- The foreign organization cannot provide the legal or financial documentation required for ED.
- The grant addresses urgent needs (e.g., disaster relief, pandemic response, humanitarian aid) where obtaining ED documentation is impractical.
- The recipient is a social enterprise or other non-traditional entity where ED is not available.
- The sponsor is contributing to a pooled or intermediary fund that will regrant funds internationally.
- ER, though more hands-on than ED, gives DAF sponsors the flexibility to support high-impact work in complex or underdeveloped philanthropic environments.

The Five Steps of ER Compliance

To fulfill ER requirements, a DAF sponsor should follow five core steps adapted from the IRS regulations applicable to private foundations:

1. **Pre-Grant Inquiry:** Conduct a reasonable investigation into the grantee's identity, leadership, financial history, and capacity to carry out the proposed charitable purpose. This inquiry should be documented, especially for grantees in high-risk jurisdictions.

2. **Written Grant Agreement:** Execute a formal grant agreement requiring that the funds be used exclusively for the stated charitable purpose. The agreement should prohibit regranting without prior written approval, specify reporting requirements, and outline consequences for noncompliance.

3. **Segregation of Funds:** The grantee must maintain the grant funds in a separate bank account or a distinct ledger entry to ensure the funds are not co-mingled with unrestricted or non-charitable resources.

4. **Ongoing Reporting:** Require the grantee to submit periodic written reports, typically annually and upon project completion, detailing how the funds were spent and the outcomes achieved.

5. **Internal Recordkeeping (990-PF Equivalency):** Although DAF sponsors are not required to file IRS Form 990-PF, the best practice is to maintain internal documentation that mirrors private foundation standards. This includes the amount, purpose, and current status of each ER grant, creating a defensible audit trail.

Risk Mitigation Systems

DAF sponsors should implement comprehensive systems to assess and manage legal, financial, reputational, and operational risks associated with international giving. This includes:

*   Screening all grantees against the U.S. Treasury Department's SDN (Specially Designated Nationals) list, maintained by OFAC. Sponsors must block any match and file a report as required.

*   Conducting Politically Exposed Persons (PEP) screening to flag high-risk associations with current or former public officials, their family members, or close associates. If a grantee is identified as a PEP, enhanced due diligence (EDD) protocols should be triggered.

- Identifying high-risk jurisdictions, using FATF guidance or internal risk scoring tools.
- Monitoring for unusual donor requests or complex funding structures that may warrant further review.
- Establishing clear escalation protocols, including when to consult legal counsel or pause grant activity.
- Documenting all risk assessments, screening results, and due diligence actions taken to demonstrate compliance and protect donor intent.

Common Pitfalls and How to Monitor Compliance

Even with strong protocols in place, sponsors may still encounter common pitfalls when managing international grants. One frequent challenge is late or incomplete reporting. To address this, sponsors should establish clear deadlines and maintain a follow-up calendar to ensure timely submission of required documentation. Another potential issue involves changes in a grantee's leadership or mission. Sponsors should require grantees to report any material changes and be prepared to reassess eligibility if the organization no longer aligns with its originally approved status.

Unapproved regranting or the use of undisclosed fiscal sponsors can also present risks. To mitigate this, sponsors should clearly outline restrictions in the grant agreement and require full disclosure of any subgranting activity. Maintaining open lines of communication, conducting site visits where feasible, and collaborating with local partners are additional tools that not only support compliance but also help build lasting trust with international grantees.

Grant Agreements and Subgrantee Provisions

Well-drafted grant agreements are central to effective ER compliance. At a minimum, the agreement should:

- Reference U.S. charitable standards, including IRC §170(c)(2)(B).
- Require written approval from the sponsor for any subgrants or material changes to the funded project.
- Specify the grantee's recordkeeping responsibilities and reporting deadlines.
- Include clear recourse provisions in case of breach or misuse of funds.

If the grantee intends to work with subgrantees, the DAF sponsor should ensure that the same standards apply to those subgrantees and other downstream recipients (the ultimate beneficiaries of the funds). This may involve requesting copies of subgrant agreements, providing reporting templates, or requiring pre-approval of the subgrantee list.

Five Steps of ER for DAFs

Step	Description	Best Practice
1. Pre-Grant Inquiry	Assess the grantee's capacity and legitimacy	Document findings and screen against watchlists (e.g., OFAC, PEPs)
2. Written Agreement	Restrict grant funds to specific charitable purposes	Use standardized ER templates; include subgrant and regranting clauses
3. Segregation of Funds	Ensure ER funds are not co-mingled with general funds	Require a separate account or distinct ledger entry
4. Ongoing Reporting	Monitor use of funds through grantee reports	Set reporting deadlines and proactively follow up
5. Record-keeping	Maintain internal documentation for each ER grant	Mirror IRS Form 990-PF-style reporting in internal systems

Sample ER Grant Agreement Clause

The following clause may be included in an international grant agreement to fulfill ER requirements. It reflects IRS guidance and language commonly used by DAF sponsors and private foundations.

The Grantee agrees to use all grant funds exclusively for the charitable purposes described in this Agreement, and not for any political or non-charitable purposes, as defined under Sections 501(c)(3) and §4945 of the U.S. Internal Revenue Code. The Grantee shall not regrant or transfer any portion of the funds to another organization or individual without the prior written approval of the Grantor.

The Grantee further agrees to:

- *Maintain the grant funds in a separate account or clearly designated ledger.*
- *Submit annual written reports detailing expenditures and progress toward stated objectives.*
- *Provide a final report upon completion of the funded activities.*
- *Retain all supporting documentation for at least four years from the date of the final report.*

Failure to comply with these terms may result in suspension or termination of the grant, and the potential return of any unused or misused funds. The grantee shall promptly notify the grantor of any material changes in governance, leadership, or project direction.

Private Benefit Risks Abroad

While ED and ER provide essential safeguards for legal compliance, they do not eliminate the risk of improper private benefit to donors, advisors, or related parties. The IRS rules that prohibit undue benefit to donors, advisors, or related parties apply to international grantmaking just as they do to domestic giving. These rules are global in scope and must be taken seriously in every jurisdiction.

Problematic situations can arise when grants are directed to overseas schools that a donor's child attends, or when funds are given to foreign nonprofits managed by the donor or their family members. In some cases, personal or business expenses may be disguised as charitable support, which violates the core intent of DAF regulations. To guard against these risks, DAF sponsors must screen for potential

Self-Dealing and Private Benefit Prohibited

conflicts of interest and require donors to disclose any personal relationships with the grantee or its leadership. These practices are not only essential for preserving the DAF sponsor's tax-exempt status; they are also critical for maintaining trust in the charitable sector as a whole.

TARGETED COMPLIANCE CHALLENGES

As DAFs increasingly engage in global grantmaking, certain compliance risks extend beyond traditional ED and ER frameworks. Two issues in particular, the use of "friends of" organizations and DAF-to-DAF transfers, require careful oversight to safeguard legal integrity, donor trust, and the DAF sponsor's tax-exempt status.

"Friends of" Organizations and Foreign Control

"Friends of" organizations, U.S.-based public charities formed to support a specific foreign nonprofit, can be valuable pathway for international giving. However, they must maintain true independence over their governance and grant decisions. If they simply act as pass-through entities, lacking discretion over funds or rubber-stamping the wishes of the foreign group, the IRS may classify them as conduits. This can jeopardize their 501(c)(3) status and result in penalties.

To remain compliant, a "friends of" organization must retain control over its mission, set its own charitable priorities, and follow its own grantmaking process. Donors and advisors should ensure that any such organization has a clearly documented board, operates under U.S. charitable law, and does not automatically regrant all donations overseas without proper review.

DAF sponsors must verify the organization:

- **Maintains Independent Governance:** The U.S. entity must have its own board with real decision-making authority, free from foreign control.
- **Exercises Genuine Discretion Over Grants:** Grants must align with the U.S. charity's mission, not merely fulfill donor or foreign directives.
- **Meets All U.S. Compliance Requirements:**
    - Federal: Files required IRS returns (Form 990, 990-EZ, or 990-PF).
    - State: Registers for charitable solicitation in states where it is fundraising (if required). 36 states + Washington DC mandate registration before soliciting donations, with some exemptions for small or religious groups.

    ◦   IRS Disclosure: Form 1023 (for new charities) requires disclosure of foreign ties; ongoing monitoring is essential.

Due diligence on these U.S. fiscal sponsors should be as rigorous as for foreign grantees. This helps ensure that the intermediary is not acting as a conduit and preserves the integrity of the sponsor's international grantmaking program. IRS Form 1023 requires new U.S. charities to disclose any control by or close relationship with foreign organizations. While not reported annually in the same way, DAF sponsors should continue monitoring whether affiliated U.S. organizations are operating independently or simply serving as conduits for foreign entities, as such arrangements may still trigger IRS scrutiny under private benefit, conduit, or misuse rules.[295]

DAF-to-DAF Transfers: Who Is Responsible?

DAF-to-DAF transfers, where one DAF makes a grant to another with the intent of reaching an international beneficiary, require special care. Sara C. DeRose , Director, Development and Philanthropic Services, Fairfield County's Community Foundation, reminds us DAF-to-DAF transfers can become important for donors wishing to make international grants from a DAF that does not offer the service:

> While donor advised funds can facilitate international giving, smaller sponsors face challenges with compliance and fees, which can limit their ability to support global philanthropy.[296]

To ensure compliance, DAF sponsors must clarify:

- Who will conduct due diligence (ED/ER or equivalent)
- Who bears the burden of reporting and recordkeeping
- Whether the downstream sponsor is acting as a true intermediary or simply following donor instructions

Best practice: Establish a formal memorandum of understanding (MOU) that outlines roles, compliance expectations, and documentation protocols. The DAF making the grant (often called the upstream DAF) should not assume that compliance is automatic.

---

[295] IRS, Instructions for Form 1023 (Rev. 01–2020), Part VIII, Line 14.
[296] DeRose, S. Interview with Ted Hart, December 12, 2024.

If DAF A grants to DAF B and the ultimate grantee is already donor-specified or known at the time of transfer, and DAF B fails to exercise genuine discretion and control over the subsequent grant, the IRS may treat this as a conduit arrangement. Under IRC §4966, this could constitute a taxable distribution, exposing the DAF sponsor to excise taxes and regulatory penalties. Sponsors should carefully document that each intermediary DAF evaluates and approves grants independently, not simply at the direction of an upstream donor.[297]

ASSESSMENT #2: DOCUMENTATION

Building a Defensible Record for Global Grantmaking

In international grantmaking, good documentation is more than paperwork; it is a protective shield. For DAF sponsors, maintaining thorough and consistent records is critical to preserving tax-exempt status, demonstrating compliance with IRS rules, and safeguarding the credibility of the grantmaking process.

Legal tools like ED and ER must be backed by a clear, complete, and verifiable audit trail. Without it, even well-intentioned grants may be questioned without proper documentation. Sponsors should approach documentation not just as a technical obligation, but as a demonstration of prudent governance and institutional integrity.

What Every International Grant File Should Include

A globally compliant grant file should document the full lifecycle of the grant, from initial validation to final reporting. Donors and advisors may wish to confirm whether their DAF sponsor maintains this level of documentation rigor. Foreign charities can use this list to anticipate what information they may be asked to provide when applying for a grant or submitting reports. At minimum, each grant file should contain:

---

[297] PPA 2006; IRS EO CPE Text 2019–03, pp. 52–54 (explaining conduit risks in DAF-to-DAF transactions and the application of IRC §4966).

Document	Purpose
Internal review or compliance memo	Documents sponsor's discretionary control and decision-making
Sanctions screening logs (e.g., OFAC, PEPs)	Verifies grant is not made to restricted entities
Translations (if applicable)	Ensures staff and auditors can assess foreign-language materials
Renewals	Ensures ED status remains valid (recommended every 2 years). ER eligibility is renewed according to protocol; if risk-based, this is likely per grant or up to every three years.
Grant proposal or application	Establishes charitable intent, scope of work, and alignment with sponsor's mission
Due diligence and risk review	Screens for legal status, reputational issues, sanctions, and country-specific risks
ED opinion or ER inquiry and agreement	Demonstrates IRS-recognized compliance methodology
Executed grant agreement	Defines purpose, restrictions, reporting terms, and subgranting clauses
Proof of disbursement	Wire confirmation, exchange rate record, and payment verification
Interim and final grantee reports	Confirms charitable use and outcomes

Acknowledgment Protocols and Donor Disclosure

Because DAF grants are issued by the sponsoring organization rather than the donor, it is essential to maintain clarity and accuracy in all related communications. Acknowledgment letters sent to foreign grantees should clearly name the DAF sponsor as the source of the grant, not the individual donor. These letters should also describe the charitable purpose of the funding and include a statement confirming that no goods or services were provided in exchange for the contribution.

To remain in compliance with IRS regulations, donors must not receive acknowledgment letters or tax receipts directly from the foreign grantee. Any language that implies donor-directed giving should be strictly avoided, as it could trigger concerns about private benefit and jeopardize the sponsor's tax-exempt status. These distinctions, while sometimes overlooked, are critically important. They help protect all parties, donors, grantees, and sponsors from audit risk, legal complications, and reputational harm.

What This Means for Donors and Foreign Grantees

To protect all parties, foreign grantees should never send tax receipts or acknowledgment letters directly to donors. Donors should expect communication only from the DAF sponsor. This protects the integrity of the grant and prevents private benefit violations.

Institutionalizing Strong Documentation Practices

While these are internal practices for sponsors, donors and advisors may ask about file retention, audit practices, and whether sanctions screening is performed. Foreign organizations can build trust by maintaining clear, consistent records of their own that align with these expectations. To ensure consistency and readiness for audits or regulatory inquiries, grantmakers (DAF sponsors) should:

6. **Standardize File Structures**
   - Use a global grant file template or checklist.
   - Organize folders by lifecycle stages (e.g., validation/agreement/ disbursement/reporting).
7. **Centralize Documentation**
   - Implement a grant management system (GMS) with:
   - Role-based access
   - Document linking

- ○ Version control and audit trails
- ○ Automate reminders for report deadlines and ED renewal cycles.

8. **Formalize Internal Policies**
   - ○ Define document retention timelines (e.g., 7 years from close).
   - ○ Assign responsibilities across departments (legal, finance, compliance).

9. **Train and Align Teams**
   - ○ Equip all relevant staff with guidance on documentation expectations.
   - ○ Use templates for legal memos, ER reports, and donor communications.

10. **Ensure Schedule F Alignment**
    - ○ Maintain consistency between what is filed on IRS Form 990 Schedule F and what is stored in the grant file.
    - ○ Create internal crosswalks between financial systems and compliance files.

11. **Conduct Regular File Reviews**
    - ○ Review a sample of files quarterly or semi-annually.
    - ○ Confirm that ED determinations remain valid, ER reports are complete, and no conduit arrangements exist.

Common Red Flags to Avoid

In international grantmaking, small lapses in oversight can lead to significant compliance problems. DAF sponsors should be proactive in identifying and addressing red flags before they escalate into violations. One common issue is relying on expired or outdated ED or ER opinions. These documents must be regularly reviewed and updated to ensure they remain valid.

Another warning sign is the submission of vague or non-substantive reports from grantees. When reports lack detail, fail to demonstrate how funds were used, or omit programmatic outcomes, sponsors should request clarification and consider delaying future disbursements. A third risk arises when sanctions screening is incomplete or missing altogether. This step is essential to ensure that grant funds do not inadvertently benefit prohibited entities or individuals.

Donor involvement in selecting grantees or influencing grant reporting can also be problematic, as it may suggest impermissible donor control. Similarly, when both the DAF sponsor and the donor receive acknowledgment letters, or when communications contain conflicting messages about who made the gift, the sponsor's tax-exempt status could be placed at risk. Even relatively minor gaps in documentation or language can undermine the credibility of a sponsor's compliance posture and invite unnecessary scrutiny.

Red Flags to Avoid

ASSESSMENT #3: PRIVACY AND DATA

Protecting Personal Information in a Global Grantmaking Environment

Cross-border grantmaking introduces not only financial and legal complexities but also profound responsibilities related to the collection, processing, and protection of personal data. As DAF sponsors work with international grantees, vendors, and sometimes even beneficiaries, they must navigate a shifting landscape of global privacy regulations that may apply extraterritorially or impose strict conditions on data transfers.

Failure to manage privacy obligations properly can expose sponsors to legal liability, reputational risk, donor backlash, and interruptions in local partnerships. This section offers a framework for compliance with global privacy laws, both well-known and emerging, and provides guidance on data minimization, risk mitigation, and secure systems design.

What This Means for Donors, Advisors, and Foreign Grantees

While this assessment is designed to guide DAF sponsors, donors and advisors can also understand how global privacy rules affect the sharing of personal data across borders. Foreign charities, especially those working in jurisdictions with data localization laws, can use this information to strengthen trust and prepare for due diligence requests that involve personal data.

The Expanding Landscape of Global Data Privacy

Many jurisdictions around the world now have comprehensive privacy regimes modeled after or stricter than the European Union's General Data Protection Regulation (GDPR). These include:

Jurisdiction	Privacy Law	Key Features
Australia	Australia's Privacy Act (Privacy Act 1988 (Cth)[298]	Consent, access rights, data minimization, regulator enforcement
Brazil	Lei Geral de Proteção de Dados (LGPD)[299]	Consent-based processing, data localization requirements
Canada	Personal Information Protection and Electronic Documents Act (PIPEDA)[300]	Data subject rights, cross-border transfer restrictions, high penalties
China	Personal Information Protection Law (PIPL)[301]	Sectoral restrictions, cybersecurity reviews, local storage mandates
European Union	General Data Protection Regulation (GDPR)[302]	Data subject rights, cross-border transfer restrictions, high penalties
India	Digital Personal Data Protection Act (DPDPA)[303]	Data fiduciaries, notice and consent, cross-border rules pending finalization

[298] Privacy Act 1988 (Cth), Federal Register of Legislation. Accessed June 4, 2025, https://www.legislation.gov.au/Series/C2004A03712

[299] Brazilian General Data Protection Law – LGPD, LGPD Brazil Info. Accessed February 26, 2025, https://lgpd-brazil.info/

[300] Personal Information Protection and Electronic Documents Act (PIPEDA), S.C. 2000, c. 5. Accessed February 26, 2025, https://laws-lois.justice.gc.ca/eng/acts/p-8.6/

[301] "The PRC Personal Information Protection Law (Final): A Full Translation," China Briefing, last modified August 26, 2021. https://www.china-briefing.com/news/the-prc-personal-information-protection-law-final-a-full-translation/

[302] GDPR Compliance for Nonprofits: How to Stay Compliant with European Privacy Laws," CharityEngine Blog. Accessed May 30, 2025. https://blog.charityengine.net/gdpr-compliance-nonprofits

Jurisdiction	Privacy Law	Key Features
Japan	Act on Protection of Personal Information (APPI)[304]	Data minimization, regulator registration, accountability principles
Mexico	Ley Federal de Protección de Datos Personales en Posesión de los Particulares (LFPDPPP)[305]	Consent, purpose limitation, data rights, security measures, penalties
Nigeria	Nigeria Data Protection Act (NDPA)[306]	Data subject rights, accountability principles, controller and processor requirements
South Africa	Protection of Personal Information Act (POPIA)[307]	Data minimization, regulator registration, accountability principles
United States (state-level)	California Consumer Privacy Act (CCPA)[308]	US-based DAF sponsors must also monitor evolving domestic privacy frameworks, with California leading and states such as Virginia, Colorado, Connecticut, and Utah forming the first wave of comprehensive laws.

[303] The Digital Personal Data Protection Act, 2023, Ministry of Electronics and Information Technology (MeitY), Government of India, last modified June 4, 2024, https://www.meity.gov.in/static/uploads/2024/06/2bf1f0e 9f04e6fb4f8fef35e82c42aa5.pdf

[304] Act on the Protection of Personal Information (APPI), Act No. 57 of 2003, as amended. Personal Information Protection Commission of Japan. Accessed May 14, 2025 https://www.ppc.go.jp/en/legal/

[305] Ley Federal de Protección de Datos Personales en Posesión de los Particulares (LFPDPPP), Gobierno de México. Accessed February 26, 2025. https://www.dof.gob.mx/nota_detalle.php?codigo=5150631&fecha=05/07/2010

[306] Nigeria Data Protection Act, 2023, Nigeria Computer Emergency Response Team (ngCERT). Accessed July 30, 2025. https://cert.gov.ng/ngcert/resources/Nigeria_Data_Protection_Act_2023.pdf

[307] Protection of Personal Information Act (POPIA)," POPIA.co.za. Accessed July 30, 2025. https://popia.co.za/

[308] California Consumer Privacy Act (CCPA), Office of the Attorney General, State of California. Accessed July 30, 2025. https://oag.ca.gov/privacy/ccpa

Importantly, even if a sponsor is not physically located in these jurisdictions, its grantmaking activities can still trigger obligations if personal data is collected from individuals in those countries.

Types of Data at Risk in International Grantmaking

DAF sponsors and intermediaries often collect or process the following data categories during due diligence or grant management:

- **Grantee contact information** (names, titles, emails, addresses)
- **Government-issued IDs** (for legal verification or ED/ER)
- **Personal financial data** (bank details, compensation disclosures)
- **Donor information** (in matching or regranting programs)
- **Staff or board profiles** (used in reputational screening or grant justification)
- **Beneficiary data** (in impact reporting or site visit evaluations)

In many jurisdictions, even basic contact data may be considered "personal data" and subject to regulation.

Key Privacy Principles for DAF Sponsors

In an increasingly regulated global environment, DAF sponsors must take data privacy seriously. Protecting personal information is not only a matter of ethical stewardship but also a legal necessity in many jurisdictions. To maintain compliance and foster trust, sponsors should adopt a clear set of privacy principles that guide their handling of personal data throughout the grantmaking process.

First, sponsors should follow the principle of data minimization. This means collecting only the information necessary to fulfill legal or operational due diligence requirements. Sponsors should avoid gathering sensitive personal data, such as information about race, religion, or health status, unless it is absolutely required and supported by a valid legal justification.

Next is purpose limitation. Personal data should be used solely for the specific charitable purpose for which it was originally collected. Repurposing that data for marketing, analytics, or unrelated communications without the individual's clear consent undermines transparency and can violate international privacy laws.

Consent and transparency go hand in hand. Sponsors should provide clear, accessible privacy notices to grantees, vendors, and any individuals whose data may be collected. Informed and documented consent must be obtained where required, particularly when personal data will be transferred across borders.

Cross-border data transfers introduce additional complexity. Sponsors must verify whether the destination country meets adequacy standards under regulations like the General Data Protection Regulation (GDPR). When it does not, legal mechanisms such as Standard Contractual Clauses, Data Transfer Agreements, or Binding Corporate Rules should be used to legitimize the transfer.

Sponsors should also establish a clear data retention and deletion policy. For example, retaining records for seven years after the close of a grant may be appropriate for audit purposes. Once that period expires, and unless required otherwise by law, personal data should be securely deleted. Secure deletion protocols must be documented and followed consistently.

Security safeguards are another critical component. Files containing personal data should be stored and transmitted using encryption. Internal access must be limited to authorized personnel only, and modern protections such as multi-factor authentication and audit trails should be implemented within grant management systems.

Finally, every sponsor should have a formal incident response plan in place. This plan should be designed to comply with GDPR and any applicable local privacy laws. In the event of a breach, legal counsel should be engaged to determine the appropriate notification thresholds and timing. A prompt and professional response can limit legal exposure and preserve the trust of donors and grantees alike.

By embedding these privacy principles into their operations, DAF sponsors can align with global best practices while maintaining the confidence of those they serve.

Local Partnerships and Jurisdictional Expertise

DAF sponsors should engage local legal advisors or trusted partners in high-risk jurisdictions to:

- Interpret local privacy law obligations.
- Customize privacy notices or grant agreements.
- Ensure consent mechanisms and disclosures align with local customs and legal expectations.

Localization is particularly important in countries with broad state surveillance powers (e.g., China) or rapidly changing legal environments (e.g., India, Nigeria).

Reviewing Privacy and Data

Privacy is no longer an optional concern in international grantmaking; it is a core element of responsible, ethical, and legally compliant philanthropy. DAF sponsors must take proactive steps to understand global privacy laws, build secure systems, and honor the dignity and rights of those whose data they steward.

By integrating privacy-by-design into their global grantmaking practices, sponsors not only avoid legal exposure, but also reinforce the values of trust, transparency, and accountability that underpin effective philanthropy.

ASSESSMENT #4: SUBGRANTING

Managing Regranting Chains and Preserving Charitable Control

International grantmaking often involves multi-tiered delivery structures, where the direct recipient of a DAF grant passes funds on to other local partners. These subgrants, sometimes known as regrants, are common in pooled funds, international intermediaries, fiscal sponsor networks, and emergency response collaboratives.

However, subgranting introduces added risk for DAF sponsors, who remain responsible under IRS regulations for ensuring that all funds ultimately support a qualified charitable purpose. Whether a grant is made through ED or ER, DAF sponsors must evaluate whether the original compliance rationale extends to all downstream recipients.

What This Means for Donors, Advisors, and Foreign Charities

Regranting arrangements are common in global philanthropy, especially in emergencies or pooled giving initiatives. Donors and advisors should confirm whether the DAF sponsor monitors where funds ultimately go and how impact is tracked. Foreign charities working through intermediaries should understand that they may be subject to additional compliance reviews or reporting expectations, even if they are not the direct recipient.

Risk: Gaps in Oversight or Due Diligence

One of the most significant legal risks in cross-border grantmaking arises when there is insufficient oversight or due diligence in subgranting relationships. When a primary grantee passes funds to secondary recipients without clear documentation or control, it can jeopardize the original donor intent

Subgranting introduces added risk for DAF sponsors.

and expose the DAF sponsor to regulatory violations. This breakdown in control may violate the terms of an ED or ER grant, especially if charitable purpose or reporting requirements are not maintained throughout the process. Such arrangements can also raise concerns about conduit activity, where the initial recipient acts only as a pass-through. This outcome is prohibited under U.S. tax law. "In addition, a failure to maintain oversight can lead to violations of the private benefit and diversion restrictions, and may trigger taxable distribution concerns under IRC §4966 and §4945. Maintaining control and documentation at each step is not simply a best practice; it is essential for compliance and public trust.

Compliance Requirements for Subgranting

To reduce the legal and regulatory risks associated with subgranting, DAF sponsors must adopt a proactive and structured approach before approving any grant that may involve regranting. The first step is to determine whether the primary grantee intends to issue subgrants. This intent should be clearly disclosed in the grant proposal, outlined in the budget narrative, or gathered through a due diligence questionnaire. If subgranting is anticipated, this information must be surfaced early in the review process.

Once the intent to regrant is confirmed, sponsors must assess whether the existing compliance framework, either through ED or ER, adequately covers the proposed subgrants. In cases where ED is used, it is important to note that the determination typically applies only to the primary grantee. Any subgrantees must be separately qualified or explicitly included in the original legal opinion.

Under ER, the initial grant agreement should include specific provisions for sub-granting. These provisions must require pre-approval of all subgrantees, impose a duty to apply ER-equivalent diligence downstream, and clearly state that the intermediary remains fully accountable for all financial and narrative reporting.

The grant agreement itself must include protective clauses to maintain transparency and accountability. It should require that subgrantees be disclosed in advance and approved in writing. The agreement must prohibit further regrants without the sponsor's explicit consent, and all subgrants should be aligned with the original charitable purpose. Reporting obligations must extend to both financial and programmatic outcomes at the subgrantee level. Throughout the grant period, the intermediary should retain oversight and control over both expenditures and activities.

Finally, sponsors should establish procedures to monitor the flow of funds. This includes requiring intermediaries to segregate subgranted funds from their general operating accounts and to maintain documentation of subgrant approvals, reports, and related correspondence. These measures are essential not only for legal compliance but also for safeguarding donor intent and sustaining the integrity of the charitable mission.

Best Practices for Working with Intermediaries

When DAF sponsors choose to partner with international regranting networks, fiscal sponsors, or pooled funds, they must take care to balance efficiency with accountability. Intermediaries can offer valuable on-the-ground knowledge and logistical capacity, especially in complex or high-risk environments. However, these arrangements introduce additional layers of compliance responsibility, particularly under Expenditure Responsibility rules.

To manage these risks effectively, sponsors should first establish a standard ER clause that clearly addresses subgranting protocols. This language should define the intermediary's obligations, require disclosure and pre-approval of any downstream subgrants, and assign responsibility for reporting across the entire regranting chain. Setting this expectation up front helps prevent confusion and reinforces the sponsor's commitment to compliance.

Sponsors may also benefit from creating a list of preferred intermediary partners. These organizations should be carefully validated for their internal compliance systems, experience managing international funds, and ability to provide trans parent reporting. Maintaining a curated list simplifies the grantmaking process while ensuring a baseline standard of operational integrity.

Periodic post-grant audits can provide further assurance that funds were used as intended. These reviews allow sponsors to verify documentation, assess risk, and learn from past activity to improve future oversight. In cases where subgrants are approved outside of the standard policies, sponsors should maintain an exceptions log. This record should capture the rationale, approval pathway, and any additional safeguards imposed to mitigate potential risks.

By adopting these practices, DAF sponsors can confidently collaborate with intermediaries while upholding their fiduciary duty and preserving the integrity of their international grantmaking programs.

Reviewing Subgranting

Subgranting is a practical and often necessary feature of global philanthropy, but it requires rigorous compliance protocols to ensure transparency, control, and adherence to IRS requirements. By embedding safeguards at the outset and maintaining documentation throughout the regranting chain, DAF sponsors can fulfill their obligations and extend their reach through trusted intermediaries without compromising legal or fiduciary standards.

ASSESSMENT #5: DONOR EDUCATION

Educating Donors and Advisors on Global Compliance

International grantmaking through DAFs is governed by strict legal frameworks and nuanced operational protocols. While DAF sponsors are legally responsible for ensuring compliance, donors and their advisors must understand how these rules shape grant eligibility, processing timelines, and reporting standards, especially when supporting international causes. Educated donors are essential partners in ethical and effective global philanthropy.

This section provides sponsors with tools to educate donors and their advisors about the realities and responsibilities of cross-border giving. A well-informed donor is more likely to align expectations with legal requirements, avoid problematic requests, and support stronger philanthropic outcomes.

Core Learning Areas for Donors

Educating donors about international grantmaking is not just a matter of compliance; it is also a critical opportunity to build trust, manage expectations, and empower donors to engage meaningfully in global philanthropy. There are several key areas where sponsors should focus their educational efforts.

First, it is important to explain the fundamental role of DAF sponsor discretion and control. While donors make recommendations, it is the sponsor who must ultimately approve all grants. This responsibility is especially important in international contexts, where the sponsor must validate that the proposed grant serves a charitable purpose and complies with IRS regulations. Sponsors are prohibited from acting as conduits or simply following donor instructions without an independent review process.

Donor education is the key to setting realistic expectations.

Another essential learning area is helping donors understand why compliance matters. When donors are informed about the purpose of ED and ER, they gain confidence that their charitable contributions are being used ethically and legally. Sponsors should also highlight real-world risks associated with noncompliance, such as reputational harm, the disallowance of tax deductions, regulatory challenges from foreign governments, or even IRS audits.

It is equally important to set expectations around timing and documentation. International grants typically take longer to process due to the need for document collection, compliance review, and local legal considerations. Donors should be educated about the steps involved in ED and ER, including delays related to currency exchange, legal validation, or foreign registration requirements.

Sponsors must also clarify the rules surrounding acknowledgment and tax documentation. Donors should not receive acknowledgment letters or tax receipts directly from international organizations. The official acknowledgment must come from the DAF sponsor to protect both the donor's tax deduction and the sponsor's exempt status.

As donors become increasingly interested in outcomes and impact, sponsors should offer guidance on transparency and reporting. While many donors appreciate stories and updates from grantees, sponsors need to clarify what can be shared under IRS rules and what must remain confidential, particularly in high-risk regions. Impact storytelling can be provided through sponsor-prepared summaries, anonymized case studies, or aggregated outcome reports that maintain compliance while satisfying donor curiosity.

Finally, for grants directed to politically sensitive or high-risk countries such as China, Russia, or Nigeria, donors should be briefed on additional legal constraints. These may include regulatory delays, the need for donor anonymity, or the use of alternate intermediaries. Sponsors should also be transparent about situations where a recommendation cannot be fulfilled due to sanctions, local restrictions, or compliance barriers.

By addressing these learning areas in a thoughtful and proactive way, sponsors can equip donors with the knowledge they need to participate responsibly and confidently in international philanthropy.

Recommended Donor Education Tools

Providing effective donor education requires more than occasional conversations. DAF sponsors should build a structured set of tools that guide donors through the unique considerations of international grantmaking. These tools serve not only to inform but also to foster deeper engagement and long-term trust.

A good place to start is with onboarding materials. Donor welcome packets and online portals should include a dedicated section that explains the process and responsibilities involved in making international grants. This ensures that global grantmaking is introduced as a core option, not an afterthought, from the very beginning of the donor relationship.

Educational events can further deepen understanding. Webinars or in-person sessions that feature compliance professionals, international advisors, or even grantees themselves can provide valuable insight into the realities of cross-border philanthropy. These events help demystify the process and make complex topics more accessible.

Sponsors should also develop a comprehensive Frequently Asked Questions (FAQ) resource. This public-facing document should clearly explain key topics such as ED, ER, common timing expectations, privacy rights, and acknowledgment rules. A well-crafted FAQ allows donors to find answers independently and reinforces the sponsor's role as a trusted advisor.

To meet donor expectations around transparency and impact, sponsors can offer annotated reports that summarize outcomes from international grants. When appropriate, these reports should be aggregated or anonymized to maintain legal compliance while still demonstrating results. They offer a compelling way to show how international giving is making a difference.

Finally, sponsors can provide donors with pre-recommendation reviews. These help donors confirm in advance whether their intended grantee is likely to meet both IRS and foreign legal requirements. By helping donors identify potential issues before a recommendation is submitted, sponsors can reduce delays and ensure smoother processing.

Together, these tools form a comprehensive framework that supports informed, strategic, and compliant international giving.

Reviewing Donor Education

Educating donors is not a luxury; it is a legal safeguard and a service to their philanthropic vision. By proactively addressing questions and setting expectations, sponsors protect themselves, their donors, and the integrity of their global grantmaking programs.

When donors understand the rules, they become champions of compliance, not obstacles. And when advisors are trained, they help amplify compliant giving rather than unintentionally undermining it.

One powerful example of international best practice comes from Switzerland, where a high-net-worth couple used DAFs not just for efficient giving, but as a tool for passing on family values and creating structured opportunities for intergenerational philanthropy. Their story illustrates how DAFs can serve as both financial instruments and vehicles for family legacy, especially when donors receive thoughtful guidance from sponsors.

CASE STUDY: PRESERVING FAMILY VALUES THROUGH DAFS

Prepared by Christoph Courth, Global Head of Philanthropy Services,

Pictet Wealth Management (Geneva)

In a private discussion with an elderly ultra-high-net-worth (UHNW) couple from Switzerland, concerns about their wealth's legacy sparked a transformative philanthropic journey. Despite their significant estate, the couple expressed a clear desire not to leave additional wealth to their three children, having already ensured they were well-provided for. Their concern stemmed from the potential negative influence of wealth on younger generations, coupled with a desire to pass on deeply held family values to their nine grandchildren.

The Challenge

The couple's challenge revolved around how to achieve their philanthropic goals while maintaining family unity. They felt their children lacked the shared interest or capacity to cohesively manage a traditional charitable foundation. Similarly, the grandchildren, dispersed across the globe with diverse interests, seemed unlikely candidates to collaborate effectively on a unified philanthropic initiative.

The Solution

After exploring various philanthropic strategies, the couple embraced the concept of DAFs as a tool to both preserve their values and empower their grandchildren. Each grandchild would be gifted an independent DAF account, tailored to their individual passions and interests, with $1 million deposited into each account. To maintain family connections and foster shared learning, they proposed a unique addition: an annual family meeting, funded through a designated provision in their will. This gathering would allow the grandchildren to share their philanthropic journeys, challenges, and successes, reinforcing family bonds and shared purpose.

Implementation

The couple engaged with experts to identify appropriate DAF providers in different countries, ensuring compliance with local regulations and maximizing flexibility for the grandchildren. In parallel, they crafted personalized letters to each grandchild, articulating their values, the responsibilities of managing wealth, and their hopes for how this philanthropic gift could serve as a tool for empathy and positive impact.

Outcome

The independent DAF structure allowed each grandchild to pursue their philanthropic interests while maintaining a connection to the broader family legacy. The annual meetings provided a platform for collaboration and learning, ensuring that the couple's values continued to influence future generations. This innovative approach to wealth transition combined individual empowerment with collective family connection, creating a lasting philanthropic legacy.

Preserving Family Values Through Philanthropy

Donor-advised funds offer a powerful platform for families navigating the complexities of intergenerational giving. In families with members living in different places or holding diverse philanthropic interests, a DAF provides centralized oversight while supporting flexible, evolving goals.

Beyond financial efficiency, DAFs help preserve and transmit family values. When donors pair charitable assets with a written narrative of their motivations, they create a lasting legacy that fosters purpose and stewardship in the next generation.

Annual family gatherings supported by a DAF or by a dedicated funding provision can deepen this engagement. These meetings create opportunities for shared decision-making, reflection on impact, and strengthening bonds across generations.

ASSESSMENT #6: LOCALIZATION

Empowering Local Leadership in Global Grantmaking

As global grantmaking expands, the future of effective philanthropy increasingly depends on local leadership. For DAF sponsors, supporting grassroots organizations is not just a moral imperative, it is also a strategic opportunity to enhance impact, legitimacy, and trust. DAF sponsors are expected to adopt grantmaking practices that not only comply with legal frameworks but also respect local knowledge and center community leadership.

Localization refers to the principle that people closest to the challenges are best positioned to identify and implement solutions. In the context of international grantmaking, it means funding local NGOs, community-based organizations, and frontline leaders, rather than defaulting to foreign intermediaries or large international nonprofits.

While localization can introduce compliance and capacity challenges, DAF sponsors that invest in local leadership and build systems to support that investment are better equipped to deepen trust with communities abroad.

Why Localization Matters

In international grantmaking, the principle of localization is more than just a strategic consideration; it is a commitment to equity, effectiveness, and accountability. Traditional models of philanthropy have often centralized decision-making in donor countries, unintentionally reinforcing global power imbalances. By contrast, a localization approach shifts funding and authority toward the communities that are most affected by the issues being addressed. This shift ensures that those with lived experience are empowered to lead, not just receive, philanthropic support.

Localization also enhances effectiveness. Local partners typically possess a deep understanding of cultural dynamics, political sensitivities, and linguistic nuances. Their contextual knowledge allows them to design and implement programs that are more responsive, adaptive, and sustainable. These insights are critical in navigating environments where outsider-led initiatives often fall short.

The future of effective philanthropy increasingly depends on local leadership.

Accountability is another core benefit. When donors and DAF sponsors cultivate direct relationships with local organizations, they lay the groundwork for long-term partnerships built on mutual trust and transparency. This moves grantmaking away from one-off transactions and toward sustained, collaborative investment.

Finally, localization is not just a best practice; it is increasingly a global expectation. Institutions such as the Coca-Cola Foundation, Conrad N. Hilton Foundation, David and Lucile Packard Foundation, Ford Foundation and several others have embraced localization as both an ethical and strategic imperative.[309] For DAF sponsors and donors committed to meaningful international engagement, aligning with these goals demonstrates a forward-looking commitment to inclusive and responsible philanthropy.

---

[309] Council on Foundations. Leading Global Foundations Join Bilateral Donors in Commitment to Locally Led Global Development. September 20, 2023. Accessed February 26, 2025. https://cof.org/news/leading-global-foundations-join-bilateral-donors-commitment-locally-led-global-development

DAF Sponsor Responsibilities in Supporting Localization

For DAF sponsors, supporting localization is both a strategic opportunity and a compliance challenge. As global philanthropy evolves, sponsors are increasingly called upon to center local voices and organizations in the grantmaking process. To do this effectively while still meeting legal obligations, sponsors must adopt practices that are both flexible and principled.

One of the most impactful steps a sponsor can take is to enable direct grants to local organizations. This involves using ED or ER to qualify grassroots nonprofits rather than defaulting to large international intermediaries. To facilitate this process, sponsors should consider offering translation support and document preparation assistance so that smaller organizations can participate fully and confidently in the application process.

Diligence protocols should also be adapted to reflect the realities of diverse operating environments. Rigid, standardized due diligence frameworks can unintentionally exclude small, emerging, or non-Western organizations that may not follow U.S. governance or reporting conventions. By allowing for cultural and organizational variations such as differences in board structure or accounting formats while still upholding core compliance standards, sponsors can expand access to underrepresented grantees without compromising integrity.

Supporting localization also means investing in organizational strength. Sponsors should encourage donors to provide general operating support or capacity-building grants, not just restricted program funds. Offering multi-year or flexible funding allows local organizations to plan more effectively, build institutional resilience, and respond to changing needs in their communities.

Finally, sponsors should monitor and evaluate their own progress toward localization. This includes tracking the proportion of international grants that go directly to local organizations versus those routed through international pass-throughs. It also means examining whether donor priorities align with the self-identified goals of the communities being served. Sponsors can help shift the conversation by prompting donors to reflect on key questions: Who is leading the work, and who sets the agenda?

By embracing these practices, DAF sponsors can align their international strategies with a growing global consensus that philanthropy should be locally rooted, community-informed, and equity-driven.

What This Means for Donors and Advisors

Donors who care about equity and sustainable impact can play a powerful role in advancing localization. Recommending grants to qualified local partners and being open to flexible, capacity-building support can create deeper and more authentic community partnerships. Advisors can help by highlighting the importance of local leadership and preparing donors for longer timelines or alternative due-diligence processes.

What This Means for Foreign Charities

Foreign charities seeking to partner with U.S.-based DAF sponsors can strengthen their readiness by preparing localized documentation, being transparent about leadership structure, and proactively communicating how they align with community needs. Clear communication, flexibility around documentation formats, and openness to capacity-building relationships can help build trust and facilitate funding partnerships that are both compliant and empowering.

Sample Language for Donor Education and Grant Agreements

- "This DAF sponsor supports localization by prioritizing direct support to qualified local organizations wherever legally and operationally feasible."
- "Grants may be structured to build capacity, promote long-term resilience, and reduce reliance on international intermediaries."
- "We encourage donors to recommend grants that elevate local voices, leadership, and solutions."

Reviewing Localization

Localization is not just a development strategy. It is a reflection of philanthropic humility, trust, and shared responsibility. DAF sponsors must balance regulatory oversight with a commitment to decentralizing power, removing barriers, and honoring the agency of those on the front lines.

By building systems and cultures that support localization, sponsors help redefine global grantmaking from something done *to* communities to something done *with and by* them.

ASSESSMENT #7: RISK MONITORING

Identifying, Assessing, and Responding to Global Grantmaking Risks

Every international grant carries some level of risk, whether related to legal compliance, political instability, reputational exposure, or financial misuse. For DAF sponsors, risk monitoring is not about avoiding complexity but managing it wisely.

This assessment offers a strategic approach to risk oversight in cross-border philanthropy. It helps sponsors move beyond assessment and toward proactive, principles-based decision-making grounded in fiduciary duty, regulatory expectations, and ethical stewardship.

Risk Monitoring Practices for DAF Sponsors

To effectively monitor and respond to these risks, sponsors should establish a structured yet adaptable approach.

Key Risk Categories in Global Grantmaking

International grantmaking offers transformative opportunities, but it also introduces a range of risks that DAF sponsors must actively manage. Understanding these risks is the first step toward building resilient systems that protect donor intent, comply with legal obligations, and uphold public trust.

One of the most critical areas of risk is regulatory noncompliance. This includes issues such as incomplete or invalid ED or ER documentation, subgrants issued without the required controls, and violations of sanctions laws. For example, providing funds to individuals or organizations listed by the U.S. Office of Foreign Assets Control (OFAC) can result in severe penalties and loss of tax-exempt status. To comply with U.S. Treasury regulations, DAF sponsors engaged in international grantmaking should screen all foreign grantees against the Specially Designated Nationals (SDN) list, maintained by the Office of Foreign Assets Control (OFAC). This list includes individuals, organizations, and countries subject to U.S. sanctions.

Sponsors should implement automated screening tools or vendor services to compare grantees against the SDN list prior to disbursing grants. If a match is identified, funds must be blocked immediately, and a report must be filed with OFAC. Routine screening and documentation of results are essential to demonstrate due diligence and maintain legal compliance.

Fraud and financial misuse represent another serious category of risk. This can take the form of funds being diverted from their intended charitable purpose, undisclosed related-party transactions, or partnerships with grantees that lack basic financial controls. Without adequate oversight, even well-intentioned grants can result in misuse that damages both the sponsor and the broader philanthropic sector.

Fraud and misuse are persistent threats to global grantmaking.

One publicly available tool that can inform an initial country-level risk scan is the Basel AML Index, published annually by the Basel Institute on Governance.

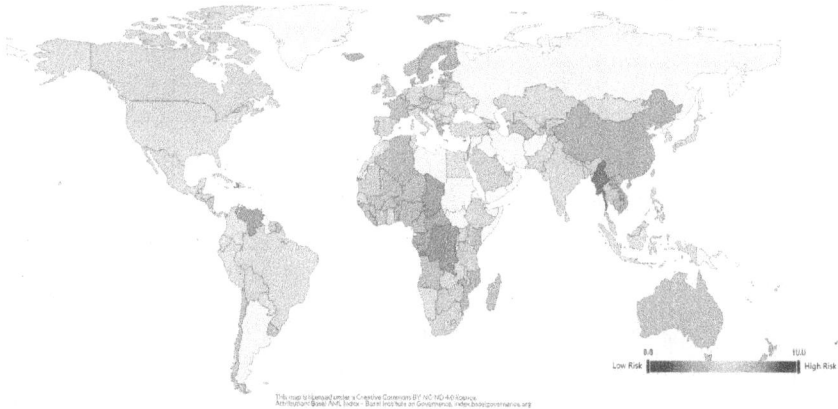

The index ranks jurisdictions on a scale from 0.0 (low risk) to 10.0 (high risk) based on their vulnerability to money laundering and terrorist financing, drawing on data from sources such as the Financial Action Task Force (FATF), Transparency International, and the World Bank. While not specific to philanthropy, it offers a valuable starting point for identifying higher-risk environments where enhanced due diligence may be warranted before making a cross-border grant.[310]

---

[310] Basel Institute on Governance. Basel AML Index 2024: 13th Public Edition. Basel: Basel Institute on Governance, 2024. https://index.baselgovernance.org.

Reputational risk is closely tied to public perception and can arise quickly. Associations with partner organizations involved in litigation, scandal, or controversy may erode donor confidence. In politically sensitive regions, grants that appear culturally inappropriate or aligned with partisan agendas can attract unwanted attention and criticism.

DAF sponsors must also be attentive to the heightened risks posed by Politically Exposed Persons (PEPs), individuals who hold or have recently held prominent public roles, such as government officials, political leaders, or executives of state-owned entities. Grants involving PEPs, their family members, or close associates may raise red flags for potential corruption, conflicts of interest, or reputational damage. While U.S. regulations do not mandate PEP screening for DAFs, many sponsors adopt this best practice to strengthen due diligence protocols and mitigate exposure. Screening tools can help identify PEP associations during the grantee vetting process and trigger internal reviews, risk escalation, or enhanced documentation. Failing to assess for PEP-related risks could expose the sponsor to public scrutiny or inadvertently enable the misuse of philanthropic funds.

As international grantmaking increasingly relies on digital systems, cybersecurity and data privacy have become central concerns. Risks include the exposure of personal data collected during due diligence, as well as the unsecured transmission of sensitive documentation across jurisdictions. Sponsors must take steps to protect both their systems and the individuals whose data they manage.

Finally, operational risks must not be overlooked. These include situations where grantees are overwhelmed by overly complex compliance demands or internal issues, such as poor recordkeeping or staff turnover at the sponsor organization, leading to breakdowns in grant administration.

By identifying and addressing these risk categories, DAF sponsors can proactively design systems that support ethical, legal, and impactful international philanthropy.

For a list of global resources to support your due diligence process, see the Appendix: Global Due Diligence Resources for International Grantmaking at the end of this chapter curated with the assistance of Upsall International.

Strengthening Oversight Through Risk-Tiered Reviews and Sanctions Screening

To responsibly manage international grantmaking, DAF sponsors must implement systems that proactively identify and mitigate risk. One of the most effective strategies is to adopt a risk-tiered grant review framework. This approach allows sponsors to categorize each international grant according to its level of risk, typically labeled as low, medium, or high, based on several key factors. These may include the jurisdiction in which the grantee operates, the size and duration of the grant, the stated purpose of the funds, and the nature of any prior relationship with the organization.

By applying this tiered model, sponsors can allocate review resources more effectively and tailor oversight procedures to match the risk profile of each grant. For example, low-risk grants to long-standing partners in stable jurisdictions may require only routine due diligence, while high-risk grants, such as those to new partners in regions under heightened regulatory scrutiny, may warrant deeper investigation and enhanced monitoring.

To further streamline this process, sponsors can configure their grant management systems to apply automated flags for known risk indicators. These may include grantees located in high-risk countries, such as those listed by the Financial Action Task Force (FATF), or organizations with a documented history of noncompliance. Other triggers might include grant recommendations involving unusually large transfers or grantees that have been flagged in prior reviews for sanctions exposure.

Sanctions and watchlist screening are another essential component of responsible international grantmaking. Before any funds are disbursed, sponsors should screen all grantees and associated individuals against the U.S. Treasury Department's Specially Designated Nationals (SDN) list. Additional layers of screening may include checks for AML red flags, adverse global media coverage, politically exposed person (PEP) status, and inclusion on FATF grey or black lists.

These tools not only help protect the integrity of the grantmaking process, but also ensure that sponsors remain in full compliance with both domestic and international legal obligations. When implemented thoughtfully, they serve as a frontline defense against regulatory violations and reputational harm, allowing sponsors to pursue meaningful cross-border giving with confidence and care.

FATF: Recommendation 8: Non-Profit Organizations

To fully understand why some jurisdictions, pose elevated compliance challenges, it's important to consider the global regulatory framework shaping national policy.

Many foreign funding restrictions and banking challenges stem from national efforts to comply with the FATF, an intergovernmental body that sets global standards for AML and counter-terrorist financing (CTF). FATF's Recommendation 8 initially raised concerns by identifying non-profit organizations (NPOs) as potentially vulnerable to terrorist financing abuse, leading some governments to impose excessive scrutiny on cross-border grants. However, following criticism that these measures were harming legitimate humanitarian work, FATF updated Recommendation 8 in 2016 and again in 2019 to emphasize a risk-based approach, urging governments to avoid blanket restrictions and ensure counter-terrorism rules do not disrupt legitimate aid. The 2019 guidance further clarified that NPOs should not face indiscriminate banking restrictions (de-risking) and called for dialogue to prevent over-regulation. Despite these reforms, some countries continue applying stringent controls, citing FATF compliance. DAF sponsors and other NGOs must still navigate this landscape by demonstrating strong internal controls, risk assessments, and due diligence procedures to mitigate perceived risks and maintain access to funding.[311]

Re-screen grantees at regular intervals, especially for multi-year or recurring grants, to ensure ongoing compliance with sanctions lists, reputational risk criteria, and eligibility requirements. Triggers for re-screening may include changes in leadership, mission, geographic focus, or adverse media coverage. Best practice is to adopt a schedule based on the grantee's risk profile, ranging from re-screening at each grant renewal to once every three years for low-risk grantees.

Incident Response Protocols

In situations where a risk event emerges after a grant has been approved, or even after funds have been disbursed, DAF sponsors must be prepared to act swiftly and responsibly. Sponsors should have documented protocols for withholding or revoking disbursements when circumstances change. These protocols should also address the documentation of compliance decisions, such as approving exceptions in consultation with legal counsel, and the escalation of high-risk issues to the board or a designated compliance committee. A clear and consistent approach to incident response ensures transparency and protects both the sponsor and the donor from regulatory exposure.

---

[311] Financial Action Task Force. "Protecting non-profits from abuse for terrorist financing through the risk-based implementation of revised FATF Recommendation 8." June 2016. https://www.fatf-gafi.org/content/fatf-gafi/en/publications/Fatfrecommendations/protecting-non-profits-abuse-implementation-R8.html

Grantee Monitoring and Reporting

Monitoring does not end when a grant is made. Through ER reporting requirements, sponsors can identify potential anomalies, such as vague activity descriptions, delayed reports, or the absence of financial documentation. Open and regular dialogue with grantees can help uncover emerging issues before they escalate. Encouraging grantees to communicate concerns early not only supports compliance but strengthens the partnership overall.

Periodic Internal Audits

DAF sponsors should also conduct periodic internal audits to evaluate the integrity of their international grantmaking processes. These reviews may include examining a sample of international grants each year to assess the completenessof documentation, the presence and resolution of risk flags, and adherence to policies related to due diligence, escalation, and approvals. Internal audits help sponsors identify gaps and continuously improve their procedures.

Balancing Risk and Opportunity

Risk should not be viewed as a barrier to international giving. Instead, it should serve as a compass, guiding decisions that balance fiduciary responsibility with philanthropic purpose. In many cases, the highest-risk environments are those where charitable support is needed most urgently. Sponsors must weigh regulatory obligations against their mission and values, and be prepared to make thoughtful, informed decisions that align with both.

Creating a culture of transparency around risk empowers staff to elevate concerns without fear and enables leadership to make deliberate, accountable choices. A risk-aware organization is not one that avoids complexity, but one that navigates it with integrity.

Reviewing Risk Monitoring

International philanthropy is never entirely risk-free. But when managed responsibly, it can be both effective and secure. With structured monitoring systems, real-time alerts, and clearly defined escalation protocols, DAF sponsors can operate confidently across borders. Risk, when viewed not as a constraint but as a strategic tool, helps sponsors extend their reach, protect their reputations, and maximize the impact their donors seek to achieve.

ASSESSMENT #8: DIGITAL INFRASTRUCTURE

Building Secure, Scalable Systems for International Compliance

Modern international grantmaking depends on far more than good intentions and legal documentation; it requires robust digital infrastructure. For DAF sponsors, technology underpins every element of readiness, from sanctions screening and document retention to ED/ER tracking, cross-border disbursements, and donor transparency.

As regulators and donors alike demand higher standards of governance, sponsors must ensure that their grant management systems, data security protocols, and reporting platforms are built to handle the unique demands of cross-border philanthropy

The Role of Digital Infrastructure in Global Grantmaking

In an era of expanding international philanthropy and heightened compliance demands, digital infrastructure has become foundational to the success of DAF sponsors. It is no longer sufficient to manage global grantmaking manually or across disconnected systems. Today, sponsors must invest in secure, scalable, and integrated digital tools that ensure regulatory compliance, operational efficiency, and donor confidence across borders.

Digital infrastructure encompasses the entire suite of systems used to track, process, and archive international grants. This includes the tools that manage ED and ER documentation, oversee due diligence and legal review workflows, and screen for sanctions, reputational risk, and anti-money laundering concerns. It also includes the secure platforms used to share sensitive data across jurisdictions and to generate reports for audits, donor updates, and required IRS filings such as Schedule F.

Supporting Donor Anonymity and Transparency

A well-built digital infrastructure should be flexible enough to support both donor anonymity and grant-level transparency, depending on the sponsor's policies and regulatory requirements. This means incorporating donor identity flags and redaction protocols for grants to high-risk countries, while also enabling public dashboards that provide aggregate data on global grantmaking without compromising individual privacy. These features help balance donor preferences, grantee safety, and the growing demand for sector-wide transparency.

From the donor's perspective, secure digital infrastructure ensures that their intent is respected and their personal information protected. From the grantee's perspective, it ensures that sensitive data is handled appropriately and that compliance processes are clear, consistent, and fair. Whether working in a stable environment or a high-risk region, both parties benefit from a well-designed system.

International philanthropy is never entirely risk-free

Preparing for the Future

As international giving grows in complexity, DAF sponsors must prepare for the next wave of digital innovation. Artificial intelligence is beginning to assist with detecting anomalies in grantmaking patterns or identifying indicators of fraud. Blockchain solutions are being explored for improving fund traceability and transparency in cross-border remittances. Natural language processing tools may soon allow compliance teams to scan grant agreements in real-time for red flags or prohibited clauses. Donor-facing portals that provide real-time status updates and self-service international checks are also emerging, offering a more transparent and user-friendly experience.

Reviewing and Investing in Digital Infrastructure

Digital infrastructure is not just a back-office necessity; it is the foundation of a sponsor's credibility in global grantmaking. It supports compliance, protects privacy, and enables the scale and flexibility that today's donors expect. As scrutiny around international giving continues to rise, sponsors who invest in secure, interoperable, and forward-thinking systems will be best positioned to lead with confidence, meet evolving legal requirements, and fulfill their mission of connecting donors with global impact.

ASSESSMENT #9: GLOBAL POLICY & COMPLIANCE

Staying Current on Evolving Laws and Reporting Obligations

DAF sponsors engaged in international grantmaking must do more than approve individual grants; they must also monitor the shifting legal and regulatory environments in which their grantees operate. From U.S. IRS disclosure rules to foreign NGO registration laws, policy vigilance is critical to avoiding legal exposure, reputational damage, and grant disruptions.

This assessment covers three interrelated obligations:

1. Tracking foreign laws and restrictions that affect grantees
2. Monitoring U.S. policy shifts impacting cross-border giving
3. Ensuring accurate and timely IRS Schedule F reporting

Monitoring Legal Compliance: Domestic and International Obligations

DAF sponsors engaged in international grantmaking must navigate a complex web of regulatory frameworks, both in the United States and in the countries where their grantees operate. To meet this challenge, sponsors must establish systems for ongoing legal monitoring and ensure that their reporting practices align with evolving IRS expectations.

Foreign Registration and Local Law Monitoring

International grantees operate in legal environments that can be volatile, restrictive, or unpredictable. These jurisdictions may impose burdensome requirements on organizations receiving foreign funding, and failing to comply can result in grant disruptions, reputational harm, or even legal sanctions. For this reason, DAF sponsors must track several key elements of local compliance.

At a minimum, sponsors should require grantees to provide proof of legal registration in their home country. This demonstrates that the organization exists as a recognized legal entity and can lawfully receive charitable funds. In high-risk jurisdictions, sponsors may need to go further by engaging local legal counsel or partnering with trusted intermediaries to validate compliance.

Key areas to monitor include laws that mandate foreign agent registration, banking and currency controls, restrictions on the activities of foreign-funded NGOs, and any required government approvals or ministry filings. For example, in Russia, nonprofits receiving foreign support may be labeled "foreign agents," a designation that imposes both stigma and reporting burdens. In India, the

Foreign Contribution Regulation Act (FCRA) places strict limitations on how international donations can be received and used. In China, organizations affiliated with foreign entities are subject to heightened surveillance and administrative scrutiny.

To manage this complexity, DAF sponsors should maintain an internal "country law tracker" that is updated quarterly. This tool should document known legal restrictions by country, flag jurisdictions under U.S. sanctions or identified by the FATF, and provide guidance for staff evaluating new international grant recommendations.

IRS Schedule F and Form 990 Reporting

Public accountability for international grantmaking is largely driven by IRS Form 990 and its accompanying Schedule F. All 501(c)(3) public charities that conduct foreign grantmaking must complete this disclosure, which serves as a transparent record of the organization's global activity.

Schedule F requires country-by-country reporting of grant totals, including the number of grants issued, dollar amounts disbursed, and the use of intermediaries. Sponsors must also indicate the purpose of the grants and identify the procedures used to ensure compliance, whether through ED, ER, or another method.

In some cases, DAF sponsors may choose to include a narrative description of their international compliance protocols in Part III or Schedule O of Form 990. This can help demonstrate proactive stewardship and may position the organization as a leader in global philanthropic compliance.

To facilitate accurate reporting, sponsors should consider integrating their grant management systems with tax preparation tools that allow for auto-population of Schedule F data based on verified grant records. This reduces the risk of human error and ensures that operations and compliance remain in sync.

Finally, sponsors must remember that Form 990 also requires disclosure of total DAF activity, including the number of accounts held and the number of grants issued. Any grants made to foreign organizations or intermediaries must be accurately reflected in both the Schedule F and the narrative sections where applicable. Coordination between finance, program, and compliance teams is essential to maintaining accuracy and credibility.

U.S. State-Level Registration for Internationally Active Charities

Charitable solicitation laws in 36 U.S. states plus the District of Columbia require nonprofits, including DAF sponsors, to register before soliciting or receiving donations from residents. DAF sponsors that host donor engagement events, promote global causes online, or publish impact reports featuring international grantees may inadvertently trigger state registration requirements.[312]

Moreover, states such as California and New York have begun requesting foreign grant disclosures as part of annual compliance reporting. DAF sponsors should consult state-level guidance to determine whether their activities qualify as solicitation, what foreign grant documentation is required, and how donor confidentiality rules may apply.

For example, California's Registry of Charitable Trusts requires completion of Form RRF-1, which may trigger additional disclosures when international grantmaking is involved. New York's CHAR500 form similarly requests detailed financial and grant information, including potential foreign grant disclosures.

Sponsors operating or soliciting in these states should review applicable instructions closely and ensure alignment between IRS Schedule F filings and state submissions.

By building strong internal systems, avoiding compliance shortcuts, and respecting donor-grantee boundaries, DAF sponsors can meet their legal obligations and reinforce the philanthropic trust that underpins cross-border giving.

International grantees operate in legal environments that can be volatile, restrictive, or unpredictable.

---

[312] COGENCY GLOBAL, "Charitable Solicitation Registration Chart by State," updated February 2025. https://www.cogencyglobal.com/wp-content/uploads/2025/02/Charitable-Registration-Map.pdf

Assessment #10: Cultural Intelligence

Cultural Awareness and Effective International Grantmaking

International grantmaking requires more than regulatory compliance. DAF sponsors operating across borders must consider how cultural differences can affect communication, expectations, and the overall success of a grant. This is not about ideology. It is about reducing risk and improving outcomes.

A working understanding of local customs, communication styles, and decision-making norms helps sponsors build trust and avoid preventable misunderstandings. Delays in reporting, for example, may result from national holidays or local religious observances that differ from the U.S. calendar. A grant agreement written in technical English may confuse a partner unfamiliar with American legal terminology. In some cultures, direct feedback is discouraged, which can limit honest conversations about project results.

DAF sponsors can take practical steps to strengthen cross-border relationships. These include translating key documents, providing cultural briefings before site visits, and including regional experts or diaspora advisors in program design. Sponsors may also benefit from inviting feedback from grantees to understand how their processes are perceived locally.

What it requires is intentionality and a willingness to ask whether small adjustments in communication and process can improve trust and impact. In international philanthropy, cultural awareness is not a soft skill. It is part of what makes grantmaking effective.

Review and Make a Plan

Focus Area	Key Focus	In Place?	Next Steps
1. Regulatory Compliance	ED/ER procedures, IRS rules	☐ Yes ☐ No	
2. Documentation	Grant files, audit trails, internal systems	☐ Yes ☐ No	

Focus Area	Key Focus	In Place?	Next Steps
3. Privacy and Data	GDPR, PIPL, LGPD, consent, data security	☐ Yes ☐ No	
4. Subgrant-ing	Regrant controls, conduit avoid-ance	☐ Yes ☐ No	
5. Donor Education	Donor onboard-ing, compliance messaging	☐ Yes ☐ No	
6. Localiza-tion	Direct local sup-port, equity, ca-pacity	☐ Yes ☐ No	
7. Risk Monitoring	Sanctions, coun-try law changes, fraud	☐ Yes ☐ No	
8. Digital Infrastructure	Systems, automa-tion, GMS tools	☐ Yes ☐ No	
9. Policy Watch/ Schedule F	Foreign law, U.S. rulemaking, IRS filings	☐ Yes ☐ No	
10. Cultural Intelligence	Ethics, humility, context aware-ness	☐ Yes ☐ No	

Completing the readiness assessment provides sponsors, donors, and nonprofit partners with a structured understanding of current capabilities, potential vulnerabilities, and future opportunities. This summary helps turn insights into action by institutionalizing best practices, prioritizing improvements, and reinforcing a culture of global grantmaking excellence.

All stakeholders are encouraged to revisit this assessment regularly, particularly after significant legal, geographic, or operational changes.

Readiness Is a Process, Not a Destination

Global philanthropy is evolving, and so must the systems that support it. By adopting this 10-part framework and revisiting it regularly, stakeholders across the philanthropic ecosystem can move from reactive to proactive, from compliant to exemplary. International grantmaking is not just possible; it is powerful. And with the right structures in place, it can be executed with confidence, care, and lasting impact.

INTERNATIONAL PARALLELS

The United States pioneered tax incentives for philanthropy, but similar approaches have taken root elsewhere. In the United Kingdom, reforms such as Gift Aid strengthened the partnership between government and the charitable sector. According to legal scholar Debra Morris, these reforms transformed the charitable tax landscape in the UK and reinforced the partnership between government and the voluntary sector. [313]

Looking ahead, Ben Morton Wright, Founder, President, and Group CEO, Global Philanthropic Worldwide Group of Companies adds,

> The shift from traditional fundraising models to DAF-driven giving requires nonprofits to adapt. It's no longer just about asking for donations directly; nonprofits need to strengthen their digital presence, use PR effectively, and build relationships in new ways to engage DAF donors. [314]

Canada has likewise developed a robust set of incentives to encourage giving. Jo-Anne Ryan, Vice President at TD Wealth, explains:

> For Canadian donors, DAFs have become a key instrument not only for tax planning but also for leaving a lasting legacy. [315]

These international models reinforce a global pattern: when governments design effective tax incentives, they drive donor engagement, encourage giving, and strengthen nonprofit support. As Sir John Low, former Group Chief Executive of Charities Aid Foundation (CAF), concludes:

---

[313] Morris, D. The Fiscal Treatment of Charitable Contributions in the UK. Published in Charity Taxation in the United Kingdom: Comparative Analysis, The Global Perspective. Charity Law Unit, University of Liverpool, 2001.
[314] Morton Wright, B. Interview with Ted Hart, November 8, 2024.
[315] Ryan, J. Interview with Ted Hart, October 8, 2024.

Cross-border philanthropy through DAFs is transformative; it allows resources to flow to communities in need globally, breaking down barriers that might otherwise prevent this kind of generosity.[316]

While the UK and Canada remain the most developed examples of DAFs outside the United States, other regions are beginning to experiment with similar models. In Australia, Ryan Ginard, Head of Advocacy for Effective Philanthropy at Minderoo Foundation, Founder of Fundraise for Australia, and author of *Future Philanthropy* observes:

We have a culture of mateship in Australia. We're generous, but giving isn't typically seen as a core part of our culture. Sub funds (what DAFs are called in Australia) really are in their infancy and they will continue to grow, especially just due to the ease of giving and the accessibility.[317]

From Singapore Usha Menon, Executive Chairman of Usha Menon Management Consultancy informs,

The next generation is looking for authenticity and impact in their giving. They're not just inheriting wealth; they're inheriting the responsibility to make a difference.[318]

Meanwhile in Geneva, Sabrina Grassi, Director General, Swiss Philanthropy Foundation, notes that,

In Switzerland, we have a high density of charitable foundations compared to our population. What I see is that DAFs provide a good alternative option to philanthropists—reducing costs, benefiting from the expertise of umbrella foundations, and mutualizing both costs and risks.[319]

These international perspectives show that DAFs are more than an American innovation; they're becoming a global movement evolving to meet the needs of modern donors and diverse communities.

[316] Low, Sir John. Interview with Ted Hart, September 12, 2024.
[317] Ginard, R. Interview with Ted Hart, November 4, 2024.
[318] Menon, U. Interview with Ted Hart, September 17, 2024.
[319] Sabrina, G. Interview with Ted Hart, September 6, 2024.

GLOBAL COMPLIANCE LANDSCAPE

As cross-border philanthropy has grown, so too has regulatory complexity in the countries where DAF sponsors seek to support charitable activity. While DAF sponsors must comply with U.S. laws, they also face growing legal, political, and operational hurdles in the countries where their grantees operate. Understanding these challenges is vital to maintaining both local impact and global compliance.

Country-Specific Compliance

Many governments have introduced legal and administrative regulations regarding the receipt of foreign charitable funds. Some notable countries include:

- **China:** The Overseas NGO Law requires foreign nonprofits to register with a domestic sponsor and restricts types of activity and geographic scope.[320]
- **Hungary:** Laws targeting NGOs with foreign support have been challenged at the EU level but continue to signal political hostility to external philanthropy.[321]
- **India:** The Foreign Contribution Regulation Act (FCRA) requires NGOs to register for permission to receive foreign funds and imposes strict banking, reporting, and governance requirements; 2023 amendments narrowed eligibility. Despite challenges, many Indian NGOs have successfully navigated FCRA restrictions through strong local governance and transparent reporting frameworks.[322]

These restrictions can delay or block grant implementation, increase grantee risk, and put DAF sponsors in politically sensitive positions.

[320] ChinaFile. "Fact Sheet on China's Foreign NGO Law." Asia Society Center on U.S.-China Relations. December 2016. https://www.chinafile.com/ngo/fact-sheet-chinas-foreign-ngo-law

[321] Transparency International EU. "Hungary's New Bill Threatens to End Civil Society and Empower the Government to Persecute with Impunity." May 19, 2025. https://transparency.eu/hungarys-new-bill-threatens-to-end-civil-society-and-empower-the-government-to-persecute-with-impunity/

[322] The Indian Express. "NGOs to lose FCRA licence over conversion, other 'violations': MHA," February 4, 2023. https://indianexpress.com/article/india/ngos-lose-fcra-licence-conversion-violations-mha-8423315/

ess. "NGOs to lose FCRA licence over conversion, other 'violations': MHA," February 4, 2023. https://indian-express.com/article/india/ngos-lose-fcra-licence-conversion-violations-mha-8423315/

Operational Barriers

Even in countries without formal laws restricting foreign funding, DAF sponsors often encounter administrative and logistical obstacles, such as:

- Local banks rejecting wire transfers from U.S.-based organizations due to missing licenses or untranslated documentation
- NGOs facing registration delays or denials simply for accepting U.S. funding
- Government requirements to file, translate, or notarize grant agreements for them to be considered legally binding

Country	Primary Barrier	Recommended Strategy
India	FCRA licensing and bank oversight	Use FCRA-registered grantees; pre-validate banking details
Russia	Foreign Agents Law and USA Sanctions	Avoid direct grants for politically sensitive causes
China	Restricted NGO registration	Partner with registered local entities or intermediaries
Brazil	Data protection and NGO tax classification	Ensure grantee compliance with LGPD; confirm tax ID
Nigeria	AML/KYC compliance enforcement	Confirm grantee legitimacy and verify reporting ability

These challenges can delay or derail grant implementation, increase risks for local grantees, and place DAF sponsors in politically sensitive positions. To mitigate these risks, sponsors should consult local legal counsel and banking intermediaries, especially when working in countries under financial sanctions or those scoring poorly on Transparency International's Corruption Perceptions Index.

DAF sponsors must not only comply with the letter of the law but also exercise diplomatic sensitivity and cultural intelligence. Donna Callejon, former Chief Executive Officer at GlobalGiving, reminds us:

> Cross-border philanthropy is essential, but compliance isn't just about following the rules; it's about respecting the communities we're aiming to help.[323]

The global regulatory landscape is dynamic, and risk profiles can shift quickly. DAF sponsors are advised to monitor legal changes through reliable country advisories, collaborate with experienced intermediaries, and develop internal risk matrices to guide foreign grant approvals.

The Future of International Grantmaking

Global grantmaking through DAFs is poised for continued growth, but not without disruption. The landscape ahead will be shaped by geopolitical pressures, technological evolution, and shifting norms around power, equity, and trust in philanthropy. For DAF sponsors, staying ahead of these trends is not only strategic; it's necessary for legal compliance, reputational integrity, and mission relevance.

Robert Collins, Global Managing Director at TrustBridge Global Foundation, strengthens this statement by noting:

> Global philanthropy is within reach, but compliance must be our priority to ensure every dollar has a clear, positive impact overseas.[324]

One of the most important shifts in global philanthropy is the move toward localization. Increasingly, funders are encouraged, or required, to direct resources to organizations based in the communities they serve, rather than routing support exclusively through large international intermediaries.

This trend, accelerated by the COVID-19 pandemic and growing attention to community leadership, reflects broader efforts to:

- Elevate local voices and leadership in project design and delivery.
- Reduce delays and costs from long subgranting chains.
- Build sustainable capacity within partner communities.

---

[323] Callejon, D. Interview with Ted Hart, September 16, 2024.
[324] Collins, R. Interview with Ted Hart, September 16, 2024.

DAF sponsors can support localization goals by:

- Establishing trust-based, long-term relationships with community-rooted organizations
- Supporting capacity-building alongside project funding
- Ensuring donor priorities are informed by, rather than imposed upon, local expertise and context

Advising funding to community-based organizations may raise additional regulatory, linguistic, or cultural considerations. The key challenge is not whether to localize, but how to do so with humility, accountability, and adaptability. Sampriti Ganguli of Ganguli Associates, LLC, and former CEO of Arabella Advisors, puts this in perspective by sharing:

> When it comes to cross-border giving, compliance isn't just about checking boxes. It's about understanding the cultural and regulatory nuances of each region.[325]

GLOBAL GOALS

Alignment with Sustainable Development Goals

The 17 UN Sustainable Development Goals (SDGs) offer a shared global blueprint for addressing issues like poverty, health, education, climate, and justice. Increasingly, donors and DAF sponsors are aligning international grant portfolios with these goals.[326]

Philanthropy and Global Goals

The launch of the SDG Philanthropy Platform in 2015 further accelerated the alignment of philanthropy with the global goals.[327] This initiative, a collabo-

The SDGs offer a blueprint for addressing global issues.

---

[325] Ganguli, S. Interview with Ted Hart, September 11, 2024.
[326] United Nations. "The 17 Goals." Sustainable Development Goals. United Nations Department of Economic and Social Affairs. Accessed June 20, 2025. https://sdgs.un.org/goals
[327] SDG Philanthropy Platform. "SDG Philanthropy Platform." Accessed December 11, 2024. https://sustainabledevelopment.un.org/partnerships/SDGphilanthropy

rative effort between organizations like the Gates and Ford Foundations, brought together philanthropic entities, businesses, and governments to ensure that their resources were strategically directed towards achieving the SDGs. Although the SDG Philanthropy Platform is no longer active as a standalone initiative, its resources and influence continue to shape philanthropic engagement, including through successor efforts like SDGfunders.org and integration into broader UN SDG partnership platforms.

Yet as philanthropic ambitions expanded globally, so too did scrutiny, by both the public and regulators, over how effectively these vast resources were being governed. This shift from inspiration to oversight marked a pivotal turn in modern philanthropy's structure and accountability.

Philanthropy's role in advancing the SDGs underscores its capacity to foster innovation. DAFs, with their ability to support cutting-edge solutions, from renewable energy initiatives to microfinance programs, demonstrate the power of targeted, strategic giving. By aligning their investments with the SDGs, DAFs amplify their impact and contribute to long-term, sustainable progress.

As the SDGs illustrate, philanthropy is evolving to meet the complexities of a rapidly changing world. DAFs`, with their adaptability and alignment with donor values, embody this revolution, bridging the timeless human desire to give with the modern need for strategic, impactful philanthropy.

DAF sponsors increasingly use SDG tags to:

- Help donors align personal values with global priorities
- Track portfolio impact across thematic areas
- Improve transparency in Form 990 disclosures and donor reports

While SDG frameworks are not a legal requirement, they offer a credible and internationally recognized way to signal mission alignment and measure results.

KEY TAKEAWAYS

DAFs offer powerful flexibility for global giving, but international grantmaking requires more than good intentions. IRS-recognized frameworks such as Equivalency Determination (ED) and Expenditure Responsibility (ER) remain essential to ensuring compliance, protecting tax-exempt status, and fulfilling donor intent. Sponsors who master these pathways, including approaches like ER-Lite, risk-tiered ED, or in-house determinations, can confidently navigate the legal landscape and reduce audit risk.

Effective cross-border giving also depends on strong operational systems. The Readiness Assessment Framework introduced in this chapter provides a practical guide for sponsors to evaluate grantee vetting, documentation, sanctions screening (including OFAC and PEPs), monitoring, staffing, and technology. While automation and AI can support due diligence, cultural intelligence and local trust remain irreplaceable. Sponsors who combine disciplined compliance with values-based strategies, such as community-driven grantmaking, pooled funds, and alignment with global development goals, can deliver impact that is both lawful and lasting.

APPENDIX FOR CHAPTER 7

GLOBAL DUE DILIGENCE RESOURCES FOR INTERNATIONAL GRANTMAKING

Developed with assistance from Upsall International

UN AND INTERNATIONAL SANCTIONS LISTS

- **UN Global Compact:** provides access to "Our Participants," listing participating organizations in the UN Global Compact.
  https://www.unglobalcompact.org/what-is-gc/participants

- **UN Partnerships:** describes the UN Partner Portal as a platform to connect UN Agencies and civil society for partnership opportunities.
  https://www.unpartnerportal.org/landing/

- **UN Sanctions List:** includes all individuals and entities subject to Security Council measures.
  https://main.un.org/securitycouncil/en/content/un-sc-consolidated-list

- **Interpol List:** allows users to view and search public Red Notices issued by Interpol.
  https://www.interpol.int/en/How-we-work/Notices/Red-Notices/View-Red-Notices

DATA PRIVACY & CYBER RISK

- **DLA PiperData Protection Laws of the World:** an interactive tool providing a country-by-country overview of privacy and data protection laws, including regulatory enforcement and breach notification requirements.
  https://www.dlapiperdataprotection.com/

- **UNCTAD Global Cyberlaw Tracker:** a United Nations resource that monitors legal frameworks in electronic transactions, data protection, consumer protection, and cybercrime laws across all countries.
  https://unctad.org/topic/ecommerce-and-digital-economy/ecommerce-law-reform/summary-adoption-e-commerce-legislation-worldwide

COUNTRY-LEVEL RISK SCORES

- **Freedom HouseFreedom in the World Index:** annual assessments of political rights and civil liberties in 195 countries and 15 territories, used by governments and NGOs for democracy and human rights due diligence.
  https://freedomhouse.org/report/freedom-world
- **The Risk Advisory Group:** a premium intelligence and security consultancy offering country risk analysis, political stability forecasts, and geopolitical briefings. Subscription-based but widely used by multinational organizations for reputational and operational risk validation.
  https://riskadvisory.com/

CORPORATE & NONPROFIT FINANCIAL DISCLOSURES

- **Bloomberg:** provides business & markets news, data, and analysis globally.
  http://www.bloomberg.com/
- **Hoovers:** business research and company information platform.
  http://www.hoovers.com/
- **NASDAQ Company Financials:** o ffers company financials, fundamental data, stock quotes.
  http://www.nasdaq.com/quotes/company-financials.aspx
- **Charity Commission (UK):** UK regulator for charities, ensures public confidence.
  https://www.gov.uk/government/organisations/charity-commission
- **CRA Charities Directorate (Canada):** the official government database of registered Canadian charities, offering financial data, compliance status, and annual filings.
  https://www.canada.ca/en/revenue-agency/services/charities-giving.html
- **ACNC Charity Register** (Australia): maintained by the Australian Charities and Not-for-profits Commission, this register includes detailed compliance, financial, and governance information for Australian nonprofits.
  https://www.acnc.gov.au/charity
- **Charity Register of Ireland (CRA):** a searchable registry of charities operating in Ireland, including governance, annual returns, and regulatory status.
  https://www.charitiesregulator.ie/en

- **NZ Charities Services Register (New Zealand):** managed by the Department of Internal Affairs, this registry includes financial information, officer listings, and activity summaries. https://www.charities.govt.nz/
- **FCRA Online (India):** the official government portal listing all Indian NGOs registered under the Foreign Contribution Regulation Act (FCRA), including registration status, compliance history, and annual return filings, essential for verifying legal eligibility to receive foreign grants.
- https://fcraonline.nic.in/
- **Charity Navigator:** provides ratings and research tools to evaluate charities. http://www.charitynavigator.org/?bay=search.alpha
- **Candid Foundation Center/990 Finder:** provides access to nonprofit tax forms to help identify funders. http://foundationcenter.org/findfunders/990finder/

Business and Human Rights

Business Human Rights Link (Resource Center): a global NGO that promotes corporate accountability, tracks human rights impacts, and provides detailed profiles of over 10,000 companies. http://www.business-humanrights.org/en/companies

- **OECD WatchComplaints Database:** searchable database of complaints filed under the OECD Guidelines for Multinational Enterprises, tracking company-level grievances related to human rights, labor, environment, and corruption. https://www.oecdwatch.org/complaints-database/

Corporate Social Responsibility (CSR), Governance and Sustainability

- **CorpWatch:** a watchdog organization providing investigative research, company profiles, and campaign tools focused on environmental justice and corporate accountability. http://www.corpwatch.org/

AccountAbility: a global standards and consulting organization that helps businesses and nonprofits improve ESG performance, governance practices, and stakeholder engagement. http://www.accountability.org/

- **FTSE4Good Index Series:** a family of ESG investment indices maintained by the London Stock Exchange Group, tracking companies that meet rigorous environmental, social, and governance standards.
  https://www.lseg.com/en/ftse-russell/indices/ftse4good
- **Dow Jones Sustainability Indices (DJSI):** global benchmarks assessing the long-term sustainability performance of publicly traded companies across economic, environmental, and social dimensions.
  https://www.spglobal.com/spdji/en/index-family/sustainability/sustainability/
- **S&P Global Corporate Sustainability Assessment (CSA):** an annual evaluation of over 12,000 companies' sustainability practices, serving as the foundation for DJSI inclusion and ESG benchmarking.
  https://www.spglobal.com/sustainable1/en/csa
- **Open Sustainability Index:** a community-edited, open-source platform offering global ESG data for companies, designed to enhance transparency and stakeholder access.
  https://www.opensustainabilityindex.org/

ENVIRONMENTAL RESOURCES

- **Greenpeace International:** a global network of independent national and regional Greenpeace organizations collaborating to protect forests, oceans, and environmental justice through direct action, advocacy, and research.
  https://www.greenpeace.org/international/
- **Environmental News Network (ENN):** a trusted, long-standing online publication offering a global perspective on environmental issues. ENN informs, educates, and enables action regarding climate, wildlife, and sustainability trends.
  https://www.enn.com/
- Environmental Defense Fund (EDF): a leading science-driven non-profit that delivers bold, game-changing climate, ecosystem, air quality, and public health solutions grounded in economics and policy.
  https://www.edf.org/
- **World Wildlife Fund (WWF):** the largest global conservation organization, dedicated to preserving biodiversity, reducing human impact, and promoting wilderness resilience. Known for the Living Planet Reports and high-impact campaigns such as Earth Hour.
  https://www.worldwildlife.org/

FRAUD AND CORRUPTION

- **Transparency International:** a global civil society organization dedicated to ending corruption and promoting transparency, accountability, and integrity at all levels. Known for the Corruption Perceptions Index and Global Corruption Report, Transparency International is widely used for country-level due diligence.
- https://www.transparency.org/
- **Organized Crime and Corruption Reporting Project (OCCRP):** an international investigative journalism network exposing transnational corruption, organized crime, and money laundering through high-impact reporting and in-depth case studies.
  https://www.occrp.org/

HUMAN RIGHTS

- **Amnesty InternationalCountries:** a global human rights movement present in over 150 countries, offering in-depth country-by-country human rights reporting and real-time research.
  https://www.amnesty.org/en/countries/
- **UN Guiding Principles on Business and Human Rights:** full text and implementation guidance: outlines the "Protect, Respect and Remedy" framework, detailing expectations for both states and businesses to prevent and address human rights abuses.
  https://www.business-humanrights.org/en/big-issues/governing-business-human-rights/un-guiding-principles/
- **Human Rights Watch (HRW):** an international NGO that investigates and advocates for victims of human rights abuses across more than 100 countries, covering issues such as war crimes, torture, discrimination, and children's rights.
  http://www.hrw.org

Continuing The Revolution: The Future of DAFs

EXECUTIVE SUMMARY

To explore the future of donor-advised funds (DAFs), I interviewed more than 120 of the field's most prominent experts, including philanthropic advisors, nonprofit and foundation leaders, DAF sponsor executives, legal scholars, financial professionals, and global innovators. Their collective insights, referred to throughout this chapter as the DAF 120, reveal five defining themes shaping the road ahead: generational shifts, regulatory pressures, technological transformation, collaborative giving models, and the globalization of donor intent. This chapter distills their perspectives into a forward-looking roadmap that challenges donors to engage more intentionally, Data subject rights, accountability principles, controller and processor requirement, and sponsors to lead with transparency, innovation, and stewardship. The DAF revolution is still unfolding. Its future will be shaped by the choices stakeholders make today. The call is clear: build trust, empower participation, and unlock the full potential of DAF philanthropy for a more inclusive and impactful future.

LEARNING FROM THE DAF 120

The philanthropic landscape is undergoing a profound transformation, with DAFs at the center of this revolution. Once viewed as a niche giving vehicle, DAFs have grown into a major philanthropic force, driving record levels of charitable contributions and offering donors unprecedented flexibility in how and when they give. As these funds continue to gain momentum, they are also facing increased scrutiny, shifting donor demographics, and the challenge of balancing flexibility with accountability.

Throughout this book, many of the most accomplished leaders, advisors, executives, scholars, and innovators in the DAF space have shared their insights. This chapter brings their perspectives together. Referred to here as The DAF 120, these voices offer a uniquely informed and cross-sector view into the future of donor-advised funds. Their collective insight reveals emerging trends, shared concerns, and bold ideas that may shape the next era of philanthropic practice. The strength and elegance of DAFs is summed up so well by Jo-Anne Ryan, Vice President of Philanthropic Advisory Services at Royal Bank of Canada Wealth Management:

The beauty of DAFs is that they simplify the process of philanthropy, allowing donors to focus on the causes they care about while delegating the administrative burden to professionals.[328]

DAFs take on the administration of philanthropy, often providing services with unmatched speed, deploying grants within hours or days. This agility makes them especially vital during humanitarian crises and global emergencies, when rapid response can save lives and catalyze immediate impact. In fact, Beth Kaufman, Partner and National Chair of Private Client Services, Lowenstein Sandler, LLP, and former Associate Tax Legislative Counsel at the U.S. Department of the Treasury, shares:

I think you really only need a private foundation if you're going to provide direct services or make grants that cannot be made through a donor-advised fund.[329]

Kaufman's comment reflects a broader trend in modern philanthropy. DAFs are increasingly central to a wide range of giving strategies, combining immediate tax benefits, simplified grantmaking, and long-term charitable planning. This makes them attractive not only to high-net-worth individuals and corporate donors but also to next-generation philanthropists who value transparency, engagement, and measurable impact. As Millennials and Gen Z donors gain influence, they are helping reshape the DAF landscape toward greater accountability, values alignment, and participatory giving.

Meanwhile, regulatory debate continues. Policymakers, sponsors, and nonprofit leaders are actively discussing reforms that could reshape the sector. Despite these pressures, most DAFs already exceed the minimum payout required of private foundations. Still, critics persist. The core tension between donor flexibility and nonprofit funding stability remains a defining issue for the sector.

Another major theme emerging from The DAF 120 is the globalization of giving. More donors are seeking to support international causes, but cross-border grantmaking involves significant complexity, including foreign registration laws, local tax rules, and currency restrictions. Leading DAF sponsors increasingly partner with international grantmaking experts to navigate these challenges, providing donors with secure, compliant pathways to support global impact.

[328] Ryan, J. Interview with Ted Hart, October 8, 2024.
[329] Kaufman, B. Interview by Ted Hart, November 5, 2024.

Technology is also accelerating change. Innovations in digital platforms, data analytics, and real-time reporting are enhancing both domestic and international philanthropy. These tools are improving grantmaking efficiency, enabling better donor engagement, and powering more strategic and transparent giving programs.

This chapter explores these trends through the lens of The DAF 120. Their collective wisdom has been synthesized into five major themes that serve as a forward-looking framework for the next decade of DAFs. What follows is not just a forecast. It is a roadmap shaped by the voices of those closest to the field's evolution, grounded in experience and motivated by a shared commitment to impact, integrity, and innovation.

FUTURE FOCUS AREA #1: THE NEXT-GENERATION DONOR

Across the DAF 120 conversations, no theme emerged more consistently than the influence of Millennial and Gen Z donors. Their insistence on personalized, impact-driven, tech-enabled giving is the lens through which every other trend must now be viewed.

These younger philanthropists are not simply modernizing past practices. They are bringing a revolution within the DAF revolution. Their expectations for transparency, measurable impact, values alignment, and seamless digital experiences are reshaping every corner of the philanthropic sector. Sir John Low, former Group Chief Executive of Charities Aid Foundation (CAF) informs:

> If we want philanthropy to thrive in the future, we need to find ways to engage the younger generation, not just as recipients of wealth but as active participants in giving.[330]

Giving with Purpose, Not Just Dollars

For this generation, philanthropy is a direct expression of personal values. They want to solve problems, not just write checks. Their giving is shaped by social movements, climate urgency, and a deep concern for global equity. They expect results and want tools that support thoughtful, strategic decision-making. Frances Sheehan, President, The Foundation for Delaware County, helps us see the future by sharing:

---

[330] Low, Sir John. Interview by Ted Hart, September 12, 2024.

To engage the next generation of donors, we must highlight how DAFs can be used for innovation and meaningful, sustained impact.[331]

Sheehan's insight reminds us that innovation is not optional; it is the language of trust for the next generation of givers. For this generation, flexibility is not about deferring decisions. It's about customizing giving to match evolving interests and emerging needs.

Digital Expectations Are Non-Negotiable

Digital tools are no longer optional for DAF sponsors. Younger donors expect intuitive online platforms with the same quality and speed they experience in banking, investing, and retail. From fund setup to impact tracking, they want clarity and access at their fingertips. As Jacqueline Valouch, Head of Wealth Planning and Philanthropy at Deutsche Bank Wealth Management, explained:

> Technology is key. It's made DAFs more accessible and easier to use. Donors expect seamless experiences.[332]

Sara C. DeRose , Director of Development & Philanthropic Services at Fairfield County's Community Foundation, adds:

> The future of donor advised funds lies in intuitive technology and deeper, more meaningful connections between donors and the causes they champion.[333]

Some DAF sponsors are responding with AI-powered recommendations, mobile-first grantmaking, and real-time dashboards that show how funds are deployed and what results they achieve. Importantly, younger donors are data-savvy and expect evidence, not just promises. Many are also more comfortable contributing diverse assets, including appreciated stock, cryptocurrency, or other illiquid assets, further expanding the range of tools used for philanthropy.

From Parking Lot to Launchpad

Traditional donors may have viewed DAFs as a place to hold charitable dollars until they were ready to act. That mindset is expanding. Tomorrow's donors want to move quickly and create change in real-time. DAFs are becoming launchpads for issue-driven, rapid-response philanthropy resources added to longer-term problem solving and legacy planning.

---

[331] Sheehan, F. Interview with Ted Hart, September 26, 2024.
[332] Valouch, J. Interview with Ted Hart, August 8, 2024.
[333] DeRose, S. Interview with Ted Hart, December 12, 2024.

This shift is evident in the rise of pooled giving funds and collaborative campaigns, often amplified through peer networks and social media. Some are also drawn to influencer-led philanthropy and online campaigns, where peer networks and social platforms play a central role in amplifying reach and mobilizing action.

Tools for Family, Legacy, and Innovation

DAF platforms are for multigenerational learning, values transmission, and innovative social investment. Today's wealth creators are bringing their children and grandchildren into giving conversations earlier than ever before, using DAFs as living classrooms for civic responsibility, purpose-driven finance, and impact strategy. Steve Latham, CoFounder and CEO at DonateStock, forecasts:

> Future DAF donors will prioritize platforms that offer easy, seamless user experiences and the flexibility to contribute diverse asset types, reflecting the evolving expectations of modern philanthropy.[334]

At the same time, younger donors are pushing families to expand beyond legacy institutions. Many show lower trust in large, established charities and prefer supporting grassroots organizations or social enterprises aligned with their values. Mitch Stein, Head of Strategy, Chariot Giving, Inc. (www.givechariot.com), captured this shift well:

> DAFs offer a bridge for people who may not see themselves as traditional philanthropists. It can be a way to ease into giving with flexibility.[335]

These donors are increasingly exploring blended approaches, combining grant-making with impact investing or social ventures. They want to use DAFs not only to give but also to deploy capital in ways that deliver both social and financial returns.

Implications for Sponsors and Nonprofits

The rise of next-generation donors is not a distant trend. It is already transforming how philanthropy works. Those who innovate will thrive. Those who hesitate may become irrelevant. The most successful DAF sponsors will prioritize deeply personalized giving tools that align with donor values, build seamless digital platforms optimized for mobile use, and invest in education and engagement that delivers real-time impact.

---

[334] Latham, S. Interview with Ted Hart, November 22, 2024.
[335] Stein, M. Interview with Ted Hart, September 13, 2024.

Flexibility remains essential. But it must support both immediate action and long-term legacy. Sponsors that cultivate collaborative giving environments, where donors learn from peers and co-create solutions, will be best positioned to meet the expectations of tomorrow's philanthropists.

Nonprofits must evolve as well. Younger DAF donors are not interested in transactional relationships. They seek compelling narratives, measurable outcomes, and meaningful opportunities to stay involved. Organizations that embrace transparency and provide clear, ongoing pathways for partnership will be the ones that earn lasting loyalty.

Research from the Bay Area Millennial Giving Report reinforces this shift. Millennials approach giving with an investor's mindset. They want their philanthropy to create visible, lasting change in social, environmental, and civic outcomes. They prioritize causes like climate resilience, democratic integrity, local equity, and systemic justice. Many prefer unrestricted, multi-year gifts that empower nonprofits to act strategically.

They also expect their DAF sponsors to help bring this vision to life. They want digital tools to track impact, opportunities to participate in pooled or collaborative funds, and guidance that connects personal values with strategic decisions. For these donors, giving is not separate from life planning. It is central to it.

As wealth shifts to the next generation, these donors are bringing new expectations to the table, prioritizing transparency, flexibility, and values alignment. Beth Harper Briglia, Philanthropic Advisor, notes:

> As the next generation inherits wealth, they are looking for tools like DAFs that align with their values and offer flexibility. This is where the future of giving lies.[336]

FUTURE FOCUS AREA #2: ACCOUNTABILITY AND REGULATION

As DAFs grow in popularity, influence, and assets under management, the call for stronger accountability has become one of the most urgent topics shaping their future. With more than $250 billion now held in DAFs and the percentage of assets granted annually surpassing those of private foundations, stakeholders across the philanthropic, legal, and policy sectors are asking critical questions

---

[336] Briglia, B.H. Interview with Ted Hart, October 2, 2024.

about the pace and transparency of grantmaking. Reynolds Cafferata, Partner at Rodriguez, Horii, Choi & Cafferata, LLP, observes:

> As we look to the future, DAFs must evolve with societal needs, perhaps moving towards a model where there's an even greater emphasis on transparency and proactive community impact."[337]

Scrutiny and the Payout Debate

One of the most persistent criticisms of DAFs centers on the absence of a mandatory payout rate. Unlike private foundations, DAFs are not subject to federally mandated minimum distributions.

Angela Moloney, President and CEO of The Catholic Foundation of Michigan, pushed back on this perception:

> One of the biggest misconceptions about donor-advised funds (DAFs) is the idea that they hold back charitable giving. In my experience, the opposite is true. When we established the Catholic Foundation of Michigan, donor-advised funds were the first tool donors wanted to use because they enable money to move into the community quickly and effectively. While some question whether DAFs delay grantmaking, the reality is that they provide a structured way for donors to be both strategic and responsive in their philanthropy. The key is ensuring that donors understand how to actively engage with their funds, making thoughtful and timely distributions that maximize their impact.[338]

Empirical data supports this view. Most years, DAFs report payout rates above 20%, significantly higher than the 5% required of private foundations. Still, critics note that aggregate data can obscure the inactivity of some individual accounts. Proposals that have surfaced include setting a minimum annual payout, imposing time limits for distributions, or requiring account-level reporting. As Kirk Hoopingarner, Partner at Quarles & Brady, LLP, and Chair of the Evanston, Illinois Community Foundation, cautions:

> By converting complex assets such as farmland or real estate into charitable funds, DAFs empower donors to support smaller charities that might lack the capacity to manage these types of gifts.[339]

---

[337] Cafferata, R. Interview by Ted Hart, September 11, 2024.
[338] Moloney, A. Interview with Ted Hart, March 5, 2024.
[339] Hoopingarner, K. Interview with Ted Hart, December 4, 2024.

Balancing Oversight with Innovation

Policymakers, sponsors, and nonprofit leaders must ensure DAFs serve the public good while preserving the innovation and speed that make them effective.

Alan Cantor, Principal, Alan Cantor Consulting, LLC, acknowledges the unparalleled flexibility and accessibility that DAFs offer but emphasizes the need for accountability to unlock their full potential. His concerns center on the imbalance between the immediate tax benefits DAFs provide and the delayed charitable impact when funds remain inactive. He also points to transparency gaps, such as "dark money" grants and limited reporting, as risks that could foster public skepticism and erode trust.

Importantly, Cantor advocates for constructive solutions, urging proactive engagement among regulators, sponsors, and donors, along with clearer reporting standards. He highlights the value of empowering nonprofits to collaborate more directly with DAF donors, aligning donor intentions with community needs through thoughtful grantmaking and legacy planning.[340]

At the same time, many philanthropic advisors emphasize that regulation must reflect DAFs' real-world contributions. For example, during the COVID-19 pandemic, DAFs facilitated record-breaking emergency relief, with grants mobilized in days rather than months, a speed that could be compromised under rigid regulatory frameworks.

New IRS Proposals and Sponsor Responsibilities

Emerging IRS proposals, including the Proposed Regulations issued in November 2023[341], are addressing potential conflicts of interest by disqualifying personal investment advisors from managing DAF assets if they also oversee the donor's personal investments. Under the proposed rules, such dual roles would automatically trigger an excess benefit transaction, subjecting both the donor and advisor to financial penalties.

Dave Shevlin, a Partner at Simpson Thacher & Bartlett, LLP, emphasizes that while these regulations are still under review, they reflect a growing focus on ensuring the independence and accountability of DAF asset management. To navigate these emerging compliance requirements, Shevlin advises DAF spon-

---

[340] Cantor, A. Interview with Ted Hart, December 17, 2024.
[341] U.S. Department of the Treasury, Internal Revenue Service. Proposed Regulations on Donor-Advised Funds and Related Issues under Section 4966 and Section 4958. REG-142338–07, 88 Fed. Reg. 80556 (November 17, 2023).

sors to establish and enforce clear internal policies, especially regarding the use of personal advisors and the management of dormant accounts. He also recommends that sponsors review advisor compensation practices to ensure they align with the proposed regulations. Most importantly, Shevlin underscores the need for sponsors to stay informed and adaptable, given the likelihood of regulatory changes and the potential for further clarifications or re-proposals.[342]

One area frequently mentioned by DAF 120 experts is the limitation on using Qualified Charitable Distributions (QCDs) from retirement accounts to fund DAFs. As Matt Nash, Executive Director of the Blackbaud Giving Fund, observed:

> I wish that the qualified retirement distribution could go into a DAF... It's a good way to hopefully use it.[343]

This sentiment reflects a growing consensus in the philanthropic advisory community. Allowing QCDs to be directed to DAFs would give retirees greater flexibility in aligning their giving with long-term charitable goals while still enjoying tax benefits. It also underscores the need for thoughtful regulatory modernization that empowers more Americans to engage in strategic philanthropy.

Transparency as a Trust Imperative

The push for transparency is not coming just from regulators. Donors increasingly want to understand how their funds are used. Nonprofits are eager to connect with the DAF donors supporting them. And the public expects confidence that charitable tools are advancing the public good. Hillel Korin points out,

> The transparency and accountability mechanisms that DAFs have in place are often misunderstood, but they are crucial for building public trust.[344]

Some sponsors are meeting this demand through innovations such as real-time grant dashboards, enhanced donor education, and optional public-facing profiles for fundholders. Many DAF sponsors are also adopting voluntary measures, such as setting internal payout targets or offering public dashboards, to demonstrate accountability and build trust. Dien Yuen, CEO of Daylight Advisors, remarks,

> I think the sponsoring organizations do need to report on what organizations they're supporting, and they do need to be much more transparent... There needs to be guiding principles or some ethical standards.[345]

---

[342] Shevlin, D. Interview with Ted Hart, November 22, 2024.
[343] Nash, M. Interview with Ted Hart, August 8, 2024.
[344] Korin, H. Interview with Ted Hart, September 11, 2024.
[345] Yuen, D. Interview with Ted Hart, August 22, 2024.

The challenge is building systems that enhance transparency without discouraging thoughtful, strategic philanthropy. The sector needs both clarity and flexibility in a delicate balance that requires careful design.

DAFs as Vehicles for Strategic Capital

Despite ongoing skepticism, DAF 120 experts across sectors broadly reject the notion that DAFs serve primarily as tax shelters. Instead, they highlight how DAFs help donors act with intention, flexibility, and inclusion. As Rick Mills, Senior Counsel at Smith Haughey (www.shrr.com) points out:

> One of the biggest misconceptions about donor-advised funds is the idea that giving to a DAF is somehow less charitable than giving directly to a nonprofit. Critics argue that DAFs act as a warehouse where money sits unused before being deployed for charitable purposes. But that's simply false. When a donor contributes to a DAF, the money is irrevocably dedicated to charity, forever. The data is clear: DAFs often have higher giving rates than private foundations, frequently surpassing the 5% minimum payout requirement. It's essential for those of us in the DAF community to dispel this myth and emphasize the true impact of DAF philanthropy.[346]

DAFs provide the infrastructure to accept complex assets, deploy capital rapidly in emergencies, and support innovative or community-based initiatives that may be overlooked by traditional funders. For many donors, DAFs offer a way to blend immediacy with long-term impact, strengthening both donor engagement and nonprofit outcomes.

Looking Ahead

The regulatory conversation is not going away. But neither is the innovation that has made DAFs one of the fastest-growing tools in philanthropy.

The path forward requires thoughtful compromise. Reform efforts should be guided by evidence, designed with flexibility, and grounded in a clear understanding of how DAFs function. The goal is not merely compliance; it's credibility.

Nonprofit leaders also emphasize that greater visibility into DAF donor flows can help strengthen stewardship, tailor engagement strategies, and ensure that grantmaking aligns with community needs.

---

[346] Mills, R. Interview with Ted Hart, February 27, 2025.

FUTURE FOCUS AREA #3: TECHNOLOGY AND DONOR ENGAGEMENT

The future of DAFs will be shaped not only by policy and accountability, but also by how effectively the sector responds to changing donor expectations. Digital-native donors will demand seamless platforms, real-time feedback, and values-based real engagement. To meet these expectations, DAF sponsors and the broader philanthropic ecosystem will embrace a full digital transformation.

From Passive Giving to Real-Time Engagement

Younger donors are not content to contribute and step away. They want to log in, track their grants, see measurable outcomes, and receive personalized recommendations, all from their phones. In this context, the days of quarterly statements and batch-processed grant approvals feel outdated. Joe Fisher, CEO at REN predicts,

> AI will make philanthropy hyper-personalized. Imagine an AI agent recommending grants, tracking impact, and educating donors in real-time, like a financial advisor for giving.[347]

This expectation is shaping how leading DAF sponsors design their platforms. Custom dashboards, grant tracking, and even real-time impact updates are becoming the norm. In turn, these tools are encouraging deeper donor engagement and more frequent giving. These tools are not only deepening donor engagement but also equipping philanthropic advisors with insights, allowing them to guide donors toward more meaningful, data-informed choices. By providing advisors with accessible data and user-friendly tools, platforms help them serve next-generation donors with confidence, even without deep technical or philanthropic expertise. Building on this, Sunil Garga, Executive Advisor at Fairshare Ads and former CEO & President at Foundation Source, explains:

> Data is the new currency in philanthropy. It's what allows us to connect with donors on a deeper level and to measure real impact.[348]

AI and the Age of Intelligent Philanthropy

Artificial intelligence is poised to become one of the most transformative forces in the DAF landscape. Algorithms can already suggest giving opportunities based on donor history, regional needs, and global events. In time, AI will likely do more, helping validate charities, flagging high-impact opportunities, and even

---

[347] Fisher, J. Interview with Ted Hart, February 13, 2025.
[348] Garga, S. Interview with Ted Hart, September 16, 2024.

modeling giving outcomes over time. Miki Akimoto, Chief Impact Officer, National Center for Family Philanthropy (NCFP), states:

> Technology has allowed for asynchronous giving that's much easier to facilitate than with a traditional foundation's grantmaking process. Particularly for the next generations, who expect everything at their fingertips, DAFs have adapted more rapidly.[349]

AI is making that bridge more intuitive. It provides personalized giving pathways that are data-driven yet accessible to all levels of wealth and experience. Still, many DAF 120 experts caution against relying solely on automation. Human judgment and relationships remain essential. The future is not about replacing philanthropic intent, but about augmenting it with better tools.

Blockchain and the Pursuit of Radical Transparency

One of the recurring critiques of DAFs is their perceived opacity. Who gives? Where does the money go? How long do funds sit before being granted? Elaine Rasmussen, Founder & CEO of Social Impact Now and On Air Host of Do.Different.Better., envisions an even more transformative future:

> The future of DAFs might look very different with the increasing use of AI and technology. I think there will be fewer intermediaries, and donors will be able to connect directly with causes, bypassing traditional structures like community foundations.[350]

Blockchain technology offers a potential solution. By recording grant activity in an immutable ledger, DAF sponsors could allow donors, and perhaps even the public, to trace how charitable dollars move from contribution to impact. This is especially promising for cross-border giving, where regulatory hurdles and documentation gaps often create friction and delay.

While adoption is still early, several DAF 120 experts acknowledged blockchain as a promising tool for boosting confidence in the DAF model. Its value lies not in replacing current systems, but in reinforcing them with layers of verifiable accountability.

Mobile-First Platforms: Meeting Donors Where They Are

Today's donors manage their bank accounts, investments, and even tax filings on mobile devices. Increasingly, they expect the same from their philanthropy.

---

[349] Akimoto, M. Interview with Ted Hart, August 30, 2024.
[350] Rasmussen, E. Interview with Ted Hart, August 19, 2024.

Forward-thinking sponsors are already delivering mobile apps that let users recommend grants, track fund balances, and receive nonprofit updates on demand. This is particularly important for younger donors, who view mobile access as a basic requirement rather than a premium feature.

The result is a shift from episodic giving to integrated philanthropy. Giving becomes part of everyday digital life. Many platforms are also simplifying the contribution of complex assets, such as appreciated stock or cryptocurrency, making it easier for donors to deploy diverse forms of capital toward their chosen causes.

Technology-Enabled Impact Investing

The rise of AI and digital platforms is further fueling this shift. Tools now exist to help donors screen for values-based factors, automate portfolio adjustments based on impact goals, and receive real-time reporting on the performance of their investments. This new generation of tools empowers donors to align their philanthropic intentions with the full life cycle of their charitable assets.

In practice, this means that every dollar in a DAF, whether granted or invested, can work toward advancing a donor's mission. This is a profound change from the old model, where ungranted funds sat idle in traditional portfolios.

Technology plays a key role here, simplifying the transfer and management of complex assets, which might otherwise overwhelm smaller nonprofits. John Bennett, Partner at Simpson Thacher & Bartlett, LLP, observes,

> Donor-advised funds are a significantly misunderstood part of the nonprofit sector, but I believe they are net beneficial to charitable giving. DAFs encourage charitable giving, including assets that are more complex and often overlooked. They allow donors to be thoughtful about their philanthropy without being rushed.[351]

Digital Equity and Philanthropic Accessibility

Technology can be a great equalizer. While early DAF adopters were typically high-net-worth individuals advised by wealth managers, today's platforms are lowering the entry barrier.

This democratization of philanthropy expands the reach and relevance of DAFs. It also introduces new voices, values, and priorities into the conversation, es-

---

[351] Bennett, J. Interview with Ted Hart, November 13, 2024.

pecially those of underrepresented communities who may previously have felt excluded from structured giving vehicles. Courtney Murphy, Senior Director, Head of Strategy and Grants, Global Impact Citizenship, BNY, states,

> I think one aspect of the next generation of DAFs is the trend of democratization. DAFs shouldn't just be for the super wealthy; they could become a tool for everyone, similar to a 401K for charitable giving.[352]

For donors navigating sudden wealth or new access to capital, DAFs provide an invaluable tool to align giving with values without making rushed decisions. When powered by inclusive technology, that alignment becomes even more powerful. Kendra Onishi, Chief Development Officer (CDO) at PolicyLink, shares:

> For donors experiencing windfall wealth, DAFs serve as an invaluable tool, enabling thoughtful philanthropy without the pressure of rushed decision-making.[353]

A Future Fueled by Innovation and Intention

Technology is not just changing how people give; it is changing what they expect from the experience. The next generation of donors wants flexibility, visibility, and meaning. They want their giving to be efficient, but also impactful. And they expect the tools they use to reflect the sophistication of their values.

For DAF sponsors, the challenge is clear. Those who invest in innovation will thrive. Those who resist it risk becoming obsolete.

Tomorrow's DAF platforms will not merely be transactional. They will be transformational. Built on AI, powered by blockchain, and delivered through intuitive, mobile-first experiences, they will help redefine what it means to be a philanthropist in the digital age. Jake Wood, CEO of Groundswell, reflects,

> I think we're just beginning to see how DAFs can be integrated into broader financial planning tools. As more people recognize that DAFs can be a flexible tool for long-term planning, we'll see innovation that brings DAFs closer to the core of wealth management.[354]

[352] Murphy, C. Interview with Ted Hart, August 13, 2024.
[353] Onishi, K. Interview with Ted Hart, December 5, 2024.
[354] Wood, J. Interview with Ted Hart, September 6, 2024.

FUTURE FOCUS AREA #4: COLLECTIVE POWER OF DAFs

As philanthropy becomes more interconnected, the next evolution of DAFs is being shaped by collective strategies, where individual generosity is amplified through cooperation. From pooled funds to corporate giving platforms and issue-based collaboratives, DAFs are increasingly being used as tools not just for private philanthropy, but for community alignment and systemic change. Doug Miller, Founder Chair of EVPA, AVPN, and IVPC, captures this vision:

> It's not just about individual giving anymore; the future is in collaborations—where DAFs can pool resources to drive systemic change.[355]

From Individual Action to Collective Impact

A very strong theme across the DAF 120 expert interviews was the growing recognition that DAFs have untapped potential as collaborative engines. While most DAFs are modest in size, their cumulative power is immense. As Jane Peebles, Partner Emerita at Karlin & Peebles, observed:

> Even though most DAFs are quite small, the collective power of it is huge.[356]

This insight captures a broader trend: donors are increasingly seeking ways to align their giving with others, either by joining pooled funds, participating in giving circles, or supporting thematic collaboratives designed to address large-scale challenges.

The Rise of Pooled Giving and Thematic Funds

DAF sponsors are now curating issue-specific funds focused on causes like climate action, racial equity, and public health, that allow donors to contribute into shared pools with strategic deployment. This structure combines the flexibility of DAFs with the strategic heft of foundation-style grantmaking, enabling donors of all levels to participate in initiatives with measurable goals and professional oversight.

Pooled DAF funds also offer an answer to a frequent donor concern: how to make a meaningful difference when individual grants may feel small. In collective models, donors can be part of something bigger, joining efforts where scale, coordination, and research drive greater impact.

[355] Miller, D. Interview with Ted Hart, September 17, 2024
[356] Peebles, J. Interview with Ted Hart, August 7, 2024.

Corporate DAFs: Expanding Workplace Philanthropy

Another area of rapid growth is the corporate DAF, which allows companies to centralize charitable efforts and engage employees through matching, advisory privileges, and payroll deduction options. Mid-size businesses that may not have private foundations are increasingly turning to DAFs as a cost-effective way to structure their philanthropy. Workplace giving platforms like Benevity, Bonterra, and Blackbaud are integrating DAFs into employee benefits, positioning them alongside tools like 401(k) accounts to encourage everyday philanthropy across a broad base of donors. These programs can foster a culture of generosity and strengthen corporate identity, particularly among younger employees who seek purpose in the workplace.

Benevity's DAF-based giving accounts grew almost fivefold between 2017 and 2023, reaching approximately 680,000 accounts. Since launching in 2020, the Blackbaud Giving Fund has distributed over $2 billion to around 200,000 non-profits. These developments signal a shift in how employers and employees engage in charitable giving, making DAFs more accessible, recurring, and embedded in modern workplace culture.[357]

DAFs and Nonprofits: Partnership

Historically, nonprofits have struggled to build consistent relationships with DAF donors due to perceived anonymity or lack of direct communication. Leading nonprofits now treat DAF donors like major donors, offering personalized stewardship, timely impact reports, and invitations to collaborate on long-term projects. As Sampriti Ganguli of Ganguli Associates LLC, and former CEO of Arabella Advisors, noted:

> Nonprofits sometimes feel left out of the DAF conversation. The real challenge is to make DAFs a collaborative force where both nonprofits and donors feel equally empowered.[358]

This shift requires effort on both sides. Nonprofits should proactively engage DAF donors, while DAF sponsors should support more transparent, relationship-friendly systems.

---

[357] Lindsay, D. "Next for DAFs? Accounts as Tools for Regular Folks, Not Just the Wealthy," Chronicle of Philanthropy, January 14, 2025.
[358] Ganguli, S. Interview with Ted Hart, September 11, 2024.

CASE STUDY: COLLECTIVE GIVING IN CRISIS

The power of collaboration through DAFs becomes most visible in times of crisis. During recent disasters, from hurricanes to humanitarian emergencies, DAF sponsors created pooled rapid response funds, allowing donors to contribute quickly to validated organizations on the ground. These funds were often mobilized before traditional foundation grants could be processed.

National-level data reinforces this trend. As highlighted in the U.S. Senate Finance Committee's 2022 hearing, Examining Charitable Giving and Trends in the Nonprofit Sector, household giving for COVID-19 relief surged by more than 9% from May 2020 to May 2021. Donations to health, basic needs, racial justice, and cross-border humanitarian causes grew sharply, with many donors leveraging pooled funds, impact investments, and collective giving platforms to accelerate response. This real-world surge mirrors the DAF sector's strength in aggregating donor dollars, streamlining due diligence, and deploying aid rapidly.[359]

These examples demonstrate how DAFs can operate as a philanthropic infrastructure, not just as donor accounts, but as platforms for community action, aligned with urgent social priorities.

Strategic Collaboration, Not Competition

As the DAF sector matures, its future will depend on how well stakeholders embrace strategic partnership. DAF sponsors, nonprofits, corporations, and donors must increasingly operate as collaborators with shared goals.

CASE STUDY: DOMESTIC STRATEGIC DEPLOYMENT

The following case demonstrates how successful entrepreneurs in the U.S. used both an Opportunity Fund and a DAF to reduce tax liability and advance a deeply personal philanthropic vision, a powerful model of domestic strategic investing.

Strategic Migration from Private Foundations to DAFs

Foundations that once operated independently are increasingly choosing to terminate into donor-advised funds, not just to reduce administrative burdens,

---

[359] U.S. Senate Committee on Finance. Examining Charitable Giving and Trends in the Nonprofit Sector. Hearing, March 17, 2022, 117th Congress, 2nd session.

but to adopt a more flexible, responsive, and future-ready model of philanthropy. DAF sponsors offer modern platforms for grant processing, compliance, and collaborative giving, providing a streamlined alternative to the complexity of private foundation governance.

This strategy enables families to preserve donor intent and engage younger generations in a structure that supports shared values and long-term participation. While the foundation must relinquish control over the assets, it may still suggest purpose restrictions and offer advisory input, making the DAF a compelling successor vehicle for multigenerational family philanthropy.

As legacy structures give way to tools that are centralized, technology-enabled, and mission-aligned, this migration signals a broader shift in how philanthropic capital is managed for lasting impact. As Tim Deatrick, CAP - Director of Professional Services & Giver Engagement, MortarStone.com observes,

> The most engaging aspect of DAFs for givers is presenting them as personal, low-cost family foundations that foster a legacy of giving across generations.[360]

FUTURE FOCUS AREA #5: GLOBAL REACH AND INVESTING

DAFs are no longer confined to local or even national borders. As donors become increasingly global in their outlook and more strategic in their approach, the future of DAFs will be shaped by their ability to enable international giving and maximize impact through innovative investment strategies. This evolution is not about growth for its own sake; it reflects the deeper desire among modern philanthropists to see their charitable dollars work actively, intelligently, and globally.

Expanding Beyond Borders

International grantmaking through DAFs has grown dramatically in recent years, spurred by advances in compliance infrastructure and the increased availability of intermediaries. DAF sponsors now offer validated pathways for donors to support charitable causes around the world, with many collaborating directly with organizations like Myriad USA and GlobalGiving to ensure legal compliance and secure fund delivery. As Steve Mark, Head of Strategic Account Relationship Management, Fidelity Charitable, remarked:

---

[360] Deatrick, T. Interview with Ted Hart, November 22, 2024
[361] Mark, S. Interview with Ted Hart, August 12, 2024.

DAFs are a great vehicle for cross-border philanthropy... Doing international grantmaking through an organized vehicle is a better approach because of the risk management and structure around it.[361]

The appeal of global philanthropy is no longer limited to ultra-wealthy donors. More individuals are using DAFs to respond to humanitarian crises, fund grassroots international initiatives, and support global development goals. This cross-border activity requires diligent oversight, but it also opens the door to high-impact giving in regions where philanthropic capital is scarce.

Strategic Deployment of Capital

DAFs are increasingly being used not just to make grants, but to strategically invest in change. Many DAF sponsors now offer mission-aligned portfolios that reflect donors' values, whether that's investing in clean energy, affordable housing, education innovation, or racial equity. These investment pools allow ungranted DAF assets to generate social and financial returns while they await deployment. Gregory A. Schupra, Co-Founder, Co-Manager, Member, and COO, Spring Arbor Group, LLC, notes:

The ability to gift hard-to-value assets, such as real estate, through DAFs remains an underutilized yet powerful tool, offering donors unparalleled tax advantages and simplifying complex charitable transactions.[362]

This strategic flexibility is particularly valuable in under-resourced or high-impact environments, including international contexts where traditional funding mechanisms may be limited or inefficient.

The Future: Purpose-Driven Portfolios with Global Impact

Looking ahead, the most influential DAF platforms will be those that offer seamless, values-driven investment options alongside robust international grantmaking capabilities. Donors will expect not only efficiency and transparency but the ability to curate global portfolios of giving and investment that reflect their most urgent values.

As philanthropic capital becomes more mobile and impact-conscious, DAFs are uniquely positioned to help donors deploy that capital wisely. Whether through grants to refugee programs in Eastern Europe, microloans in sub-Saharan Africa, or equity investments in mission-aligned startups, the future of DAFs lies in their ability to think globally and act strategically.

---

[362] Schupra, G. Interview with Ted Hart, December 3, 2024.

For the DAF 120 experts who directly contributed to this book, the message is clear: DAFs will continue to evolve as dynamic engines for innovation and global good.

KEY TAKEAWAYS

The donor-advised fund is no longer a quiet corner of philanthropy. It is a dynamic force at the heart of a global movement that is reshaping how generosity is practiced, how impact is measured, and how change is scaled. Drawing on insights from the DAF 120, this chapter identified five defining areas of evolution:

- The next generation is leading now. Millennial and Gen Z donors are shaping the philanthropic landscape with demands for transparency, digital access, measurable results, and giving strategies that reflect personal values.
- Technology is transforming the donor experience. Artificial intelligence, mobile-first platforms, and blockchain tools are redefining how DAFs engage donors, build trust, and track charitable outcomes.
- Collaboration is a catalyst for greater impact. Giving circles, pooled funds, corporate DAFs, and thematic initiatives are helping donors join forces and scale solutions through shared purpose.
- Global giving is accelerating. DAFs are enabling more secure, compliant, and timely international grantmaking, empowering donors to support causes beyond borders with confidence and clarity.
- DAFs are becoming platforms for innovation. Donors are using recoverable grants, mission-aligned portfolios, and strategic investments to drive social and financial returns while amplifying long-term impact.

Across these five areas, one truth is clear: DAFs are not passive accounts. They are powerful platforms for intentional, strategic, and values-driven philanthropy. The future belongs to those who use them boldly, creatively, and with purpose.

CONCLUSION: THE DAF REVOLUTION CONTINUES

The DAF revolution is no longer an emerging trend. It is an active movement reshaping the future of philanthropy. As we face rising donor expectations, technological transformation, and evolving regulatory landscapes, one truth stands out: this is a revolutionary moment. It is a call to leadership, to intention, and to innovation that serves the public good.

DAFs are more than tax-efficient tools and charitable bank accounts. Today, they are platforms for action. They connect wealth to values, provide speed without sacrificing strategy, and unlock new possibilities for urgent generosity and lasting impact. As Salo Serfati, CEO of Chariot, sees it,

> Philanthropy is no longer just about giving; it's about innovation, collaboration, and creating solutions that are sustainable and scalable. DAFs are leading this transformation.[363]

Donors transform capital into purpose. Advisors guide with clarity and care. DAF sponsors invest in transparency, teams, and tools that meet the moment. Nonprofits become strategic partners by offering measurable outcomes and shared vision. Policymakers build frameworks that protect the public interest while preserving and promoting the good that has been built.

At the center of this revolution is a powerful promise: when donors relinquish legal control of their charitable contribution, they receive something valuable: the ability to give with flexibility, preserve their anonymity if desired, and remain meaningfully involved in shaping impact, all without taking responsibility for the administrative details required to make it all work. This structural trust is not a loophole; it is the design. And it is the reasons DAFs are trusted, adopted, and championed across generations.

What began as an innovation born of the Great Depression is now a cultural force for good. What was once a secret of charitable planning is now a robust platform for everyone.

To everyone holding a stake in this movement, you are not an observer. You are a participant. You are part of this revolution. **It's now yours to lead.**

---

[363] Serfati, S. Interview with Ted Hart, October 1, 2024.

THE DAF REVOLUTION GLOSSARY

How to Use This Glossary

Philanthropy, donor-advised funds (DAFs), and charitable giving operate within a dynamic and sometimes complex landscape of financial, legal, and regulatory frameworks. This glossary offers clear, accessible definitions of key terms used throughout The DAF Revolution: Making a Difference in Our Modern World. Each entry has been carefully crafted to reflect current industry standards, ensuring clarity and usability for philanthropic leaders, nonprofit executives, financial advisors, donors, and policymakers.

A

- **Accelerating Charitable Efforts (ACE) Act:** A proposed U.S. legislative bill, reintroduced in 2021 and 2023, that seeks to impose payout requirements on DAFs. The ACE Act offers two options: (1) a 15-year payout requirement, where funds must be distributed to charities within 15 years, with donors receiving an immediate tax deduction; or (2) a 50-year payout option, where distributions can occur over 50 years, but donors defer their tax deduction until funds are distributed.
- **Adjusted Gross Income (AGI):** A taxpayer's total income minus allowable deductions, used to calculate taxable income. AGI is significant in philanthropy as tax-deductible charitable contributions, including those made to DAFs, are subject to percentage limits based on AGI (e.g., 60% of AGI for cash contributions to public charities). Contributions exceeding these limits can be carried forward for up to five years.
- **Almsgiving:** The practice of giving to the poor, often rooted in religious or moral traditions, as seen in Christianity, Islam, and Buddhism. Almsgiving is typically informal and direct, focusing on immediate relief for those in need.

B

- **Bifurcated Gift:** A donation that includes both charitable and non-charitable components, such as a fundraising gala ticket that provides a meal (non-charitable) alongside a charitable sponsorship. DAFs may not fund the non-charitable portion under IRS rules.
- **Bundling:** A tax strategy that consolidates multiple years of charitable donations into a single tax year. Bundling is commonly used by donors to exceed the standard deduction threshold, making itemizing deductions more advantageous under U.S. tax law. This approach increases immediate tax benefits while allowing grant disbursements over time through vehicles like DAFs.

C

- **Capital Gains Tax:** A tax on the profit from the sale of appreciated assets. Donating such assets to a DAF avoids this tax, maximizing the donor's philanthropic impact.
- **Carryforward:** A provision in the U.S. tax code that allows donors to apply unused charitable deductions to future tax years. When a contribution exceeds the allowable deduction limit, typically 60% of adjusted gross income (AGI) for cash and 30% for non-cash donations, donors may carry forward the excess amount for up to five additional years, optimizing long-term tax planning.
- **Charitable Deduction:** A tax benefit that allows donors to reduce their taxable income by the amount of a qualified charitable contribution, such as a gift to a DAF.
- **Charitable Lead Trust (CLT):** A philanthropic vehicle in which charities receive financial distributions for a set period before the remaining assets pass to heirs or other beneficiaries. CLTs offer tax benefits, such as reducing estate taxes or providing income tax deductions, and can be structured as grantor or non-grantor trusts.
- **Charitable Remainder Trust (CRT):** A financial tool that provides donors with income for a set period, after which the remaining assets are donated to a charity. CRTs offer tax benefits, including an immediate income tax deduction and the avoidance of capital gains tax on appreciated assets, and are commonly used for estate planning and generating retirement income.

- **Charitable Trust:** A legal arrangement where assets are held and managed by a trustee for charitable purposes, often with specific donor intentions. Charitable trusts include Charitable Lead Trusts (CLTs) and Charitable Remainder Trusts (CRTs) and are commonly used for tax planning and long-term philanthropic goals.
- **Collaborative Philanthropy:** Giving models where donors pool funds, expertise, or decision-making to address shared goals, amplifying collective impact. Particularly relevant to DAF sponsors curating thematic funds or pooled campaigns to maximize donor engagement and sector-wide outcomes.
- **Compliance:** Adherence to legal and regulatory requirements governing charitable giving and financial management, including tax reporting, anti-money laundering regulations, and donor disclosure requirements. Compliance is essential for maintaining tax-exempt status and public trust in philanthropic organizations.
- **Component Fund:** A separately identified fund held within a public charity (typically a community foundation) that aggregates donor contributions while retaining the charity's legal control. This structure underpins many DAF arrangements.
- **Conduit Arrangement:** A grantmaking scenario in which a DAF sponsor passes donor recommendations through an intermediary DAF (or DAF-to-DAF transfer) without exercising independent discretion or control, risking IRS treatment of the downstream grant as a taxable distribution under IRC §4966.
- **Crowdfunding:** A fundraising method where individuals pool small donations through online platforms to support charitable projects, social causes, or emergency relief efforts. Crowdfunding can be donation-based, reward-based, or equity-based and is often used for grassroots initiatives and rapid response to crises.

D

- **DAF Sponsor (Sponsoring Organization):** A 501(c)(3) public charity that manages DAFs. Sponsors handle administrative tasks such as investment management, compliance, and grant distributions.
- **Dāna (Dana):** A foundational concept in Hinduism and Buddhism, meaning generosity or charitable giving. It is often considered a spiritual practice and a path to personal virtue or enlightenment.
- **Democratization of Philanthropy:** A shift in charitable giving that makes structured philanthropy accessible to a broader range of donors, beyond high-net-worth individuals.
- **Donor-Advised Fund (DAF):** A charitable giving account managed by a DAF sponsor, allowing donors to contribute assets, receive an immediate tax deduction, and recommend grants to nonprofits over time.
- **Dormant Fund Policy:** Internal policies adopted by DAF sponsors to address accounts with no grant activity over a defined period. These policies may trigger outreach, donor advice, or fund reallocation to active charitable use, preventing warehousing of assets.
- **Due Diligence:** The thorough evaluation and verification of an organization's eligibility and compliance before making grants or investments.

E

- **Endowment:** A financial donation made to an institution where the principal remains intact, and investment earnings fund ongoing charitable activities.
- **ePhilanthropy:** The use of digital tools and online platforms to facilitate charitable giving, fundraising, and donor engagement.
- **Equivalency Determination (ED):** A legal process confirming that a foreign nonprofit is functionally equivalent to a U.S. public charity, allowing a DAF sponsor to grant funds without additional regulatory burdens.
- **Expenditure Responsibility (ER):** A due diligence process required by the IRS when a U.S.-based DAF sponsor makes grants to foreign organizations that are not recognized as U.S. public charities.

F

- **Fiduciary:** A person or institution legally obligated to act in the best interest of another party. Financial and philanthropic advisors with fiduciary duties must prioritize their clients' goals over personal or institutional gain.
- **Financial Action Task Force (FATF) Recommendation 8:** A global anti-money laundering/counterterrorism financing (AML/CTF) standard that flagged nonprofits as vulnerable to abuse, initially prompting broad scrutiny of cross-border grants. It was updated in 2016 and 2019 to promote a risk-based, proportionate approach that guards legitimate philanthropy against blanket "de-risking."

G

- **Giving Circle:** A form of collective philanthropy where individuals pool donations and collaboratively decide how funds are granted, increasing community engagement and impact.
- **Grantmaking:** The process of awarding funds to nonprofit organizations or projects to support their activities and achieve philanthropic goals.
- **Grant Recommendation:** Suggestions made by donors to DAF sponsors on which charitable organizations should receive grants from the fund.
- **GuideStar Seal of Transparency:** Recognition by Candid of a nonprofit's commitment to transparency. The Platinum level indicates comprehensive sharing of goals, strategies, and performance.

I

- **Impact Investing:** Investments made with the intention to generate positive social or environmental impact alongside a financial return. Some DAF sponsors offer mission-aligned investment options for ungranted assets, enabling donors to advance values alongside financial stewardship.
- **Impact Measurement:** The process of assessing the social or environmental outcomes of philanthropic activities, often used by DAF sponsors and nonprofits to demonstrate effectiveness.
- **Inactive Fund Policy:** See Dormant Fund Policy
- **Internal Revenue Code (IRC):** The set of U.S. federal tax laws, including

provisions governing charitable organizations, foundations, and DAFs.

- **Internal Revenue Code §4944(c) (Program-Related Investments [PRIs]):** A provision defining investments made primarily to accomplish charitable goals rather than to produce income. Although originally applicable to private foundations, PRIs inform recoverable grant practices within some DAF programs.
- **IRC §4945 (Expenditure Responsibility Rules):** IRS regulations require private foundations and DAFs to verify that grants to foreign charities are used for legitimate charitable purposes.
- **IRC §4966 (Taxable Distributions):** A rule imposing excise taxes on improper grants from DAFs to individuals or non-qualified entities.
- **IRC §4967 (Donor-Advisor Benefits):** A U.S. tax code provision that prohibits donors and their advisors from receiving personal benefits from their DAF contributions.
- **IRS Compliance:** Adherence to regulations and guidelines set forth by the Internal Revenue Service (IRS) for charitable giving and tax-exempt organizations.
- **IRS Form 8283:** An IRS form used by donors to report non-cash charitable contributions over $500, often required when contributing assets like stocks or real estate to a DAF.
- **IRS Notice 2017–73:** IRS guidance outlining limitations on using DAFs for pledge fulfillment and bifurcated gifts, reinforcing restrictions on donor benefits.
- **IRS Publication 561:** Guidance on how to determine the fair market value of donated property, used when reporting complex assets donated to DAFs.
- **IRS Publication 1771:** A document that details the IRS rules for substantiating charitable contributions, including receipt requirements and donor acknowledgment practices.

L

- **Legacy Planning:** A long-term philanthropic strategy in which donors use DAFs, private foundations, or estate planning tools to ensure charitable giving continues beyond their lifetime.

M

- **Mission-Driven Philanthropy:** Charitable giving focused on advancing specific social, environmental, or humanitarian goals.
- **Multigenerational Philanthropy:** The practice of involving multiple generations of a family in charitable giving and decision-making to create a lasting philanthropic legacy.
- **Mutual Aid Society:** A community-based organization, historically formed by workers or immigrants, to provide social and financial support during times of need.

N

- **Next-Generation Donors:** Millennial and Gen Z philanthropists whose giving emphasizes personalization, social impact, digital engagement, and collaborative models. Future generations (such as Gen Alpha) are expected to continue and expand these trends
- **Nonprofit:** A tax-exempt organization created to serve the public good through charitable, educational, scientific, or religious activities. Nonprofits must be validated by DAF sponsors before receiving grants.

O

- **Office of Foreign Assets Control (OFAC) Regulations:** U.S. Treasury rules prohibit charitable funding to organizations or individuals on the Specially Designated Nationals (SDN) list to prevent support for terrorism and financial crimes.

P

- **Payout Requirement:** A mandated percentage of assets that private foundations must distribute annually (currently 5%). Unlike private foundations, DAFs do not have a federal payout requirement, though some policymakers advocate for one.
- **Pension Protection Act of 2006 (PPA):** A U.S. law that established the first legal definition of DAFs, imposing restrictions on self-dealing, payout structures, and grant distributions.

- **Politically Exposed Person (PEP):** An individual holding a prominent public position (or a close associate), considered higher-risk for potential corruption or misuse of funds. Used in global DAF compliance and anti-money laundering screening to protect charitable assets.
- **Pooled Giving Fund:** A shared fund where multiple donors contribute, often within a DAF structure, to collectively support specific causes or initiatives.
- **Predictive Analytics in Philanthropy:** The application of AI and data modeling to forecast giving trends, donor behavior, and impact measurement in charitable organizations.
- **Private Benefit Doctrine:** A legal principle in U.S. tax law stating that tax-exempt organizations must operate exclusively for public benefit and may not confer disproportionate benefits on private individuals or entities.
- **Private Foundation:** A tax-exempt nonprofit organization, typically funded by a single donor or family, that is required to distribute a minimum percentage of its assets annually for charitable purposes.

Q

- **Qualified Charitable Distribution (QCD):** A tax-free transfer of funds from an IRA directly to a qualified charity, available to donors aged 70½ and older.

R

- **Recoverable Grant:** A grant structured as a low- or no-interest loan or equity investment, with the expectation that funds will be repaid and re-deployed for future charitable use. These grants combine philanthropy and financial sustainability, often used in DAF impact investing.
- **Revenue Act of 1913/1917:** U.S. laws that introduced the federal income tax and later established charitable tax deductions, incentivizing philanthropy and laying the groundwork for modern structured giving.
- **Risk-Tiered System:** A compliance framework where DAF sponsors classify grantees by risk level (e.g., high, medium, low) to determine the appropriate level of due diligence and monitoring.

- **Roth IRA Conversion:** A financial strategy involving the transfer of assets from a Traditional IRA to a Roth IRA, which triggers taxable income in the year of conversion. Donors often offset this taxable event by making charitable contributions, such as to DAFs, in the same year, thereby reducing their overall tax liability while advancing philanthropic goals.

S

- **SDG Philanthropy Platform:** A collaborative initiative that connects philanthropic organizations with global policymakers to align charitable efforts with the UN's Sustainable Development Goals.
- **Self-Dealing:** Prohibited transactions where donors or related persons benefit personally from the use of DAF assets.
- **Shared Services Model:** A structure in which DAF sponsors centralize administrative, investment, and compliance services to reduce costs and extend professional philanthropic tools to donors of all income levels. This model expands access to high-quality giving strategies.
- **Socially Responsible Investing (SRI):** An investment strategy that considers environmental, social, and governance (ESG) criteria.
- **Structured Giving:** A formalized approach to philanthropy using vehicles like DAFs, charitable trusts, or foundations to achieve long-term, strategic impact with tax and planning advantages.
- **Successor Advisors:** Individuals designated to recommend grants from a DAF after the original donor's death or incapacity.

T

- **Tax Cuts and Jobs Act (TCJA) of 2017:** U.S. tax legislation that significantly increased the standard deduction, reducing the number of taxpayers who itemize charitable contributions.
- **Tax Deduction Limits (for DAF Contributions):** IRS regulations cap the percentage of a donor's Adjusted Gross Income (AGI) that can be deducted for charitable contributions. The limits for U.S. federal tax law are generally 60% of AGI for cash contributions and 30% of AGI for appreciated assets. Note: These limits apply specifically to U.S. federal tax law; tax treatment of DAF contributions may vary in other jurisdictions.

- **Tax Reform Act of 1969:** A pivotal law that established regulations for private foundations, including the 5% payout rule, restrictions on self-dealing, and new tax compliance measures that distinguished DAFs from private foundations.
- **Tithing:** A religious practice, common in Christianity and Judaism, in which individuals donate a portion of their income (typically 10%) to support religious institutions or charitable causes.
- **Tzedakah (Judaism):** A Hebrew term meaning "justice" or "righteousness," which denotes charitable giving as a religious and ethical obligation rather than voluntary generosity.

U

- **Unified Registration Statement (URS):** A standardized form used by nonprofits, including DAF sponsors (501(c)(3) public charities), to register for charitable solicitation across multiple U.S. states, streamlining compliance with state fundraising laws.
- **Uniform Prudent Management of Institutional Funds Act (UPMIFA):** A U.S. legal framework adopted in 2006 that governs how nonprofit institutions manage investment assets, emphasizing sustainability, donor intent, and prudent investment, key to DAF fund management.
- **United Nations Sustainable Development Goals (UNSDG):** A global framework for addressing social and environmental challenges, with philanthropy playing a key role in funding initiatives aligned with these goals.

V

- **Values-Aligned Investing:** Investment strategies that align charitable assets (including DAF holdings) with the donor's social or environmental priorities, often through ESG or impact investing.

W

- **Waqf:** A charitable endowment in Islamic tradition used to fund religious, educational, or social welfare programs, structured to generate long-term support.
- **Wealth Management:** A comprehensive service that includes financial planning, investment management, estate planning, and charitable giving. Advisors incorporate philanthropy into these plans to benefit their long-term clients.

Z

- **Zakat:** One of the Five Pillars of Islam, requiring Muslims to donate a fixed portion of their accumulated wealth (not just income) to the poor and those in need as an act of faith and social responsibility.